UNDER THE PARSON'S NOSE

Revd Benjamin Armstrong about the time of his arrival at Dereham

Under the Parson's Nose

Further extracts from the diary of

The Revd B.J.Armstrong M.A. (Cantab)

Vicar of East Dereham 1850-1888

Edited by his Great Grandson

C. S. Armstrong B.A. (Hons)

with a foreword by

Professor Sir Diarmaid MacCulloch,
Kt., D.D., F.B.A.

The Larks Press

Published by the Larks Press
Ordnance Farmhouse, Guist Bottom
Dereham NR20 5PF

01328 829207
Larks.Press@btinternet.com
Website: www.booksatlarkspress.co.uk

September 2012

British Library Cataloguing-in-Publication Data
A catalogue record for this book is available
from the British Library

ACKNOWLEDGEMENTS
Sincere thanks are due to Professor Sir Diarmaid MacCulloch for his delightful Introduction, to Canon Leslie Morley for his help with the Glossary, and especially to David Sharp for his encouragement and wise counsel.

ISBN 978 1 904006 62 6

FOREWORD

It gives me a particularly personal pleasure to welcome this splendid new edition of one of England's great clerical diaries, because I have known the existing and less comprehensive editions since I was twelve years old. In 1963 my father (like Benjamin Armstrong, an East Anglian clergyman) bought the newly-published selection from the diaries, and I have that volume beside me as I write, still in its agreeable dustjacket so redolent of East Anglia in the 1960s, as well as East Anglia a century before. I read it voraciously, and it inspired me to keep a daily diary in emulation; I have done so every day over the last half century. So I owe much to the Norfolk diarist.

The qualities in Benjamin Armstrong which I admired then, still seem admirable now: his shrewd and clear-sighted observation; his keen intellectual curiosity; his wickedly sharp humour balanced by kindness, especially to the poor and vulnerable; his firm convictions, maintained in the face of unsympathetic and unimaginative bishops, and put into practice with tact and pastoral sensitivity; finally, the results that his patience eventually obtained. He was a good and faithful parish priest, in the multifarious ways that were then demanded of Anglican clergy, who were as much local governors and social workers as spiritual pastors. In Armstrong's time, the Church of England was undergoing one of those seismic shifts which are often at the time mistakenly seen as a sign of its imminent demise; *plus ça change.* The C. of E. ended up being very different from the Church into which Armstrong was born in 1817, theologically, socially and politically – and none the worse for the change.

One symptom of the transformation I remember well from first reading. Mr Armstrong had real worries when he decided to erect a cross on the grave of his daughter Gertrude in East Dereham churchyard: would it be vandalised as an object of popish idolatry by Protestant locals? He braved the disapproval, and now crosses on graves are part of the English landscape. That memory always provokes me to fury when I watch costume drama on television. TV producers go to endless trouble to get right the last frill and furbelow of every Regency bonnet, but they couldn't care less about the ecclesiastical detail. On more than one occasion I have had to restrain myself from hurling a volume of Tractarian pamphlets at the screen, at the egregious sight of some early Victorian hero posturing beside a grave with a cross in some rural churchyard. Armstrong, a man of pleasingly strong intolerances, might have cheered me on.

There are so many riches to be savoured in this volume – not least Armstrong's first sighting of a Christmas tree in 1856. Now the need for personal discretion has been reduced by the passage of time, we can meet more of the private and emotional life of this engaging man and his family, but there is also a wider picture of a vanished society to enter and explore. Every page contains multiple delights for laughter, surprise, musing or admiration. We are greatly in Chris Armstrong's debt for continuing and expanding the work which his father and brother commenced in bringing these diaries to a wider public: an act of family piety perhaps, but also a great gift to a wider public through the delight of meeting one of the most attractive personalities of small-town Victorian life.

Diarmaid MacCulloch
St Cross College, Oxford
June 2012

The Diarist and the Diaries

Benjamin Armstrong was born on 11th Nov. 1817, and educated first at Great Ealing School (whose alumni include such diverse characters as W. S. Gilbert and Cardinal Newman), and then at King's College, London, before going up to Caius College Cambridge. Ordained Deacon in 1841, and priest in 1842 he became Vicar of East Dereham in 1850, remaining in post until 1888.

He was an organised, energetic and committed parish priest, living at a time of great upheaval in the Church. As what might best be described as a 'pragmatic ritualist' he needed both to exercise discretion and show courage in the face of the strength of anti-ritualist feeling in some parishes at that time. His discretion ensured that controversial practices were introduced gradually and at a pace commensurate with maintaining a degree of amity within the parish. The success of this policy is clear: over the years he was able to make practically all the changes he desired, while there is only one occasion listed in the diary when he landed on the carpet at the Palace, and that was in respect of a sermon preached by his curate. He needed courage too – not only was there a clearly identified group of opponents for many years, but also his views were not calculated to commend themselves to the successive Low Church Bishops under whom he served.

His determination and nerve were evidenced in an incident in his youth when, as a member of the Queen's Staghounds, he found himself confronted by the Great Western Railway while in full pursuit. *The Times* (14th January 1839) reported that while most of the riders diverted to cross a bridge those of 'higher blood', he being one, leaped the fences. One of the other riders had the misfortune to fall, his horse being killed by an oncoming train that was thus de-railed, but Armstrong and his future brother-in-law, William Duncombe, cleared the obstacles successfully. *The Times* concluded its report with the hope that:

'these gentlemen of the higher blood will be prosecuted for this feat. They are at liberty to break their own necks if they please; but they are not justified in breaking other folks' necks by riding over a railroad. Someone should endeavour to give these gentlemen an inkling of the fact that, though they may have no brains of their own to be knocked out, other people have.'

Perhaps it is just as well that Armstrong later concluded that hunting was not an appropriate pursuit for a clergyman, or his time in

Dereham might have been limited. He did, however, continue to fish, and occasionally to shoot.

Woodforde's Weston Longville is only a few miles from Armstrong's Dereham, but their lives were worlds apart. In some ways this is a consequence of the enormous change that occurred in the half century between Woodforde's death and Armstrong's appointment. Developments in communication and travel meant that Armstrong had a broader experience; he travelled widely on the continent and his frequent visits to his father in London gave him ample opportunity to experience both the high and low culture of that city. But the differences are more than just a matter of different times. Their parishes were very different too. Weston was a tiny village, Dereham a growing market town. The centrality of the Church to town life was absolute in Dereham, where there was barely a pie into which the Vicar was not expected to put a finger. Local Boards, Health Boards, Schools, Charities, even disputes about the street lighting – all these were grist to Armstrong's mill. His energy and his commitment to the wellbeing of his parishioners were immense, and the range of duties he performed is clear from the diaries.

The diaries themselves remained largely unread until my father turned to them during the Second World War when the blackout began to curtail his evening parish work. He quickly became alive to the level of interest that might exist in such a record and the first volume of extracts he selected was published in 1949. This was followed by a second volume, also edited by my father, but published in 1963 after his death, by my brother. When the latter passed all eleven hand-written volumes on to me, I read them in their entirety for the first time, and recognised the extent and interest of the unpublished material, hence this third volume.

I have taken a slightly different approach to the responsibilities of editorship than did my father. First, as a priest his particular interest was with matters of the Church – I have focussed as much on the record of secular events. Second, I have not felt constrained in my selections, as I know he was, by an anxiety not to cause offence to the immediate descendants of those mentioned in the diary. It is now roughly 150 years since the events recorded – long enough I hope to ensure that no offence can reasonably be taken. The result is a record which more completely reflects the words and thoughts of the diarist, and which affords, I believe, a wealth of unwitting testimony as to the mores of mid-Victorian country life.

As was the case with the earlier volumes the spelling has been modernised to make the diaries more comfortable to read. One change is the provision of extensive background notes, grouped at the back of the book. While no effort has been spared to ensure their accuracy, the responsibility for any errors is entirely mine.

Those who are familiar with the earlier published diaries may recognise a few entries, but most are appearing in print for the first time, or for the first time using the exact words employed by the diarist. Of the remainder some have been included because they are needed to give a context to other entries, others simply because to exclude them would be to deprive the new reader of some entertainment.

Although the diaries cover his entire life, much of the early content is more autobiographical reflection than contemporaneous recording of events, and of interest mainly to his descendants. It is really only after he had settled in at Dereham that it becomes of wider interest and this volume deals exclusively with those years.

There are some signs in the diary that my great grandfather expected his words to be read by others, if only by his family. I am sure that he would have been as delighted as I was, on visiting St Nicholas, Dereham, this year, to discover that he is not forgotten and that an entry from his diary appears regularly in the Parish Newsletter, more than 120 years after his death. If nothing else this new volume will afford an extra resource for that publication!

C. S. Armstrong
Bodham, Norfolk
April 2012

Dramatis Personae

Benjamin John Armstrong – the diarist. Born 1817. Educated Great Ealing School, Caius College Cambridge. Ordained Deacon 1841 and Priest 1842. Became Vicar of East Dereham in 1850.

Ann Rebecca Armstrong (née Duncombe) (Nelly) – the diarist's wife. Daughter of William Duncombe, senior, of Lagley, Northchurch, Herts.

Benjamin John Armstrong, D.L., J.P. – the diarist's father. Lived in Upper Wimpole Street and Southall.

Ann Armstrong – the diarist's mother.

Annie Emma Challice (née Armstrong) – the diarist's sister. Novelist, and author of various works on French culture.

John Challice – Annie's husband, a medical practitioner deeply involved in public health issues. An inveterate investor in flawed enterprises.

William Duncombe – the diarist's brother-in-law.

Helen Armstrong – the diarist's eldest daughter.

Louisa Marion Armstrong (Lilly) – the diarist's second daughter.

Arthur Nelson – Lilly's husband, a ne'er do well.

Benjamin John Armstrong – (John, Jack) the diarist's elder son.

Mary Penrice Armstrong (née Bell) – John/Jack's wife

Herbert Duncombe Armstrong (Bertie) – the diarist's second son, an Officer in the Royal West Kent Regiment.

Gertrude Mary Armstrong – the diarist's youngest daughter who died in infancy.

Challices various – the 8 children of John and Annie. Most frequent mention is of Roger (the family black sheep) and John (a Naval Officer who was admitted to the Naval Hospital on the grounds of insanity).

Glossary of Terms and Organisations

Church Association (CA)

An organisation set up in 1865 with the purpose of opposing Anglo-Catholicism and the use of ritual. It was behind some of the instances of legal action taken against incumbents under the provisions of the PWRA (q.v.). It continues today as the Church Society, a strongly evangelical body.

District Visiting Society

An organisation comprising a group of lay visitors working under the auspices of the Church. The visitors' role included identifying suitable cases for moral or financial support and the distribution of a portion of parish funds to alleviate hardship. Visitors were expected to encourage attendance at church, and by children at Sunday School, as well as seeking to improve cleanliness and responsible budgeting amongst those upon whom they called.

English Church Union (ECU)

Founded in 1859 as the Church of England Protection Society to support and further the spread of High Church principles. It was essentially an Anglo-Catholic grouping that became strongly committed to the defence of those prosecuted under the terms of the PWRA. Armstrong was an active member, and the complete diary frequently refers to his attendance at its meetings. It continues to this day as the Church Union.

Established Church

The Church of England is an established church. This means that it is not just a voluntary movement, but a part of the state, and that its laws form part of the wider law of England, and that the appointment of its Bishops is subject, in practical terms, to political selection and, in law and theory, to Royal selection. At the time the diary was written the church in Ireland was, as in England, established, but Gladstone's government disestablished it in 1869. One key issue relevant to the period of the diary relates to the use of secular courts to deal with ecclesiastical matters. It was judgements of these courts that resulted in the imprisonment of those who disregarded its strictures with regard to ritualism. This caused great unrest and led some, who might have been expected to be strongly opposed to it, to question whether there was a case for disestablishment.

Liberation Society

Originally known as the British Anti-State Church Association, this group was committed to the disestablishment (see Established Church) of the Church of England. To this end it worked for the election of dissenting Members of Parliament. Although it had some success in this tactic, it was never able to secure a parliamentary majority in favour of disestablishment.

Oxford Movement

A movement established as a response to the perceived growth of liberalism in theology and a decline in church life. Committed to re-energising the Church of England, its leading members were influential theologians. While most of its leading adherents did not seek the re-joining of the Anglican Church with the Church of Rome, but rather to establish a middle course between Roman Catholicism and evangelical Protestantism, some were eventually received into that Church.

Papal Aggression

The term given by opponents of the re-establishment by the Roman Catholic Church, in 1850, of a structure which mirrored that of continental countries. An Archdiocese of Westminster was created and 12 other Bishops appointed, creating fears of a full scale Catholic attempt to supplant the Established Church. In part this fear was caused by an open letter from Dr Wiseman, the newly appointed Archbishop of Westminster, which appeared to suggest that such was the intention. It turned out that the letter had not been drafted with sufficient care, giving an impression of seeking to establish a diocesan structure for the whole nation, rather than for the Catholic population, which had been Wiseman's intended message.

Public Worship Regulation Act 1874 (PWRA)

This was a private Bill introduced by the then Archbishop of Canterbury, Archibald Tait, as a means to put an end to the accelerating move towards Ritualism (q.v.) in the Anglican Church at the time. It was enthusiastically supported by Disraeli, and empowered, amongst others, a Churchwarden or other lay parishioners, to make a representation to the Diocesan Bishop alleging a breach of a set of prescribed rules. Actions arising from such representations (which the Bishop had discretion to prevent) were heard in a secular rather than in an ecclesiastical court. This led to a number of prosecutions, and several clergy were imprisoned for contempt of court when they continued to follow ritualistic practices. Armstrong was appalled by the Act, and there are frequent diary references to some of those imprisoned. Wilson (2002, p.370) cites statistics to suggest that the Act was counter-productive in that some of the core elements of ritualism grew in the following 5 years.

Puseyism

After Edward Bouverie Pusey, who became leader of the Oxford Movement (q.v.) in succession to Newman some time before the latter was received into the Catholic Church. Although not a committed Ritualist himself, Pusey adopted some of their practices and was a firm defender of those challenged under the terms of the PWRA (q.v.). Appointed Regius Professor of Hebrew and Canon of Christ Church, Oxford, he attracted some opposition to his support for the spiritual value of Confession and for advocating the doctrine of The Real Presence i.e. that the body and blood of Christ are actually present as opposed to symbolically so in the Sacrament.

Ritualism

The term refers to a series of practices to which there are frequent references in the diary. These included the wearing of eucharistic vestments, the adopting of a position eastward facing the altar when celebrating Communion, the use of incense, the burning of lights and the use of water mixed with wine at the celebration of communion, and even a robed choir. These were seen by Ritualists as positioning the Church close to its pre-Reformation practices. There was strong resistance in many quarters to these practices and a perception that their proponents were moving towards Roman Catholicism. This resistance found its extreme outlet in riots and other disturbances.

Vestry

A type of parish meeting with a history going back to the 14th century. By the mid 19th century it was essentially a meeting to regulate church matters and elect parish officials, such as the Churchwardens, its responsibility for the relief of the destitute having been transferred to separate elected Boards or Unions responsible for the administration of the Poor Law. Those entitled to vote comprised not just members of the congregation, but also other ratepayers. This meant, for example, that dissenters could seek to influence decisions about who was the elected Churchwarden in the Parish Church.

Early Plans and Impressions

At the time of his appointment to Dereham, Armstrong set out in his diary the agenda he proposed to follow:

'I class the entire management of the Parish under three heads. First, the Church, second the Schools, and third the Poor, and have printed and published a programme for each division. Under the first come the Sunday, weekday and festival services, catechising, monthly sacrament etc. Under the second, the management and clerical inspection of Schools for boys, girls and infants. Under the third, the division of the parish into two large Clerical and 25 lay districts. The Clergy distribute the Offertory and endowed charities, and the lay visitors an annual fund of £150 collected by subscription – they meet monthly and are provided with books for information, a stock of Bibles, Tracts, Prayer Books and private devotions.'

By 1853 he had recognized that his role gave him a rare insight into the ways of his parishioners:

November 26th
'Concluded my visitation to the families of Tradespeople, Farmers, & those classes which are not so easy of access as the cottage poor. No one who has not thus seen behind the curtain, can form an idea of the discordant elements of a country town, & the numerous feuds, jealousies and rivalries therein prevailing.'

The Diary

1852

1852 undated

Driving through Longham I perceived the posts and wires of an electric telegraph stretching across the fields from the chief farmer's house to the Parsonage. Fearing that a Railway was in contemplation, I enquired of a labouring man a solution of the enigma. 'Sir', he replied, with a most knowing look, and indicating the houses with his forefinger, 'There is a gentleman as lives <u>here</u> and a lady as lives <u>there</u> and they tell me (looking incredulous) that they talk to one another by means of them wires'.

1852 undated

Travelled here (Oxford) to meet my father. Nothing worthy of note occurred on the journey save that the engine burst at Winslow and enveloped us in steam. This detained us for an hour, while they telegraphed for and obtained a fresh one.

May 9th (at Harrow Weald)

I dined and slept at Mr Hales' beautiful place 'The Hermitage' and Lord Ebrington dined with us. The conversation turned upon provincial peculiarities, when I took occasion to inform the company that 'the right of sanctuary' (instituted in the 'City of Refuge' and adopted by the church in the Middle Ages) was still in vogue in Norfolk. It is not uncommon when a man has been ejected from his tenement to remove his goods and family into the Church Porch – to make his house there, cook, and sleep. Once having taken up this position no one attempts to remove him, except by the bribe of a fresh domicile.

July 18th

The following story in connection with this (weather) vane is, from its similarity to other cases, likely enough to be true. On reading the Trustees' accounts for our handsome Church Fund, considerable sums were at various times appended to this item. 'Greasing the buck'[1] – so much. This meant a dinner out of the church funds. Thus under the pretence of repairing a weather cock, these men of the 'good old times' not only lied, but robbed the church for their own selfish ends.

July 27th

On my way to Norwich had Stanfield Hall indicated to me, where one Rush shot a Mr Jermy & his son dead, & severely wounded Mrs Jermy and her maid, so that the former was compelled to suffer amputation of one arm and the lives of both were despaired of. The lady, by recently marrying a son of Sir John Beauvoir, her first love, has caused as much interest to be taken in her, as when her life was attempted by the villain Rush.[2]

September 4th

Our town in a state of excitement consequent upon the entry of a 'troupe' of horse riders. Bands of music, a man driving 'ten in hand', carriages drawn by reindeer, elephants, & one by an ostrich added not a little to the novelty.

September 7th

Dined with Mr & Mrs Gurdon of Letton Hall.[3] They are people of great style, & the lady is daughter of Lord Colbourne who is staying there. Lord & Lady C. are very agreeable persons, but, as is generally the case among grandees, no opportunity presented itself for intellectual converse.

September 9th

Made up a party to view the restored churches of Reymerstone and Cranworth in company with the Squire, Mr Press, & concluded with dinner at the Vicarage. Mr Press although the son of a clergyman was, formerly, but a first rate farmer. He came to the Reymerstone Estate through the bequest of a very distant relative, and unexpectedly. It seems that Mr P's brother, who is a Whig, was always regarded as the probable successor to the property & to this end was unceasing in his attentions to the sick relation. Our friend, on the contrary is a Tory, & never expecting anything had not seen him for some years. Notwithstanding all this, old Mr Mann bequeathed him all his estate, on the ground that he 'would never give a farthing to any Whig!' It is satisfactory that, irrespective of political bias, our Mr Press is in all respects worthy of this accumulation of fortune.

September 14th

The Papers record, what all must regard as a great national calamity, a circumstance so full of interest as to demand notice in every private diary. The Great Captain of the age, & conqueror of Waterloo has breathed his last! May he rest in peace!

September 15th

Completed a domiciliary visitation to certain outlying parts of the Parish, consisting of 100 families. The statistical result of my enquiries is this, that out of the 100 families only 13 are dissenters, only 2 families are without Bibles, only 14 children (chiefly belonging to dissenters) are unbaptized, but alas only 15 have ever received the Holy Communion. The people were cleanly, frugal and glad to see me. Many of them expressing their thanks, although my visit was not accompanied with any gift.

September 20th

Completed a second visitation to 50 poor families living in Northall and Etling Green. The statistics differ from the last tour, inasmuch as the proportion of Dissenters is greater, and yet that of the communicants is also greater. They stand thus: 10 are dissenters (chiefly Mormonites), 11 are communicants at the Parish Church, 1 only is without a Bible, and 17, chiefly the children of dissenters, are unbaptized.

September 24th

Completed, in conjunction with my curate, a similar visitation of the parish of Hoe. It consists of 34 poor families, all of which possess a copy of the Holy Scriptures, and all are baptized. The whole of them belong to the Church, except two families who are Mormonites & there are 15 communicants. As for the farmers in Hoe, there is very little to be said in their favour. They contribute to no charity, and, like many of their class, are the dogged and determined opponents of every moral and religious improvement. I much doubt whether the liberal British farmer, with a hearty welcome and a good tap of ale, is not like the British lion, or his determined antagonist, the Unicorn, simply a fabulous and apocryphal animal, but their wives are always superior to them.

October 5th

Dined at Col. Mason's to partake of a haunch of venison weighing two stone. During dinner it was remarked that the swan was a county dish, and that a man in Norwich obtained his livelihood as a swan-fatter. The owners of the birds pay him £2.2.0d for fatting them, in which operation, among other things, each bird consumes a Coomb of corn. One of the party had seen the birds a few days before and described them as inhabiting an area wondrously small, & having a tank of water for their common benefit. When brought to table they are stuffed with rump steak, and eaten with a currant jelly.

October 21st

Employed the whole day in visiting the people in that part of Norwich Road between the station and Etling Green. This completes my visitation of the entire parish. Considering the unconsciousness of the English poor, & their want of character and intellectuality, it is not to be wondered at how little of interest occurs, even in so large a Parish as this. I discovered, in this visitation, that our exertions have closed the Meeting House in Etling Green & that several are in the constant habit of using the Prayers I published for the poor.

November 13th

Went to London by rail, partly to see my dear father's new residence in Upper Wimpole Street and partly to witness the magnificent public funeral of the Duke of Wellington.

November 14th

Attempted to see the lying in state of the Duke at Chelsea Hospital. The crowd, however, was so great that I gave up the attempt. My watch glass was broken in my pocket by the pressure. The day but one previously two females were killed and several wounded by the crowd.

November 18th

I rose at 5.30 and proceeded to the Amicable Life Office in Fleet Street with my father (he being a director) to view the procession. Although quite dark the streets were thronged, & one unbroken line of vehicles extended from Apsley House to the Cathedral. Barriers were erected in all directions, & the streets gravelled, & the whole had a kind of revolutionary appearance, the like of which I never saw before. Temple Bar, that begrimed and ugly nuisance, was completely transmogrified, being covered with black cloth and decorated with silver cornices studded with stars of the same. Various representations of the Duke's innumerable 'Orders' were suspended above it – curtains of gold tissue decorated the centre & four immense funeral embers surmounted the whole, pouring forth volumes of red smoke. It was really worthy of any Parisian Fête. The street was kept by a double line of the 33rd (The Duke's favourite)[4] regiment, & nothing could exceed the good feeling which subsisted between them and the people, who, at a later period in the day, showered down food and money on them from the houses, so that the road was presently strewed with paper. At length the procession arrived consisting of about 9,000 soldiers and a number of carriages. Cavalry – Infantry – Rifles – Scots Regiments – Artillery with 17 guns – Marines, etc., marched past each headed by their respective Bands playing the 'Dead March in Saul'. The State Carriage of the Queen, containing Prince Albert, The Speaker & the Lord Mayor were there, also Chelsea Pensioners, pursuivants, heralds, with the 'Guidon' & 'Wellesley Banner' – the state trumpeters – the chief mourner and friends of the deceased & his charger, led by a groom. The car was very beautiful, being drawn by 12 richly caparisoned horses. The whole array took more than an hour to pass our window[5] and there was not a break in the cavalcade. The solemnity in the Cathedral is described as beyond everything grand, and 200 officiated in surplices. The Queen viewed the procession from St James' Palace.

1853

April 21st

During my collection of School Subscriptions a respectable auctioneer of the town expressed much gratification in paying, since he was once a poor boy in the same school. By dint of industry he has now become comparatively opulent. He articled his son to a solicitor, but nothing would do for him but soldiering. To this end he three times enlisted as a private and was as often bought in discharge by the father. Having however done it a fourth time, Mr G. thought to let him go. He is now at The Cape, being a corporal in the Lancers and much respected. How much better it would have been to have furthered instead of frustrating this young fellow's taste, & to have spent the money on a Commission which was thrown away upon his 'Articles'!

May 19th

Had to return to Dereham owing to my curate Gibson being laid up with an ague. I started by the 8 am train [from London] and by 3pm was carrying on the routine of parish work as though it had never been interrupted. It is only such practical examples that teach us what a wonderful thing the railway is. Time and space are annihilated by it.

May 22nd

Trinity Sunday. The Cooper family were absentees today. This arises from an affaire de coeur between my curate and their daughter in which I got implicated about a year ago. Mrs Cooper consulted me about Gibson's intentions. Having privately exhorted him not to trifle with the girl but to declare either one way or the other, he declared 'off'. This has never been forgiven and the family suddenly made the awful discovery of Puseyism in vicar and curate. Gibson was not to blame and is a valuable coadjutor.

May 23rd

The Provisional Committee of the Institute, of which I am Chairman, brought their labours to a close and sent their Rules & Report to the printer. We have fixed the Subscription at 6/- a year, and want to establish a Reading Room – a Library – and occasional lectures.

May 25th

Whit Monday. Came up to London with my wife and children in an excursion train. It consisted of nearly 40 carriages and vast crowds availed themselves of the privilege.

Went with my father about painting a shield on his chariot. This is the first time his arms would be mounted, in full, with my dear mother's, the sort of carriages they have hitherto driven not being of a sufficiently State character to demand it.

May 28th

After entering my wife and children at the Zoological Gardens, I went to hear Albert Smith's account of Mont Blanc[1]. It consists of a humorous lecture largely embellished with anecdotes, instrumental music, a real St Bernard dog, and a Panorama very prettily painted. The alternatives from light to dark, & the lighting the Camp Fires on the 'Grand Mulets' was very effectively managed. There was a view of the famous convent, & the lecturer said that the effect of the atmosphere at so great an elevation (the highest habitation in the World) was such, that the lungs of the Monks were to use his own expression 'cut to pieces', by the age of 34 or 5. They then died, or exchanged their convent. He rather under-rated the sagacity of the famous dogs, & indeed rather threw an air of ridicule on their powers. On the whole it was a very pleasant way of whiling away a couple of hours on a wet day.

June 6th

Went to a Ball at Mrs Burchall's in Harley Street, with my parents. It was splendid enough, but I do not dance, or play cards, or talk to turbaned wallflowers, & always feel to be out of place. I did not stay to supper.

June 7th

Visited Mr Wylde's model of the Earth[2] in a large building recently erected by him in the centre of Leicester Square. The various portions of the earth are depicted on a gigantic scale, and all the rivers, lakes, mountains etc. seem to be delineated with great accuracy. The volcanoes are distinguished by being tipped with red foil. The size, however, of the model, & the surface being concave, prevent one's having so good an idea of the earth, as is obtainable from a common globe, & the more so because the galleries erected for the convenience of visitors, so block up the centre, as to prevent one's viewing the relative proportion of the parts. On the ground floor were a variety of models etc, & the chief objects of interest seemed to be a number of 'nuggets' from the newly discovered gold regions, some of which were worth as much as £400! Their size, colour, & value, & the fact that they may be taken out of the rocks by hand, without any machinery but a common hammer – these considerations are certainly enough to whet the ardour of many. How wonderful is this discovery, nearly simultaneously, of gold, in California, Australia and other places.

June 8th

Had agreed to go with my father to Paris...when a letter comes from my wife to say that the Lagley[3] party have determined to visit Ascot Races tomorrow, and that she will not go unless I accompany them. Notwithstanding my want of interest in races, & my grave doubts that it be right for a clergyman to visit them, it would be selfish of me to deprive my wife of a pleasure who is so thoroughly unselfish herself.

June 9th

At eight o'clock we started in an open Barouche for Ascot, a distance of above 28 miles – a proof, if it were needed of what toils people will not undergo in the pursuit of pleasure. The ride was lovely in the extreme, the trees were in their full foliage, & sparkling with innumerable sparkles from the rain of last night. There were steep hills, rushing streams, hanging woods, & village churches, & the lark 'carolling at Heaven's gate'. We changed horses at Chalfont, where Milton lived and wrote, & passed Stoke, in whose lovely churchyard Gray wrote his famous elegy. Shortly after, Windsor's magnificent pile came in view – and now all these beauties were to be exchanged for the turmoil and excitement of a racecourse, the frequenting of which I have long abjured, & only came on this occasion for other's sake. The number of vehicles, from the aristocratic four-in-hand to the dogcart was immense – the dust excessive – the crowd, vast. Her Majesty came on the course in the usual style. Prince Albert and the Royal children and the Duke of Genoa were in the Royal party. On the course I was recognised by a poor woman whom I had often tended at Whitchurch; her blessing, and the ride, were the only points in the day which there is any satisfaction in recalling to memory. It was nearly midnight when we reached Lagley.

June 16th [London]

Took the nurse and the children to see Tussaud's celebrated exhibition of waxworks, which The Times describes as 'one of the best in the Metropolis'. When I last saw it, some fifteen years ago, it scarcely exceeded the travelling waxworks which Dickens so admirably hit off in the 'Old Curiosity Shop', but now one is amazed at the size and sumptuousness of the saloon, & the gorgeousness of dresses & uniforms, arranged with admirable taste & judgement. As the rooms are lighted by a vast number of pendant lamps, the exhibition must have a truly brilliant effect at night, when music adds its charm to the scene. The figures, each mounted on a gilded pedestal, are very appropriately costumed, & the countenances are more human than artificial. In some cases it is really difficult to distinguish between the real & the unreal, as in the case of a certain (wax) old gentleman who sits, nodding his head, on the seat appropriated to visitors, and inspecting the Coronation group.

In the evening accompanied my father to dine with the Lord Mayor at the Mansion House 'to meet the Bishops' as the invitation was worded. We were first ushered into the presence of the Lady Mayoress who sat on a minute throne surrounded by her lady friends. This office was performed by a gentleman clad in purple velvet whom I thought was the Mayor, but was soon undeceived when that high functionary presented himself in a gown covered with gold and an enormous number of chains around his neck. He was exceedingly affable, & said he would invite me again. After this a great number of prelates, D.D.s and dignified clergy were presented, wearing their gowns and cassocks, the Bishops carrying their three cornered hats, and the clergy their college caps. Among them I observed the Archbishop, the Bishops of London, Winchester, Oxford, Bangor, Chichester, Salisbury, Worcester, S. Asaph, Manchester, Nova Scotia, Adelaide etc. The dinner was of the most sumptuous character. Real turtle and champagne were in profusion, & the tables were tastefully decorated by bouquets of flowers in gold and silver epergnes. The loving cup was sent round after dinner. In proposing and replying to the toasts, the speaking was below par. I thought the Bishop of London, the Archbishop and the Bishop of Winchester very vapid.

June 18th

Went with my dear father to see the military camp at Chobham. Our route was by the Southampton rail to Chertsey. It was enlivened by an extraordinary fellow traveller who entertained us with ventriloquism, songs, anecdotes and imitations of all kinds. When the train stopped at a station he astonished the Guards by feigning to be an aged lady in distress – or by bleating like a sheep or crowing like a cock thus inducing the authorities to inspect the carriage with the view of ascertaining whether any such contraband travellers were in the carriage.

Chobham had assumed the appearance of a fair, & though there was not to be any military display the road, cut to pieces by the artillery & baggage trains, was crowded with vehicles of every description. The "Camp" consisted of a vast sea of tents, the plan of which was by no means clear at first. Ascending a hill, however, I found it to be in the form of a crescent, of which the Life Guards occupied one extreme end, & the Artillery the other. A pavilion for Her Majesty's use occupied the centre. It was a most picturesque and interesting scene, exhibiting the business side of military life & being the nearest approach to actual warfare I am likely to witness. The men sleep in small round tents, on clean straw, their feet meeting in the centre, like the spokes of a wheel. The stables were most orderly, & composed of rough tents made of fir poles. The kitchens consisted of trenches cut into the earth with a chimney at the end, at intervals in the trench, through which the fire passes, holes are cut for the saucepans. It is needless to add that so motley an array produced many unconscious tableaux; the naked-legged Scot, the superb Guardsman, the dingy Rifleman, the gay Lancer, contributing to this effect. The drums, muskets, standards etc, were beautifully arranged. I regretted the substitution of the 'shell jacket' for the officer's neat blue frock. One can hardly distinguish them from the men, & Mr Fitzgerald of the Marines, who dined with us yesterday, says, that our officers never get saluted on account of sentinels being unable to discriminate between the two.

June 21st [en route to Boulogne]

We left London Bridge station at 1.30, and arrived at Folkestone at 5.20. At Sydenham we caught a glimpse of our old friend, the Crystal

Palace, looking none the worse for its new position. On board the 'Princess Helena' our passage was charming, a fresh wind blew and the moon shone brilliantly. First we saw the light on Cap Gris Nez – then the return boat went screaming past & then the lights of Boulogne appeared. Soon we were marched off to the Douane, which, though a scene of some confusion, was in reality well managed. We then trudged off to the Hotel du Nord – a fine mansion, an extensive 'salle à manger', a large yard embellished with orange trees, & a conservatory. After a bottle of good 'ordinaire' & a cigar, we retired to rest.

June 23rd [Boulogne]

Before commencing our second peregrination of Boulogne, I tried in vain to account, by means of any rational theory for the French smell. I call it the French smell because it is common to every part of France I have ever visited. It assails your nostrils on the coast and inland – in Paris or in country town – in the best streets or what we should call the slums. It greets you directly you set foot on the Gallic shore & never leaves you till you embark for home. It is not the drainage because the smell is not disagreeable.

Undated [staying in Boulogne]

At the table d'hôte we were entertained by the conversation of a young English officer of Engineers, one of those easy-going devil may care fellows who, like cats, always seem to come down on their feet, & to get clear of any mess in which they may be implicated. He had not only visited most parts of Europe, but had been in Persia and Siberia; had hunted the chamois in the Alps & had ascended Mont Blanc. What is more, he was now on his road, knapsack on his back, to Constantinople, where he intended to volunteer to the Sultan to fight against the Czar who is supposed to be meditating an attack on the Turkish dominions, but had been recalled to his regiment and was on his way home.

July 5th

An old sailor with a wooden leg came to me, and with many tears expressed his remorse at having taken too much beer at the Fair last week. He had been a regular attendant at daily service & Communion, but had abstained from both these few days for fear of bringing a scandal on religion. Prevailed on him to come again this evening.

July 6th

After taking a funeral I strolled for a while among the tombs. There is, I am glad to say, a paucity of those singular and joking epitaphs which disgrace many churchyards. One runs thus: 'Be thou what you think I ought to have been'. This is very epigrammatic & ironical.

The Institute was opened today, and a considerable number of members enrolled themselves. I hope by this means to get some little hold on apprentices, mechanics, & those sort of people who are for the most part out of the Clergyman's reach.

July 15th

Wrote to Lord Leicester for a day's fishing, and dined at Mrs Wollaston's to meet several parishioners and a Mr Weston, our new doctor, whom we liked very well. The experiment of table moving, now so much in vogue was tried, without success.

July 18th

A day of recreation consequent on W. Duncombe being with us. Had a successful day with the trout at Bilney during which I bagged two and a half brace, and Duncombe several more. Took one with the fly, but the rest being caught with worms were heavier fish. Should have taken more, but having unfortunately lost my worm-box, had to find others from the ground, which were scarce and very inferior. Returned for evensong.

July 22nd [After a fruitless day's fishing with his brother-in-law at Castle Acre]

During our hedgerow dinner, in sight of the old church & ruined castle, we fell into conversation with a gingerbread baker who was on his way, he said, to Harpley Fair. He told us he had no home but his cart, and baked his nuts at the baker's 'offices', as they call them here, in the various towns he went through. Fell in with the gamekeeper – a very rough but civil fellow. On our saying that we thought the river must be poached, he said it was, and that he had caught the Revd J. N. at it the other day, & who was to be prosecuted on the ground of being an old offender. He is a poacher, I know.

August 16th

The Annual School Feast, which was attended by 317 children, being one more than last year. The procession, with the flags and banners as last year, started from the Schoolhouse at 2.30 & making a really imposing appearance, created a great sensation in the town. They were headed as usual by a band which ceased playing when the procession arrived at the Church. The children entered by the great door & took the flags up the middle aisle, which had a picturesque effect & even more so when they stood guard over them in the side chapel whither they had filed off. After church the procession re-formed to the Vicarage grounds, where many of the parishioners & some neighbouring Clergy & Gentry were assembled. Here a beautiful repast was provided for them & also vast numbers of toys contributed chiefly by the subscribers to the Schools. No sooner was the tea and cake demolished than down came the rain & continued without inter-mission the whole evening. The parishioners filled the Vicarage, where a handsome dessert was provided for them, & the children adjourned to the Tythe Barn where dancing was kept up until dark.

August 17th

Occupied my time on parish work, calling on some of the middle classes, who are sometimes overlooked, as not coming so readily into our 'sphere' as the peasantry or the rich.

Called with my dear wife and Helen on the Smiths of Brisley Rectory. They have just returned from a three month's tour & spent the Holy Week in Rome. They said that the Rev. G. Nelson, son of a neighbouring clergyman, was at Rome with them, & one day was foolish enough to speak politics very freely in a public conveyance. He had not long reached his lodgings, when he was served with a notice to leave Rome in 24 hours!

August 22nd

Resolved on a drive to Col. Mason's at Necton Hall. Found the host, and his interesting sister, Miss Mason, at home, who, with his usual condescension showed us his pictures & curiosities, and also the grounds. The latter are tastefully laid out, and most of the trees planted by himself. There are great numbers of curious trees and shrubs, among them the Cork and India rubber trees, also hickories, pomegranates and curious oaks. He pointed out one 'Lord of the Forest' for which the Admiralty (who, the Colonel said, had lists of all the estates where the finest oak is grown) had offered his father £180 for shipbuilding purposes. Mrs Sumner also was there, of whom the story is told, that when a girl she went to see David Fisher's respectable theatrical company[4] perform at the neighbouring town of Swaffham and, falling in love with the stage hero, offered, by letter, to

26

marry him. Upon which, the said David, called upon the lady's Papa, so the story goes, with the letter and warned him of his daughter's folly, at the same time exonerating himself & declining the honour.

August 23rd

Notwithstanding it being the height of harvest the daily service is well attended. It is curious to observe just how rapidly harvest work is completed in Norfolk. The farmers send such numbers of labourers into the fields that a district which was begun on a Monday is finished by Wednesday.

August 25th

Mr Drake, my Churchwarden, drove me to Carbrook to see a Lectern in the Church there, for the Clerk, which he proposes as the new model for one in Dereham. The parish Clerk, is, without exception, the most conceited of his learning & self-satisfied fellow I ever met with.

August 30th

Was spent in visiting the poor & sick. Am often struck with the little of interest one meets with in this sort of work, arising from the nature of the English poor. They are so quiet and 'every-day', so unexcitable, and have so little consciousness of action, so apathetic & reserved, that it is really trying work to probe them in the one thing needful. They seem all alike.

Dined with the Langtons of Fransham to meet some friends of theirs from Lincolnshire. When it is added that the lady guest was wholly given to Homeopathy, her husband to Mesmerism, and our host to Hydropathy, it may easily be imagined what was the subject matter of conversation. Langton said, speaking of table moving, that some Misses Blake, the daughters of a neighbouring clergyman, had walked upstairs with a small table through the sole medium of magnetism.

September 8th

Dined at Col. Mason's – Venison, champagne & other luxuries in profusion. Conversation turned on poaching. I attempted to show that nature made us poachers, & that all understand 'Punch's' assertion, viz. the least pleasurable shooting is where you preserve your own game & sport on your own ground – the next best is where you take a licence & shoot, by permission in other's ground – but the best of all where you have no licence or leave, and shoot in the face of a notice to trespassers.

September 22nd

Accompanied my father into Suffolk to see some land he has come into possession of through Mrs Meynell. As the tenant was out shooting with some friends we walked on to the land, which was very picturesque in scenery, but not first rate, I fear, in quality. At length we met the sportsmen who were a larger party than we anticipated, & with whom we returned to dinner – an excellent farmhouse repast with good wine and superb ale. There was a lawyer & a doctor from Ipswich, a miller, a farmer or two, and a young man who had married one of the daughters, was in the militia, & was cultivating an incipient moustache on the strength thereof. I observed that the company seemed to award the palm, in all respects, to the Norfolk farmers over themselves, & indeed it is not difficult for the amateur to perceive the inferiority of the Suffolk farming, the hedgerows being suffered to grow to great heights & the fields being small & rough in appearance.

September 28th [Cromer]

Walked on the shore till noon, thinking what an idle place the 'sea side' is, & watching the people on the sands. The Mamas looked all happiness with their children digging sand & themselves armed with a portable stool and a novel.

October 8th

A very fatiguing day with the local Board of Health, which I have been instrumental in forming, being occupied with them in personal visitation. Was astonished, in this, one of the prettiest & cleanest towns in England, to find such fearful nuisances at the back of some of the houses. Attempts at pig and cow keeping in a town must be always injurious, and, added to a defective drainage, must be pestiferous. The parish officers divided themselves into three companies, taking as many sections of the town, & in mine we noted down 19 cases to be reported to the Board of Guardians.

October 10th

The annual dinner of the Book Society at which I presided as President as my predecessors have done since it was established in 1810. Ten members dined & Mr Hastings & Mr Thompson took coffee at the Vicarage. During dinner a youth from Northampton completed the feat in the marketplace of running 10 miles within an hour. He had recently walked from Lynn to Dereham, & back, daily for six consecutive days, being 60 miles a day. All this he undertakes for the sake of any 'encouragement' he can get from bystanders.

Having solicited this from us, we had him into the room, & on examination found his muscles to be hard as iron.

October 12th
The day chiefly employed in visiting the poor in Hoe, & inducing several parents to send their children to the Schools. As they were mostly in the fields 'dropping' [probably sowing potatoes] I had to follow them to their work. Dined with the Gurdons at Letton Hall, & enjoyed an evening enhanced by many attractions. One is loath to leave where wealth, taste, family and accomplishment lend their combined aid.

October 13th
Was chiefly spent in casting up accounts and paying them, endeavouring to turn this opportunity with tradespeople to their spiritual account.

October 26th [at Crowle, Lincs]
In the evening went to a regular country party at the Churchwarden's, a rich farmer. There were 10 present, consisting of the Vicar, the Curate, the Lawyer, the Doctor, and some wealthy yeomen like the host. The eating and drinking began at 7 and continued without intermission until 1 in the morning. First there was wine & dessert, then tea, accompanied by innumerable cakes, then wine and spirits with a pipe, then supper, of an excellent but heavy kind, & finally spirits and tobacco again. The conversation was about farming & local matters, & the only two things I heard, which are worth remembering, are that 6,000 wild ducks had been taken at a neighbouring decoy, and, that more opium was consumed between Boston & York than in any other part of the country.

November 2nd
Called on the Gurdons of Letton Hall & the Misses Bullock of Shipdham – a Miss Hart, staying at the latter house, was recently robbed of her diamonds in Paris through keeping them in a carpet-bag through which a hole had been cut & the valuables detracted.

November 3rd
Was surprised to see a Chelsea Pensioner in the garden, in all the glories of cocked hat and scarlet coat. It turned out to be old Nicholas Peake, late a parishioner of Hoe. He had left the Hospital for a holiday & had brought me some flower roots as a present in acknowledgment of former kindnesses.

November 9th

A ridiculous onslaught of domestic troubles, the following being announced in rapid succession - the well fallen in, the pump out of order, the tax-collector in the study, and my younger son with nettle-rash.

A day of much interest among the artisans of Dereham in consequence of the inaugural lecture being given, in connection with the Institute. Lord Sondes, our President, took the chair & was accompanied by two of his daughters, the Misses Mills. No less than 297 persons attended. The Lecturer was the Rev. Bath Power of Norwich, & the (large and rather high-sounding) subject 'Physical Science, in its relation to the Arts & conveniences of Life'. I did not think much of the lecture. It wanted point & clearness. Moreover it was rather too deep for the audience. In proposing a vote of thanks to Lord Sondes, at the conclusion, I could not resist detaining them for 20 minutes with my speech – people seemed more interested during its delivery, than during the learned disquisitions of the lecturer. It was followed by prolonged applause. Mr Power gave an interesting exhibition of the Hydraulic Piers and of the Electric Telegraph, and had he confined himself to these subjects, his lecture would have been a very fair one.

November 16th

Rode on horseback to visit some outlying farms towards Shipdham. These little 'Masters' are often worse off than the labourers on a large farm. Man & wife both work very hard to 'make ends meet', their anxiety is of course very great, & being holders of land they are excluded from charitable & parochial funds.

Finished Lieutenant Osborne's Arctic Journal, being an account of the expedition after Franklin......in this expedition a carrier pigeon was despatched from Lat 74° N & 92°W to the meridian of Greenwich, & actually competed its flight of 3,000 miles! The bird had some help, however, though of a precarious kind. 'He was put in a basket' says the author 'which was attached to a balloon in such a manner, that, after combustion of a certain quantity of match' the carrier pigeon would be launched into the air to commence its flight. ...Alas, I fear poor Franklin will never be heard of more![5]

November 17th

Called on Mrs Gilbert, a good churchwoman who leads a 'quiet & peacable life' on a small maintenance. I was told by her that Lord

Sondes was actively engaged in the Battle of Waterloo & that he and the present Emperor were in the same batch of 'specials' on the memorable 10th April[6] when the Chartist display was made. It is singular that he should have fought against one Emperor Napoleon, & was ready to fight, side by side, in the same cause with another.

War has commenced between Russia & Turkey, and England & France are, of course, implicated.

November 21st

Attended, as a Trustee, a Meeting of the Headboro's[7] to take into consideration the feasibility of erecting a corn exchange in substitution of our present shambles. If we can get something architecturally good, this would be the finishing stroke to, what the 'bagmen'[8] say is one of the prettiest towns in England.

November 26th

Concluded my visitation to the families of Tradespeople, Farmers, & those classes which are not so easy of access as the cottage poor. No one who has not thus seen behind the curtain can form an idea of the discordant elements of a country town, & the numerous feuds, jealousies and rivalries therein prevailing.

November 30th

Received by Post the Act of Parliament relating to Savings Banks[9], the passing of which has suspended our plan of forming one in this town. Called on Mr Thompson in order to put this matter in motion.

December 1st

At a Vestry it was unanimously resolved to pull down the Shambles which much disfigures our otherwise handsome Marketplace. It is an eyesore with which I was much struck on first seeing Dereham, but hardly hoped to get the nuisance removed with so little trouble. In the evening took my dear wife to the Assembly, which, as usual, was a very brilliant affair, though the numbers (114) were somewhat thinned by deaths in Lord Sondes & Lord Paget's families. Nothing could exceed the taste of many of the dresses, & as we now know all the families for miles around, the meeting was pleasant enough.

December 2nd

Dined at Mrs Lee Warner's for the first time since the death of the Squire, & sat in the place of the host. There were present the Hon. Mr Harbord, brother to Lord Suffield, & reputed to be the handsomest man in the Eastern Counties, Mr & Mrs Dashwood, (sister to Lord Hastings), Mr Maugham of Stretton & the Lee Warners of Walsingham Abbey. Mr Dashwood told the story of a visit of the Dukes of Sussex & Cambridge to Holkham. When shooting, notwithstanding game was most abundant, one of the Dukes did not touch a feather. The keeper, however, who was also shooting, floored them right & left, and continually ascribed the success to the Duke, saying 'Your Royal Highness' bird'. At last old Mr Coke lost all patience, & running up to the keeper, administered a kick in his rear, saying, 'you are a lying humbug, he hasn't killed one, and you know it'.

December 7th
After prayers went for a ride on horseback with Mr & Mrs Weston, and afterwards selected a number of aged and deserving poor as recipients for the soup to be given at periods during the winter at the Vicarage.

December 9th
After Matins, visited a sick man & baptized a dying child in a distant portion of the parish. The afternoon chiefly occupied in the distribution of soup, for which purpose, I caused a famous copper to be erected in the back kitchen. There are 40 heads of families on my list. The poor man above adverted to has quite lost his reason, & it is wonderful how many instances have occurred in this parish, of partial & complete insanity. Surely it would be beneficial if our poor had more amusement wherewith to enliven the monotony of toil. Why can't the English amuse themselves like the French, Germans, and (as I have seen) even the phlegmatic Dutch? But we are certainly very prosy & unimaginative, & can scarcely wonder at the poor being heavy & dull, when their superiors are not always very much better. Our countrymen like a serious and exact deportment and are generally incapable of appreciating wit. There is truth in what Dr Challice once said to me 'I find' said he 'that joking don't pay'.

December 15th [London]
In the evening my dear Father, Fothergill & myself went to see the 'Irish Tourist's Ticket'. A poor imitation of Albert Smith's Mont Blanc entertainment. There was a panorama, songs, anecdotes, and a portfolio of sketches, but nothing worth seeing except two or three of the latter.

December 16th

While purchasing some things to take into the country saw a vast crowd of poor persons at a door opposite. It was a public soup kitchen, & the headman very civilly explained everything connected with it. They sell 600 portions per diem, consisting of an excellent pint of pea soup, and a good-sized piece of bread, for which they charge one penny. I'm told they purchase the 'waste' from the Clubhouses for this purpose. Nothing could exceed the cleanliness of the place & of the waiters, who, when they handed a ration & took the penny from the voracious unwashed, passed a wooden ball along a wire, as a tally. The soup coppers were heated by gas. Although many of the applicants were of the poorest class, I could see some citizens there to whom it was no charity, and the thought immediately suggested itself that when soup is sold, even at a nominal price, there is no means of preventing the abuse of a superior class availing themselves of a privilege they do not need, & which was not intended for them. The manager of the kitchen confessed to this.

December 17th

After breakfast, accompanied Fothergill to the Zoological Gardens to see the new 'Vivarium' & also to see the Ant Eater, which arrived this year. There is something of a connection between the hideous 'Ant-Eater' and the feathered tribe, his head being like a vulture, with a long beak, & his feet half-hoofed & half-clawed. This monster is somewhat like a porcupine with an enormous tail. The keeper said that in America, his home, the animal protrudes his long tongue near an ant-hill & when they have covered it, he suddenly draws it in and devours them. Singularly enough he will not eat English ants, & is fed on bread & milk.

Returned [from London] by the 5 o'clock express, & left Fothergill at Ely. About 7 miles further, the wheel of the tender broke, threw the carriage off the line & dragged it along ploughing up the earth at a fearful rate. It then came to a standstill and we all got out. Providentially no accidents happened, & we were near Mildenhall Station, where we waited two hours while the carriage was righted, & the telegraph set in motion in all directions. Arrived home at 11 instead of 8.30.

December 26th

Today is a general holiday on account of the Great Festival falling on a Sunday. All the shops shut, & the people standing about with their

33

hands in their pockets evidently not knowing what to do with themselves.

December 28th

Got out a quantity more coal tickets, & was besieged by the poor for alms. I have great apprehensions for them this winter, as provisions are very dear in consequence of the late harvest having been below par & the war with Russia being imminent... The Russians have thoroughly beaten the Turks at sea, but the Anglo-French squadron has not yet been in action.

1854

January 1st

Drove to Hoe this morning in a sleigh, the snow being too deep for wheels. Had some difficulty in getting through a drift where the horse was above the knees in snow. The sensation of this mode of travelling was very novel & pleasing, so that what would appear a great hardship, was in fact a source of enjoyment. There were 19 communicants, though I can hardly tell how they got through the snow to church.

January 3rd

In the evening went to a party at Mr Aufrere's. Very slow – small rooms, piano out of tune, bad wine, and stupid people.

January 5th

Collected a committee at the Vicarage consisting of the Church-wardens and some others to take into consideration the propriety of raising a special fund for the poor during this unprecedented & severe season. Some fears were expressed that to ask for contributions might damage the Dis. Vis. Society which is increasing in usefulness, & the weather showing a slight disposition to give, we deferred our meeting till next Monday. Gave soup to 50 poor persons.

Helped my dear wife to string up her harp which has been long mute.

Rev. Armstrong's wife, Ann, with her harp

January 6th

These are rather sad, I had almost said, awful times. The papers are full of war, murders, fires, railway accidents, shipwrecks, and even yet cholera. Yesterday four persons were killed, & 20 hurt by a collision near Attleborough.

January 9th

Visited the sick and the Schools, & dissolved the Relief Committee in consequence of the thaw. After Evensong attended a gentleman's evening party at my curate's for an hour. Was sorry to see cards the order of the evening, which, like dancing, may be innocent enough in itself, but to my mind incompatible with the clerical character.

January 11th

Arranged with Mrs Norton of Hoe to bring the children of that hamlet to Dereham School daily, in a 'dickey [donkey] cart'. Our annual Parochial Christmas Party, which was kept up till 4 in the following morning. We consider ourselves fortunate, amid all the private feuds of a County town, to get together nearly 50 of our parishioners, & my heart was sensibly touched & felt very grateful at seeing their enjoyment under the vicarage roof. My dear wife exerted herself to the utmost in entertaining them, & the whole affair went off with much éclat.

January 18th

In the evening to a party at Mr Weston's, who, as a comparative stranger, had unwittingly invited some discordant elements of Dereham Society. Happily we were on such good terms with both sides as to be able, with a little tact, to keep things comfortable.

January 19th

In the evening to a large party at Necton Hall, at which all the neighbouring clergy & gentry were present. As it was partly 'juvenile' dearest Helen accompanied us, and it was quite a novel feeling I underwent on seeing my daughter dancing at a large Ball.

January 25th

After Church, rode off to Etling School & catechised the children, remounted my high-mettled nag, & galloped, not cantered, for exercise sake down the green-sward lanes, to see old John Flowers, who lives in the very 'Ultima Thule' of the Parish. He is a pious, and, in person, a beautiful old man who, notwithstanding he lives 3 miles from the Parish Church, sits regularly every Sunday on the pulpit steps, in devout attention, & occasionally in the sermon murmurs approbation. His absence convinced me he was ill, and so he is. Away again to some new cottages which have arisen, mushroom-like, on Badley Moor, to visit the inhabitants who I found to be dissenters.

January 31st

A good day's work. After Catechising the central schools and tutoring my sweet child, I had a good half day among the poor at Etling Green – I am happy to say that they are much improved since I last saw them. Their cottages are cleaner, & one or two desperate cases of filth and concubinage have been transformed into clean & married homes. Almost all the children go to school, & there are very few dissenters.

February 4th

Met a small farmer who has been 'minded' for years to come to the Holy Communion, but was held back by scruples. Had heard lots of sermons but they did not meet his case etc. Reasoned with him a long time & have hopes he will receive the Sacrament.

February 5th

Was rejoiced to recognise, among the 150 communicants, my friend the Farmer. I thank God for this, & am the more persuaded of the usefulness of domiciliary visitation to the whole as well as the sick.

February 7th

A day of excitement in the Parish in consequence of Miss Dingle's wedding, & of her wearing a veil supposed to be the first ever seen in Dereham. The Church was crowded. All weddings are alike. The mind reverts to new well-fitting white gloves, & bouquets imported from Covent Garden – postboys with huge favours & smirking servant girls – a handsome breakfast with lots of champagne – wretched speeches on the part of the men, and tears on the part of the women. Then come the corded boxes, the bridegroom takes another glass & winks at the men, an old shoe is thrown into the carriage for luck, & off they go. The seniors then mumble philanthropic blessings, the juniors say that A. B. or C. is a capital fellow, & all go home under the consciousness of a day lost, and in a maudlin state of sentimentality caused partly by the champagne, & partly by that innate tendency which God has planted in all our breasts. For my own part I dislike weddings & would sooner attend a funeral!

February 8th

Dined at the Lee Warner's where one is sure to meet first-rate people. The Keppels, the Gurdons, Mr Pratt, Mr Haggard etc were there. I must say, however, that the conversation of the Squirearchy, though no longer exceptionable, as in days of yore, is not superior to those smaller fry, the 'professionals' & small gentry. They were laughing, good-naturedly enough, at the Times often speaking of the 'Booby Country Squires'. Although I am always on the qui vive to learn something, I gleaned nothing on this occasion beyond the satisfactory statement of Mr Gurdon, who said that, when he first frequented 'Brookes', they used to be playing cards all day, as well as half the night, at 30£ the rubber which was not considered high. Now there is very little playing seen in the evening, & that restricted to 10/6 points, High enough too!

February 10th

Some time back, an old lady bequeathed £126 each, to two sisters, parishioners, living in Dereham, & this money had caused nothing but misery in all directions. Thus a respectable young man who was engaged to marry my excellent little schoolmistress at Etling Green, jilted her, & married one of the rich sisters. But it is with the other that we have chiefly to do. On hearing of her good fortune another young man, as unprincipled as the former was weak, was accepted as her future husband. He persuaded her to transfer the £126 from the Colchester to the Norwich Bank & accompanied her to the former place to draw it, for that purpose. He had it in sovereigns – and quickly disappeared therewith. Thus the unfortunate girl lost her husband & perhaps more than that. Meanwhile the Papers are full of the wreck of an emigrant ship in Dublin Bay, in which 400 souls were suddenly called to their last account. Among the names of the deceased was Schilling, who was found with the total £126 in sovereigns in a bag round his neck! Yes, it is the same man! [1]

February 15th

Dined at Mr Collison's, Bilney Rectory, & met the Keppels, the Lee Warners etc. Sir Thomas Curtis was there, an old beau past eighty, but who had come eight miles to the party in an open gig. He prides himself, like most old beaux of his day, in being remarkably like George IV, & not without reason, as he almost reproduces the curly wig and flabby cheeks of that monarch. This knight was 'silver stick' to George IV, William IV & Victoria, & the following is related of him. On some occasion during the Prince of Wales'[2] popularity he was repeatedly called for by the crowd to appear in the balcony of the room in which he was dining. The mob, however, shouted in vain, for the truth was, the Prince was far too drunk to appear. Upon this it was proposed that Sir Thomas should impersonate H.R.H. which he did, & was loudly cheered by the people who never for a moment suspected the trick which had been played on them.

February 16th

Active preparations for war. 10,000 of our troops sail for the East this week & London is said to be full of Fathers, Mothers, Sisters & Lovers, bidding adieu to those they hold dear. France sends 30,000 men. Three magnificent fleets are formed – one for the Channel, one for the Black Sea, and one for the Baltic. They say the latter will be in Yarmouth for a time.

February 25th

George Nelson came to dine in order to help me tomorrow. Said that, while in Rome, the Pope had been ordered by his physicians to play at billiards, in order to prevent corpulency, to which His Holiness has a tendency. Also that the Pontiff is a great snuff taker & that while his fingers are reached forward, in the Apostolic mode, to confer the blessing, there is always some of that material the French call 'Tabac en poudre' between them.

February 28th

Barry & Walter Girling, their sister, & Miss Goldson dined with us, and afterwards attended Evensong. Walter says Caius College, of which, like myself, he is an alumnus, is now called 'Fishmonger's Hall' in consequence of the Tutor having a brother of that trade in the town. He says the Tutor & the College Cook were also at school together, the Cook the highest in the School.

March 3rd

Visited all the small farms & cottages on Northall Green. I often think, & circumstances seem to bear out the supposition, that one's footsteps seem specially guided on such occasions. Thus in a certain cottage, I was expostulating with the inmate, on the absurdity of Mormonism, to which she had addicted herself, when a fine tall young fellow entered the room with a good-natured and amiable smile, said 'Well sister, how are you?' He was dressed in a green shooting coat, pink check shirt open at the throat, & had a carpet bag slung over his shoulder by means of a stick. What was my surprise to find that this truly un-ecclesiastical character was a veritable Mormon Elder, & that Mrs Butters, the owner of the cottage, was his sister 'in the Lord'. Of course, we got to polemics, in which he maintained that no ministry was genuine which could not work miracles, & cited the 'signs' which Our Lord said should 'follow them that believe'. He advocated a plurality of wives, denied infant baptism, & maintained that God the Father had 'parts & passions'. He seemed thoroughly in earnest, & was by no means wanting in shrewdness.

About two hours after our meeting I encountered him trudging on the road, and we had ten minutes more chat. He said his sphere of labour comprised about ¼ of the county of Norfolk, & that in it there were about 250 Mormonites.[3] He lived on what the faithful chose to give him, & prided himself on being exactly like the original disciples. This is a sad delusion, but the preposterous claims it makes proportionately incline the ignorant to it. The dissenters & Low Church are very irate against the poor Mormons, but for my part, I do not see they are worse than other dissenters; the written account of their migration to the Salt Lake is wonderful, and reminds me in some particulars of the exodus of the Israelites.

March 19th

I have long had reason to expect that a power was working against my schools, and today the cat came out of the bag. I had ridden over to Toftwood Common to present some books to two 'Dames' who keep schools there, to enable them to impart better instruction to their scholars, when it came out that certain ladies are so fearful & jealous of my 'Tractarian' influence in those establishments, as to say that, if the Dames allowed the Vicar to catechise etc. in them, they would withdraw all their patronage. I begged the Dame to tell those ladies that their Vicar prayed God they might be brought to a more charitable mind, which she promised to do. But alas, what a state of things is this, that the clergyman of a parish, against whom no specific complaint has ever been preferred, and who labours unceasingly among his people, should be so treated, & that because he believes in those verities of the Church, Baptismal regeneration, Apostolic Succession & the real spiritual presence at the Eucharist. I confess I was deeply grieved.

March 21st

After visiting the schools as usual, went to Mr & Mrs Halcot Cooper[4], & frankly complained to them of their conduct. The interview which lasted two hours, is not worth repeating, but I hope and pray I left them in a better mind & corrected some misapprehensions under which they were labouring.

March 24th

A letter from my beloved Father, who always, like myself, writes once a week, gave the intelligence that Dr Challice is sadly embarrassed in his affairs, chiefly through rash speculations which have turned out badly. The Dr seems to gain nothing by sad experience in this respect, & to me it is a great grief that my dear & talented sister should be brought into this trouble.

March 29th

In the papers of today, there is an extract from the Gazette, of a declaration of WAR by the Queen against Russia, in order, in conjunction with France, to preserve 'the independence of Turkey'.

Called on Rev. J. Warays, son of Dr W., for whom I entertain much respect. The Rev. W. is a Naval Chaplain, just returned from a 3 year's cruise off the African Coast. Said the duty on board ship was 'Sunday' & not daily, as it ought to be, & that great prejudice would be felt against the latter – remember that the French Chaplains say Mass on board ship every morning at 8. The pay is £160 per annum & about £60 required for Mess account. Was at the siege of Lagos, in which 10 of our men were killed, & showed me some miserable 'Fetishes' carved of rhinoceros's teeth.

March 30th
Attended a Vestry for appointing Parochial Officers – very dull & stupid as usual.

April 10th
On our way home, Girdlestone [a neighbouring cleric] said that the Clerical Life Offices were beginning to find out their mistake in the advantages held out by them on parsons' lives. Formerly, when they did nothing, it is notorious they lived beyond the average of human life, but now the wear & tear consequent from the revival of the Missionary spirit in the church, brought them below average[5]. This is good to hear.

April 14th [Good Friday]
After service at Hoe superintended the distribution of a parochial gift amounting to about 5£. On the way home a poor man expressed his thankfulness for his portion of the dole, 3/-, and said that he never envied riches, his prayer being that he might have strength to earn his daily bread, more than which he did not desire. Within 5 minutes of this talk, met a most opulent Hoe farmer of whom I entertain better hopes than I do of some. I wanted him to subscribe to the schools, & after agreeing to all I said about education, vice, crime etc, he showed me some 'hoggets' with the view of turning the conversation. Fell in with his humour, but afterwards took up the old subject, which he thought I had forgotten – alas – he hung down his head, making no reply, & walked away under the hedgerow 'as men steal away in battle'. Towards God, therefore, the poor parishioner seems the richer of the two.

April 17th
After service, the Easter Vestry when a change of the people's warden took place for the better. Mr Wigg, an opulent yeoman 'of the old school' retires for a Mr Parker. Wigg's ambition seems to be to have it inscribed on his tombstone that he died 'deeply lamented & universally respected'. Being a man of no independence of thought or feeling, his object has been to offend no one, & therefore to do nothing.

Took the Chair at the Town Dinner and consequently was speechifying all the afternoon. The toasts, songs & speeches assumed more of a martial & patriotic tone than usual.

April 18th [London]
As usual was melted with pity for the poor beings living in Spitalfields, though there is reason to believe that they would not, after all, exchange their locale for the country.

April 19th
The Rev. G. Bull – an old Cambridge friend – said, among other matters of Auld Lang Syne, that the Gyp who used to wait on us at Cambridge, had been sent to college by some benevolent person, and was now the leading physician of the place.

April 20th
The 'skeletons', one of which is said to be in every house, are rather for showing themselves. The Challice's affairs are depressing, & of course affect my parents.

April 21st
In the evening, accompanied my Father to see 'Woodin's Carpet Bag & Sketch Book' This W. is a most versatile genius, and impersonated upwards of 50 characters, sang songs & told stories for more than two hours. His imitations were really admirable, & the rapidity with which he changed his dress, marvellous. His best characters are 'The Maid of All Work', 'Sir Benjamin Bungle' the 'Greenwich Pensioner', the 'philosophical Lecturer'. He impersonated Albert Smith to the life, & concluded by imitating the Wizard of the North[6], & by actually performing the 'Wizard's' great trick viz. he placed a page boy on a table, covered him with a large extinguisher, gave the table a tap (under the legs of which we could see) & behold the extinguisher was empty & the boy gone – where to is a mystery I cannot even guess at!

April 23rd
Having for some years wished to hear the celebrated Dr Cumming[7] of the Scotch Kirk, I was pleased to find he was going to preach in Halket Street this afternoon. My Father & I therefore went there, & so crowded was it, that, had we been a minute later, we should not have got in at all. It was difficult to believe one was in the vicinity of Belgravia, to see such a beggarly & unimaginative affair. A brawny Scotchman with a fearful twang & puritanical look, gives out, and

reads all through, a psalm nine verses long. This is a duet by the Clerk, & a young woman evidently provided for the purpose. The congregation took no part, nor was there a spark of that fervour I expected. Then Scotchy read a chapter of Revelations, & then treated us to a long, unmeaning, extempore prayer, ending with another psalm as tedious as the former, to the tune of 'Cambridge New'. At last, to our great relief, the Dr ascended the rostrum & preached a most eloquent sermon of one hour.

April 27th
Took Helen to see the Ladies go to the Queen's Drawing Room, & went to Bermondsey to take home my intelligent little nieces who had been spending the day at Wimpole St. Dr Challice, notwithstanding his pecuniary troubles, was concocting a letter to Lord Palmerston on Sanitary Reform! This is very stoical, & reminds me of the adage that it is easier to reform a Nation than to reform oneself.

May 1st
Took Helen to see The Armoury at the Tower – and the regalia. It is much improved since I last saw it, as indeed are all the public works. The manner in which the arms are disposed so as to represent trophies, stars etc. is very tasteful & curious. Among other improvements I was pleased to see a French interpreter who accompanies the numerous foreign visitors who come to see the dingy old fortress. The Regalia is worth three millions of money, exclusive of our old friend the Koh-I-Nor diamond,[8] who does not look any brighter, not withstanding his new cutting, than he did in the Great Exhibition.

May 2nd
Went on to Bermondsey, & was cheered to hear that their [The Challices'] affairs had assumed a more promising turn. I trust that the Dr may now learn that speculation on the Stock Exchange is unjustifiable & dishonest where we have not the means of payment in the event of failure. My dear sister has suffered sadly, & my Father also[9] 'in mind, body & estate'.

May 10th
A chemist in Dereham showed me a huge box which he filled weekly with pills for a travelling quack, who always disposed of his stock in that time. They were made, he said, of soap & other things which could do no harm.

May 12th

Mr Drake, who took tea with us, told some anecdotes about that most unpicturesque, & yet, in some respects interesting tract, called the Fens. He says it is so prolific, that a farmer had 600 acres, which produced him 9 Qrs. an acre (an ordinary crop is about 4 Qrs.) and that the father of that man, only paid 5£ an acre for the fee simple of the land. Also that Woad is grown in that district for dyeing. The crop is a beautiful blue colour, & contrasts pleasingly with the white fields of poppies, & the yellow mustard also grown there. He mentioned that when the waters were out, in that vicinity, two years ago, & many houses were deserted by the inhabitants for higher lands, the London thieves came in punts and carried off the furniture. Some of these having been watched into one of the houses standing out of the water, the natives came up in another punt, & took the thieves boat away. They did not go for them for two days, thus almost starving them, & when they did fetch them it was only to hand them over to the tender mercies of the law!

May 18th

Found I spent every penny I received, & though this cannot be considered as living beyond your means, yet Challice's affairs, & the increased taxation we shall have on account of the war, demand some retrenchment. I fear I must cease having a footman in the house, any inconvenience being preferable to the wretched conviction that one is living beyond one's income.

May 22nd

Drake showed me some Sikh weapons which young Oakes had picked up on the field of Sobraon.[10] It was curious to see what a very small handle there is to the largest swords, indicating the smallness of the hands, peculiar to all Asiatics. There is also a bow with a double string, connected in the centre with a small piece of cloth. From this, small stones are projected, as we should shoot arrows, & though they would be poor opponents to the Minie rifle,[11] yet they kill at some distance. Talking of the Minie rifle, some German Prince, a Turkish volunteer, the other day advanced to the front, coolly took off his gloves, & picked off several men at a mile distance, with one of these instruments. At length it was thought he had killed the General, but he had hit him, & knocked off his helmet.

May 24th

Mr Drake & Clark dined at the Vicarage. The subject arose of the travels of a sheep from first to last, before railroads. Being lambed in the grass by Lynn, they were sent to Norwich Market. There the graziers bought them to go into Lincolnshire. Having had the summer sun there, sent again into Norfolk to be sold at a fair. Bought by the Lynn people again to be artificially fatted, & finally sent to Smithfield. This would make the sheep's travels somewhere about 300 miles.

May 25th

Odessa stormed by the Anglo-French fleet, but an English ship destroyed by the Russians, & crew taken prisoners.

May 30th

Wholly employed as yesterday, with examination of the schools. Found some more bad cases, chiefly importations, & the men employed at the iron foundries, of which we have one or two. Found some of their children very ragged & dirty, & have devised measures for washing, clothing, & schooling them.

June 1st

Mr Raven showed me a beautiful optical delusion by the 'Stereoscope'. It is like a double 'Launette', & is for viewing daguerrotypes. The result is that the picture thus viewed, presents itself as a round solid figure. A curl of hair quite stood off his forehead – his arms were quite round & the silk of his cassock looked perfectly real. The principle is this. If you look at an object with one eye, & then with the other there is a certain amount of difference in what you behold. By placing therefore, two portraits, under a lens (one of which we will call the right eye-one & the other the left) they become in appearance one figure, with the wonderful rotundity before mentioned.

June 6th Whit Tuesday

A gay day for Dereham – and a busy one for me. At 11 the Odd Fellows came to Church in procession with their Banners & Music. I preached to them on Christian love. After service attended the monthly meeting of the Dis. Vis. Soc. and received the money which the ladies had collected for the Clothing Club. At 4 took the Chair at the Odd Fellows Dinner, supported by Mr Drake & Dr Vincent. The Assembly Room tastefully decorated, & 'the Chair' a perfect bower of flowers & evergreens. About 300 sat down. There was a good band and some professional singers, one of whom sang 'Mr Wilkins & his

Dinah', an absurd song, but highly popular nonetheless. After dinner the table presented a complete 'Chevaux de Frise' of clay pipes. Concluded the day by attending a Committee of the Institute to revise the rules & which did not conclude until 10.30.

June 7th

A recruiting sergeant being present [at the Odd Fellows' dinner], I got him to give thanks for the Army, in the course of which he mentioned the word 'duty' at least 7 or 8 times. What a household word this is, with the British soldier! It is said to be continually used in the Wellington despatches, while the word 'Glory' so dear to the French, never once occurs.

June 20th [London]

Met my friend Mary Hales & Mr North at the Water Colour Exhibition, & took them to see the Victoria Lily at the Botanical Gardens, of which my dear Father is a 'Fellow', though scarcely knowing a rose from a tulip.

June 21st

We called to lunch with a charitable Anglo-Catholic lady, Mrs Bayne, of the Regent's Park, & in the evening went to a party at Mrs Somerville Wood's. Lord Harrington's brother & the Duc de Roussillon were there, which said Duke (who though poor is really a man of high descent) once aimed at being master of No 7 (Wimpole Street) by marrying my aunt.

June 28th

In the morning to the Promenade Band at the Regent's Park. In the evening my Father gave a grand dinner to Mr & Mrs Pownall, Mr & Mrs Burchall, Major & Mrs Elsy, Mr & Mrs Arden, Mrs Hodgkinson, Mrs Wood, Miss Hales, Mr & Miss Kemshed etc. etc. I managed to have a good German Band playing in the garden at dinner. Mrs Wood's satellyte (sic), the Duc de Roussillon, came in the evening, & hearing my dear friend Mary Hales was well off, paid her some attention. I fear he is an adventurer.

June 29th

As a climax to our gaiety, my Father, Annie, Mary & myself went to the opera. It was one of Grisi's[12] farewell nights, and wreaths & bouquets were showered at her feet. The Opera was 'Don Pasquale' & the ballet 'Une Etoile', both I thought very poor, but the singing of Grisi, Mario, Ronconi & Lablache, of course magnificent.

July 5th

Another day at the Crystal Palace with my father. Thought it more beautiful & astonishing than ever. Many more people there, being a shilling day,[13] among them several Roman Priests moving about with that inquisitiveness & stealthy grace, for which their order is remarkable. Afterward enjoyed the great luxury (to me) of a ride in a penny steamboat, & dined at the Reform Club. The class rather respectable than aristocratic & the dinner plain, but very good.

July 10th

One of our labourers went into a field to catch a mule, when it turned upon him, threw him down, knelt on him, bit off his ear, lacerated his arm, & inflicted such injuries, that no hopes are entertained of the man's recovery!

July 13th

Took a funeral after Service. The deceased, a small farmer, died suddenly & without a will. The grief of the widow at the grave, very affecting to behold. Most of the bystanders overcome, but Philo, our sententious and matter-of-fact clerk, declares that such noisy mourners speedily marry again.

July 25th

Had all my haymakers to supper at a table under the trees, they smoked and sang songs till past nine. Mrs Grigson & Mary Hales joined us. The Choirboys had their first game of cricket on the newly mown grass!

August 21st

The School Fête, which was a counterpart of those in previous years. The morning was very wet & many a council of war was held with my wife, Mary, & myself, as to the advisability of postponement. However with bread & butter cut for 300 & tea made for the same number, this seemed to be out of the question. So the procession marched as usual from the School, the band playing, but the colours rather dripping than flying. During the service the rain descended in torrents on the Church leads, & the congregation looked almost reproachfully at me for the whole affair. At the conclusion we re-formed, though the rain had not ceased, but, (mirabile dictu) when we turned into the Vicarage grounds, the sun beamed forth and there was no more rain so there were country dances, & prizes & toys & games & music & flags &

swings, & wine for all the subscribers. Mr Barwell sent up a fine fire balloon at the conclusion, no doubt to the astonishment of the natives.

August 22nd

Visited several cottages on Etling Green whose inmates are, what the Norfolk folks call 'down' or 'set fast' with Typhus Fever. As the cottages were badly drained & very dirty & dilapidated, I went on to the landlord, and begged him to so something. Being poor and ignorant I have not much hope of him.

August 26th

By a letter from my father I find he has received one, with the intimation that 'Her Majesty has been graciously pleased to confirm the recommendation of the Marquis of Salisbury to appoint you a Deputy Lieutenant.' I'm sure my dear Father will never appear in the sort of General's uniform[14] worn by Deputy Lieutenants.

September 10th

After church a shocking report came to my ears. It was to the effect that our Organist (though not he who is at this time officiating) had attempted to commit a double suicide, first by poison & then by hanging. I immediately repaired to his house, & found, to my great relief, that he was taken by a friend for a drive. I could gain no information from the servant who was in an excited state, but the reason assigned for this rash act, is the misconduct of his wife. 'Professor' Martin, as his name plate styles him is a strange character. He can play the organ, teach singing, paint a little, carve a little, & it is true that he taught the Squire's daughter how to dance. With such varied accomplishments, it is not wonderful that he excels in none of them, while his bad temper & domineering ways make him a very unpopular character.

September 12th

Morning employed in going about the town with some other inhabitants as a Local Board of Health. When dining at Mr Nelson's of Beeston, accompanied by my father, a lady said that the dead were, in London, being removed in carts, as in the time of the Plague, and that Policemen were stationed at each end of Silver St and Regent St (a healthy portion of town) to prevent anyone entering it as the cholera was ravaging it. I am told the following was done in Norwich where the pestilence is also very bad. A piece of fresh meat being attached to a kite was flown up into the air for a couple of hours. When the kite had descended, the meat was black & putrid. This would make it seem that the cause of the cholera is in the air rather than arising from noxious vapours from the earth. It is said also said that there is something so deadly in the atmosphere that in Paris, numberless swallows fall down dead.[15]

September 30th
Drove Clarke to Watton to luncheon with Geo. Nelson, the curate. Found Nelson in a comfortable little house he has taken, which reminded me of the cabin of a ship. He complains that his wealthy young Rector does nothing but play cricket. It is a family living, & he is Lord of the Manor, & a Magistrate.

October 1st
At night news came of a great victory gained by the Anglo-French army before Sebastopol. The dispatch puts the dead & wounded on our side at 2,800, & adds that probably Sebastopol itself was by this time in our hands!

October 4th
After catechising and Dis. Vis. Society, had an early dinner and afterwards joined my family at Yarmouth. Mr Dennis Hill, a clergyman of the old school in the same railway carriage. He came down in a queer little miniature Tom Thumb sort of a chariot – his own idea – drawn by a donkey. He had his double-barrelled gun with him, with plenty of carpet bags, & said he was going to a large shooting party. Although upwards of 80 he said he could out-walk most of the younger men & rarely missed his aim. The old veteran was clad in complete black with breeches & gaiters, & was a perfect specimen of a bygone class of Clergy. With all their imperfections, however, it is impossible not to respect them, just as we do a dilapidated mansion because it is ancient & picturesque, though almost useless to anyone.

The only incident (at Yarmouth) worth remarking was the arrival of great numbers of Dutch craft from the herring fishery. An intelligent coastguard man told me some peculiarities of 'Mein Herr'. They were far less enterprising, he said, than the English, and they were quite outstripped by the French fishermen of Boulogne who also come here. Also that they ran inshore at the smallest indication of bad weather, & generally smuggled some scheidam[16] and tobacco. Their heavy flat-bottomed boats are brought so close to the surf that it was quite amusing to see them land on each other's shoulders.

October 9th

It seems that at the battle of Alma, the other day, 99 British Officers & 2,000 rank & file were killed or wounded. The Norfolk officers have been particularly unfortunate, & many county families are plunged in grief. It was estimated by the Russians that nothing could take the entrenchments under three weeks, but they were carried in as many hours. Marshall St Arnaud died of an internal complaint soon after the battle. The incidents of the conflict (as must be the case with modern warfare where hand to hand combats are rare) were few. A cannon ball passed near the Duke of Cambridge's head – a dog would not leave a slain officer – a pack of cards, & some copies of the Koran were frequently found in the Russian knapsacks of the slain – Prince Menchikoff's travelling carriage fell into the hands of the victors – and a Russian general was taken who said they thought the English good soldiers but now discovered them to be red devils.

November 5th

The Siege of Sebastopol continues, but the Allies do not seem to make much impression. War & cholera has thinned them sadly. What a Pandemonium must be created by the perpetual discharge of 3,000 guns!

November 13th

Dined at Quebec [House – the home of the Lee Warners] to meet another gay party who are staying there. Among them were Capt., Mrs & Miss Fitzroy, Rev. Burney of Hockering, Mr & Mrs Marsham. Capt. F. told a story connected with the present war, which proves that chivalry is not extinct. An officer in the Guards had arranged with his senior to purchase his commission. All was agreed upon, but as the vendor was on his way to sign the necessary papers he met a friend who informed him that war was declared with Austria. To sell out under such circumstances was out of the question. The negotiation therefore went off, but, said the senior to the junior, 'We shall go out, & perhaps you may get your promotion without purchase'. This actually occurred, the Senior was killed & the Junior succeeded him as matter of right, but he sent to the widow the sum of money which had been originally agreed upon as the price of the Commission. This was noble conduct on both sides! How different from the jobbing & distrustful method in which those sort of transactions are sometimes managed!

November 14th

Dined at Mr Cooper's to meet the Thorpes & Wollastons – a very slow affair – nevertheless as invited by my chief opponents, I at once accepted.

November 17th

Dinner parties seem endless, and there is always some reason or another why it would not do to decline.

November 19th

Have been dining out too much of late to suit either my health or inclination, but, situated as I am, it is often necessary to go, nolens volens. Fortunately it has not hindered my work, from which one derives more lasting satisfaction than from worldly gaiety & excitement.

November 20th

On the 5th of this month, a most terrific combat ensued between the English & the Russians at Balaclava. The enemy lost 8,000 men, the English 2,500. No less than 102 of our officers and 3 generals – Lord Cathcart, Goldie & Strangways were slain and 5 more generals were wounded. We claim the victory, but it can scarce be called such, at so dear a purchase. Sevastopol still holds out. Grief & enthusiasm are at their height. This disaster was caused by an error of Capt. Nolan. He was sent with a message from Lord Raglan to the cavalry, to the effect they were to charge, if practicable. He forgot to add the condition & hence the slaughter of the poor fellows who bravely rushed on to certain destruction. Nolan himself was slain, & the Duke of Cambridge had his horse killed under him. May those heroes rest in peace!

November 28th

Was wholly employed in driving about the Parish, & calling from house to house for the 'Patriotic Fund' for the widows & orphans of soldiers killed in the war. Alas! Although all contributed willingly, and most as much as they could afford, it was a case of 'Quot hominis, tot sententiae'![17] One thought there should have been a tax for this object (in which I agree) – another that we – i.e. myself & Parochial officers – were very late in the field – a third that there ought to have been a public meeting, speeches etc – a fourth suggested a concert for the purpose. In the absence of any one leading character in the Parish, the Vicar has to bear the brunt of it all, although taking all the trouble &

giving 5£ to the object, which is just four times what he can afford. Then others thought sufficient respect was not shown to them because they had not been consulted earlier. I fear this has been rather a vexatious & unpopular day. We collected 90£, however, & I attribute the above irritation chiefly to two causes, first, the soreness & anxiety in men's minds concerning our affairs in Turkey & Russia, & secondly that it is a relief to vulgar minds to have something to grumble about before they part with their money – the dissenters, as usual, gave next to nothing.

November 30th
An excellent attendance at the service. Glad to see the Lee Warners there as setting a good example. Miss L.W. told us afterwards the story of the beautiful Mrs Ives I lately met at Quebec. She was the daughter of a small builder in Norwich, & when about 16 years old, was seen by Capt. Ives, a person of property & station, in great distress at the loss of her dog. The Capt. gallantly got off his horse, & set the matter right. Was captivated, sent her to school, married her, & never regretted doing so!

December 6th
Found my Father & Mother quite well and no older, the former, as usual, immersed in Committees, Trials, Public Meetings, Justices visits to Prisons & Asylums, and so forth. In fact the active work of a Middlesex magistrate is a thing 'sui generis' – quite a profession of itself.

December 7th [London]
People very gloomy & sad at the aspect of affairs in the East. So many transports lost, that it is said that such destruction has not been heard of since the Spanish Armada. The Duke of Cambridge, who has had two horses shot under him, is returning invalided, and, shocking to say, insane. The horrors of war with all its ghastly sights & sounds, has proved too much for a brain prematurely disposed for this terrible complaint. The print shops full of battle pictures, & crowds are round them all. There are an unusual number of people in mourning.

December 8th
My dear friend Mary Hales had, with her usual energy, collected 25£ for the sick troops in the Crimea, & had invested in Flannel jackets & drawers (her own making) as well as railway rugs, Hare skins etc. etc.

She is half a mind to go there in Miss Nightingale's band of nurses, but I told her she would soon be among the nursed.

December 9th

In the evening my Father & I went to the Haymarket Theatre to see some famous 'Spanish Dancers' who are creating a great sensation at this time. They are beautiful girls & most elegant in all their movements which are full of beauty & poetry. Alas, alas, the reflection always comes how sad it is that so much that is so beautiful should be so closely allied with sin. Bouquets frequently were thrown upon the stage in compliment to 'Senora Perea Nena', the principal danseuse.

December 12th

Took my darling Helen to Mr Burchall's in Parliament St to see the Queen open Parliament, which she does at this unusual season in order to pass an Act conveying powers to employ the Militia on foreign service. The Queen & Prince looked well, & in the state coach with them was the Duke of Wellington who bears a strong resemblance to his father. The cortège was the same as usual but lacked some brilliancy from the deficiency of military. So short are we of soldiers & of cavalry horses that a company of Life Guards actually went on foot, & there were very few to keep the line. Among the company at Mr Burchall's were two persons announced as 'The Indian Princes'. These Hindoos were in their coloured and flowing robes, which had a tinselly & unreal appearance in the glare of day. Their names I will not presume to write but a General 'something' who acted as their interpreter, told me they were nearly related to the King of Oude. They were greatly scandalized, being Mohamedans, at being offered a slice of pork pie at luncheon. They drank no wine for the same reason. They had never before heard Church Bells ringing - those of the Abbey were pealing at the time.

December 13th

Morning employed in executing country commissions. Met Mary Hales at the Greenwich station & brought her to Wimpole Street, where was a large dinner party of upwards of twenty people. Mrs Byrne, whom I remember as Miss Prynne at Cambridge was an agreeable addition to the evening, and we were so merry over a 'petit souper' on her account that we not only agreed it was worth all the heavy formal dinners, but kept it up till 3 in the morning, to the destruction of my appetite & the acquisition of bile for three days afterwards.

The diarist's father in his Deputy Lieutenant's uniform

December 14th

All late at breakfast & very seedy.

It seemed strange passing by Harrow & arriving at Berkhamstead, our residences having been so often changed one hardly knows what place one most belongs to. Mrs Tawell,[18] the wife of the Quaker murderer, was in the carriage.

The Rev. Smith of Norwood called and told me that eight of his niece Miss Sellon's sisterhood had gone as nurses to the Crimea. The head of this band is a Miss Nightingale – a young lady of great piety & talent, who has gone out with the blessing, as it were, of the whole nation.

December 15th

Went with my Father to Nicol's the tailor, to be measured for his Deputy Lieutenant's uniform, in order for him to be presented at the first Levée.

Returned to Dereham by the evening express. Was observing to Lord Sondes, who was riding in the same carriage, how wonderful it was to get 127 miles in 3½ hours. 'Oh' said he 'that's nothing! I left Norwich this morning – have had four or five hours in Town, & shall be home for tea'.

December 19th

The 400 loaves annually given on St Thos's day usually cause such confusion in the church and in the hurry so many get them who ought not – that I determined this year to select the most deserving persons. To this end, I took my invaluable 'Speculum Gregis'[19] in hand, & accompanied by my curate drove all over the Parish for this purpose. Without a horse it would have taken three days instead of one, for we began at 11 a.m. and did not end until 5.30 p.m.

December 20th

Employed in telling families to come on Saturday for soup – in distributing bread tickets & in visiting the sick.

Ed. Hastings dined with us. Conversation on the nature of the 'monitorial System' at Harrow. It seems that the first 10 boys, in the 6th (i.e. the highest) form, are called 'Monitors', and that they are allowed to take cognisance of the faults & delinquencies of the other boys, and to punish them accordingly. This is generally done by, in

Harrovian language, 'whopping', which is agreed upon by the Monitors in conclave. They & only they are allowed to have 'Fags', but the fag is rather an appendage of dignity to his master & is not employed in menial offices. This system has been recently defended by Dr Vaughan – the headmaster in the public prints, but it surely seems open to the gravest objections.

December 21st
St Thomas. The gifts as usual brought a large number to Church, & many who had come only for the sake of them were much disgusted when told that they had been previously given to the poor.

December 25th
My happiness on this joyful festival somewhat shaded by receiving an anonymous letter reflecting on my Curate – insinuating in fact that he was given to drink. Neither myself, the Clerk with whom he lodges, or the Churchwarden who is mentioned in the letter is cognizant of the circumstance, believe a word of it.

December 27th
After Church, rode over to Hingham with E. Hastings to call on that remarkable and catholic old clergyman the Hon. Rev. W. Wodehouse. He said that Miss Nightingale, at Scutari, had declined co-operation with Miss Sellon's sisterhood on religious grounds. Surely at such a time & under such circumstances religious intolerance should never be allowed to intrude itself.

1855

January 2nd
Dined at Quebec, & took Miss Astley, sister to Lord Hastings, to dinner. That lady very agreeable, & amusing on the subject of 'Catholics' & 'Protestants' as she called them. Told the story of a nephew of the Duke of Norfolk leaving the Life Guards to turn Roman Priest, at the instigation of Cardinal Wiseman. Described him as young, handsome, wealthy & agreeable. Had she not been an old spinster should have begun to suspect she had a penchant for him herself.

January 4th

Among the numerous characters, difficult to manage with which a town clergyman has to do – such as Clerks, Schoolmasters, singers or organist – the bell ringers are often conspicuous. With so fine a peal as ours I have long ineffectually sought to properly organise these worthies by means of rules. To this they would never submit, till I hit upon the plan of declining to bestow my Xmas box till they did. After much vapouring & fuming & threatening not to ring out the old year with the usual 'muffled peal', these worthies have succumbed, & today brought their rules signed by them all. Nothing like determination in all such cases!

January 7th

Went to Church in some wretchedness caused by influenza & anxiety about my dear wife who, early in the morning, gave indications that her confinement was not far distant. After concluding my sermon on the Magi, packed off Ray to Norwich for the monthly nurse. They did not return until 9.30 by which time a fine girl was born, & the mother doing well. So here I am, at 37 years old, & looking much younger than that, with five children, one of whom only wants a few days to complete eleven years. It seems a great jump from four to five, and as I write I feel almost Patriarchal at being the head of such a large little family.

January 10th

Our Army cannot, as yet, take Sebastopol, & are decimated by privation & disease.

January 11th

In working with one's people for the common good, what encouragement is given them – what sympathy created between them & the poor & their Pastor, & how soothing to see the same face at evening devotion! Is this sort of thing the true 'work of the Ministry' in comparison with which, the mere Sunday preaching, is but a caricature of the clergyman's duty. And yet the trifling, dandified, morning-calling priest whose forte is to stand well, through these means, with the small gentry, is sure to be the more popular character. What are the poor to our worldly lawyers & doctors, but a race too low for their consideration?

January 12th

In the afternoon walked with my two girls to Northall Green with coal tickets for the poor. Although but four o'clock, one old widow was raking out her stove and was soon going to bed to save fuel. Her delight at the 3 cwt I gave her may easily be imagined. The rich & selfish know not what gratification they miss when they can confer happiness at so small a cost, and do it not. I believe, however, many rich persons who are not selfish would gladly secure to themselves the pleasure of doing good if only they were put in the way to do it.

January 13th

My cousin Henry Armstrong, mentioned in my father's weekly note is gazetted first Lieutenant of his regiment. This is owing to the kind interest of his step-father, Dr Piper, an Army surgeon, & who has been equally kind to his pretty sister. I remember the time when I should have jumped at such a chance, and even now, next to being what I am, were I a few years younger and single, I should prefer the Army to all other professions. Its regularity & soundness would suit me – its opportunity for foreign travel – of the best introductions – of leisure for literary & occasion for artistic pursuits – to say nothing of the chivalry attached to it, pronounce it to be the profession of my taste.

January 14th

Mrs Wollaston had the Vicar, Curate & Churchwarden to dinner, & the latter told this story of Mrs Lee Warner. When Miss Dering, and living with her father in the Fen district, riots broke out, after the late war, in consequence of the price of grain. So serious were they that the houses of Magistrates were burned, and no less than nine men suffered the extreme penalty of the law, at Ely, for crimes associated with the outbreak. Mr Dering, as a Magistrate was of course a marked man. It was known while he was among the mob & away from home that his house was to be attacked. But how to get the information to him was the difficulty. The men could not be spared, the women dare not go through such a mob to get at him. On this, the spirited Miss Dering disguised as a gypsy got to her father unmolested, & saved the premises!

January 18th

Called on Jeffreys, our amicable & respectful 'Independent' Minister, about arranging as to my delivering a Lecture to the members of the Institute & the Public. Agreed to do so. Poor fellow, he ought to be a priest. I was quite touched when I saw his little library, his

Meerschaum, & his flute, & regretted from my heart that his departure from the Church prevented intimacy.

Notwithstanding the snow there were several at evensong, when I had the misfortune to lock one of the singing boys in Church. Luckily I heard his cries before I had got too far, and a lump of plum cake soon appeased him.

January 21st

Mr Haggard attended service. He has accepted a captaincy in the Militia, & appeared with a most thriving pair of moustaches, which the infantry now wear as well as the Cavalry. He gets 200 a year by his commission, 10/- a day for lodgings & other advantages. Carthew dined with me, & in speaking of the love of Norfolk people for their county, he said it was so proverbial that when Norfolk men deserted from the Army, they always sent to their homes to find them, & seldom in vain.

January 31st

Two of my junior Parishioners have just taken their degrees, & have rather exemplified the old fable of 'The Hare & The Tortoise'. David Long, the son of a yeoman is 15th Wrangler, by sheer hard work; but Harry Drake, my Churchwarden's only child, appears very low in the Poll, though he was Captain of Eton. How often is this the case!

Our army in the Crimea is decimated, are suffering unheard of privations, & cannot yet take Sebastopol. In the Parliamentary debates it appears that the whole affair has been most shamefully mismanaged, & that, to use the words of Mr B. Osborne[1] the condition of the 'British Army is rotten to the core'. Our allies seem to have managed altogether as admirably – they carry our sick, lend us 2000 greatcoats – in short do our work for us! I was sorry to hear it said, by more than one member in debate, that England must now reckon as the second European power! The majority against the government was 157, composed of all shades of political opinions.

February 3rd

Went to Norwich by the market-train to hear an oration from the celebrated Father Gravazzi[2] on the subject of 'Nunneries', in St Andrew's Hall. He was dressed in a grey cassock, with an embroidered open Bible on the breast, over which he wore a long black cloak. He paced a platform, which he had all to himself, up & down, in the style of the Tragedians in a minor playhouse, & his gesticulations & ranting were outré in the extreme. In fact he is a complete mountebank, & except for his semi-popish costume it is very doubtful if he would 'draw'. In fact, the secret of the whole thing lay in the cloak, which he cast over his shoulder, under the arm, & so on, in the approved dramatic & Hamlet style. As for his matter, it was still worse than his manner, in fact perfect trash!

February 7th
Affairs in the Crimea most wretched! The Government at home is broken up & reconstructed. Ld Palmerston is Premier, & the Duke of Newcastle, Ld Aberdeen, & Ld John Russell retire from the Cabinet. It is on this trio the popular voice visits all the disgrace of the war. At Sebastopol our soldiers die at the rate of hundreds per diem through disease, exhaustion & neglect, and to judge from a sketch in the 'Illustrated London News' are more like Esquimaux in their wigwams, than the fine soldiers of our Army.

February 8th
Took my little girls to a concert given by our Organist Mr Martin, at which Miss Alleyne & Miss Lizzy Stuart sung. I was amused how 'humbug' was reigning supreme on this occasion: thus the giver of the concert styles himself as 'Professor Martin' & 'Herr Rust of her Majesty's private Band', is no other, notwithstanding his moustache & well-cut clothes, than plain Bill Rust of Dereham, whose father shoes horses & whose mother sells cakes & fruit. Moreover he is said not to be connected with Her Majesty except as a private & legal subject. Then there was Lieutenant Hill, the çi-devant Guardsman twirling his moustache at Miss Lee Warner, whose heart he is unable to subdue, & there was young Mr Goldson the lawyer 'improving the occasion' with regard to Miss Robberds, & there was the beautiful Kate Girling, without any lover, in an obscure little nook to herself – I believe half the people thought the music (which was very good) a consideration quite secondary to their own little plans & manoeuvres.

February 10th
The following is an extract from a letter yesterday received by my parishioner Mrs Ayers from her husband:

Abydos Hospital, December 27th 1854
'My dear Wife.....'
I am better than I was, thank God for it......and have been
here six weeks about 200 miles from Constantinople, and at

60

Scutari Hospital one month, before I came down here...I suppose you heard of the Battle of Alma? I was there. It was on the 20th September. I did not get wounded. It was [as] awful a battle that ever was fought by the British. There was great slaughter on both sides. The battle lasted 3 hours and 20 minutes, & was an awful sight to behold! We could hardly step for dead bodies. There they were, lying dead & wounded for six miles around!...It took two days to bury the dead.......there have been three battles fought at Sebastopol, but I was in neither of them being sick at the time, but Thank God I am getting better....I have not had any money for this six weeks, nor do I know when I shall [perhaps not] before the war is over, & I think that will last a long while. There is Sebastopol not taken yet. It is a very strong fortified town [having] 800 guns mounted around it, & great reinforcements of Russians.....I conclude with kind love to you and child, so no more at present from your..

'*Dearly Beloved Husband*'
James Ayers 77th Regiment

February 15th

Buried the corpse of a parishioner whose weight, with the coffin, was 60 stone. There was great difficulty getting him into the large door of the church, and great numbers came to see him buried.

My curate, Mr Clark, left me this morning, not to return; so at the commencement of Lent with its additional duties, I am left alone! The causes for this sudden & unlooked for separation are these. (1) His own affairs demand his presence at home. (2) He never was a good curate, being without method, & extremely forgetful. (3) His nervous temperament is such that he is occasionally quite beside himself, especially if unlooked-for intelligence arrives. (4) There does seem to be some ground for suspecting that he indulges in stimulants, & is therefore in bad odour in the Parish. I trust there is very little truth in this report, and that either his nervousness is mistaken for inebriety, or else that in the weak state of his brain, that effect is usually produced from a small quantity. This affair has been great grief to me, chiefly because I dread the scandal to religion which is likely to ensue from the prevalence of evil reports, true or false. What a trouble Curates are! I begin to believe the incumbent was right that said that 'his Parish caused him some anxiety, but his curate a great deal more'!

February 16th

Mrs Warcup, who called this morning, said that her son, a Naval Chaplain, was at Jamaica, and had become acquainted with a Baptist Minister there, who lived in greatest style. He drives a carriage & pair, keeps riding horses for his daughters & gives grand dinners. Singularly enough this person's mother is now living in Dereham. Her name is Filippo[3] and she keeps one of the lowest chandler's shops, in the lowest part of Town.

February 18th

The afternoon congregation was excellent for such exceedingly cold weather – indeed the Thames is nearly, if not quite frozen over in London, and people are expecting another Ox Roast as in 1814.

February 20th

Occupied in calling on the respectable parishioners with the view to counteract the evil impression with respect to Clark. It will be, as with the Apostles, that 'some believed the things that were spoken & some believed not'. I fear it is pleading a rotten cause, & that he is thoroughly bad, as well as half insane; my object is, as far as possible, to avoid scandal to the Church.

February 21st Ash Wednesday

Providentially, in the Crimea, they have milder weather. Alas, our splendid Army, which performed such wonders at Alma & Inkerman, has dwindled down to 10,000 men, who are, it is said, to stand by as a corps of reserve, & to let the French have the glory of taking Sebastopol.

February 24th

There are tens of thousands out of employ – bread riots have taken place in Liverpool & London – our Army is destroyed – the Cabinet continually changing, and the impression begins to gain some ground that 'England's Day is Over'.

During the service I thought much of poor Clark, who, I fear, is a confirmed drinker, though not a confirmed drunkard.

February 27th

Wrote to the Bishop requesting him to let me give a title to Orders for Dereham, and to appoint Mr Valpy Jnr. for Hoe – by which means I could obtain the services of two curates for the stipend of one.

Called on Mr & Mrs Brooman who, having taken Toftwood Cottage, are become parishioners. Mrs B. is the daughter of a neighbouring Rector, they have only been married a few days, & they are rendered unusually 'interesting' from the circumstance of the Bridegroom having only just returned from the Black Sea, & being about to start again, in a few weeks, for the Baltic, & of course leave his 'widowed wife' behind him. Mr B. who is quite a specimen of a sailor, saw the Battles of Alma & Inkerman, & his ship took part in the fruitless cannonade of Sebastopol. He showed me part of a Russian helmet he had picked up – the ball had taken away the other part, & at the same time, deprived the wearer of life. He says that nothing could have saved us at Inkerman had the Russians been sober, but, as it was, they were drunk – so much so that they often fell foul of one another instead of the enemy. All their cans, it was found, were full of raw spirit, the drinking which, when rendered thirsty by the smoke of Gunpowder, drove them to desperation. He says the Emperor of Russia can speak French & English as perfectly as his own language – that he calculated those two nations would never combine – and he gives five years as the probable duration of the war.

March 3rd
Buried another lunatic from the County Asylum belonging to this parish. These two men's illness began with lowness of spirits, & ended in raving madness. While in the Asylum they became great friends from discovering that they came from the same Parish. One day, Boyce took a pebble and threw it in play at Howard, as they were exercising in the Yard. On this, a desperate conflict ensued between them, & the result was that Boyce died a few days after, & was brought to Dereham for burial. Today I performed the last office for his antagonist.

March 7th
My dear Father is to be presented at the Levée today, & is introduced by the Marquis of Salisbury. His presentation is on his appointment to a Deputy Lieutenancy.

March 13th
Invitation from the Coopers. After Mr Clark's vagaries, I thought a refusal might be regarded as a Pharisaical 'straining at gnats & swallowing of camels'. We were invited to meet Mr & Mrs Neville, and a Mrs Maxwell, married daughters of Rev. Mr Mason – an aged clergyman of the 'Low & Slow' school whom circumstances have brought into our parish. It was of these ladies I wanted to write. These

dark gypsies, at the party, notwithstanding that their host & hostess were known 'Low', talked about the privilege of Matins & Vespers – the order & beauty of services in Dereham etc. They sang, with or without music – played bagatelle – have been much on the continent – & even acknowledged that they occasionally smoked a cigar!

March 14th
Continued to be much annoyed about Clark's matter arranging his debts, & silencing, as much as possible, the voice of scandal.

March 18th
I have just lost my curate, & now my manservant, & both suddenly. On Market day, I saw a very smart fellow in a new, Frenchified, but admirable uniform with a set of gaping rustics round him. On enquiry he turned out to be one of the newly organised 'Land Transport Corps', to convey stores from Balaclava to Sebastopol. He was offering recruits 2/6d per day, with good rations. This was too great a temptation for my man Ray, who, having a strong turn for the army (notwithstanding his father was nearly cut to pieces by the Sikhs) at once enlisted. He asked my advice, & I could not but give it in favour of his going.

March 21st
Was appointed a day of Fasting and Humiliation, on account of the War. It does not, however, seem to be taken up by the public. The late Ministry and their officials having greatly mismanaged affairs, and their conduct now undergoing a scrutiny in the Committee of the H. of Commons, it does not seem that there is a place for an appeal to the Almighty. If we put our head in the Lion's mouth, we must expect it to be bitten off, & Providence is not to blame. Our Army has gained the glorious battles of Alma & Inkerman, & although thousands have died in hospital, it is no more than the natural result of the Russian climate at this season on those unaccustomed to its rigours, & scantily provided against them.

March 25th
I have reason to believe that my late Curate has obtained employment near Leeds, without any recommendation from me, which has relieved me from much anxiety.

March 26th
What a sad winter is this! The Church services in particular very trying, in consequence of the coldness of the church, which is intense.

I wish Lent occurred about a month later than usual, by which the aged & infirm could avail themselves of the additional services. As it is, many are kept away especially as the wind comes down the beautiful Lantern-tower like a vortex.

March 29th

The tradesmen of Dereham are very respectable, being well-off, communicants, & well affected to the Church. The wife of one of them, an ironmonger, was one of the brightest, sensible, & well-disposed women I ever knew in her class of life. She was a District Visitor, inspected the Schools, & was very pious without one morsel of cant. This morning she came down to breakfast quite well, but subsequently fell back in an apoplectic fit & expired! The event created quite a consternation in the Town.

April 8th Easter Day

The day was fine, and the weather having altered for the better the bright Easter sun seemed to dispel the Lenten care under which we have been labouring.

April 11th

The Puseyite curate is unpopular because he won't dance, play whist, or fritter his time in gossiping morning calls. On the other hand, the Low Church Curate is fastidious & dandified, & rejoices in his eyeglass, lavenders & above all his huge whiskers!

April 13th

Capt. Bulwer said he had received a letter from the French Embassy today, in which it is said, that the Embassy had received an anonymous letter to the effect that the Emperor Nap. III would be fired at, at Charing Cross, during his visit to the Queen next week. This would be the deed of some Frenchman, the Emperor being at this time highly popular in England, not only because success has, so far, attended his grasp at the throne, but on account of the energy with which he carries on the war with Russia. It is singular that he should have once predicted of himself, that his end would be assassination in the Strand!

April 16th

Two hundred & ten children in the Schools. They seem flocking back like bees after the frost & cold. Deo Gratias. Made an arrangement with Miss Pollard, a governess of excellent Church principles, to educate my darling Helen, for three hours daily. I can but ill afford it, but education is everything. My dearest wife gives part of her pin money towards it.

April 20th

An equestrian 'Troupe' being in the town our children accompanied the little Gregsons to see it. Having seen them seated I went away to my work, & returned for them towards the close of the performance. 'Papa', said darling Helen 'I do think that dirty little girl sucking the orange is she who rode so beautifully in the gauze frock'. ...It turned out that Helen was correct. The poor child told me (notwithstanding the feats she performed on the spotted but jaded charger) that she had only practiced horse riding one month, but that her 'proper business was the tightrope', & that she was 'beautiful in that': that she should have danced today only her chair & pole had 'gone to be mended'! What a little piece of precocity – a veritable infant phenomenon, only 10 years old! Alas Poor child! Are innocence & virtue possible amid such scenes as you live in? Would that you were in the homely garb, even with a dirty face, than with painted cheek & gauze!

May 5th

The flexibility of voice – the judicious emphasis – the use of the eye & sometimes of the hand – these are the knacks of effective preaching, by the use of which an indifferent sermon may be rendered palatable, whereas the finest discourse wd. lose almost all its effect by the want of these requisites. How very rare it is, though, to hear a preacher of this stamp. At the time I write, out of all the preachers I have ever heard, Manning, Bennett, Monro, the Bp of Oxford, Dr Cumming, Baptist Noel, Dr Hook (rather heavy) and Cardinal Newman are the only ones whose manner and style, though very different, have made any lasting impression.

May 9th

Gave a private reading of my lecture, originally delivered at the Institute, at the Vicarage to which 30 of our better sort of parishioners were present. The evening, from 7–12, appeared to pass quickly enough, & all expressed themselves much pleased. Our object was to introduce a better sort of thing than country evening parties usually are – something in the 'At Home' and 'Conversazione' style. This however is very difficult with those who have not seen much of the world, & whose idea, in going to a party, is that they are to be amused, & need contribute nothing towards amusing one another. With the view to improving the taste in this matter I introduced a verbal picture of the sort of evenings of this sort we used to enjoy in Paris & it certainly had the immediate effect of putting people at their ease, & making them feel at home, which is the first lesson in the art of behaving at evening parties. Illustrated my characters by producing a French Shako, a pair of Sabots, and a Russian helmet, taken by Capt. Bulwer at the Battle of the Alma.

May 11th

In the afternoon was minded to have an hour's trout fishing at Bilney. The earlier part of this diary will show that I was once a keen sportsman in my little way, but I gradually saw that such pleasures are incompatible with our sacred calling, & so first shooting & then hunting were abandoned. For some reason, however, fishing does not seem to labour under this disadvantage. Either Isaak Walton's book, or the fact of the Apostles being fishermen, or the solitude & quiet implied by the practice of the art, have exculpated the fishing rod, while the ramrods & the Nimrods have been found guilty. Nevertheless I am losing some of the intense gusto with which I used to handle even this harmless weapon, & want the additional inducement of the company of a friend to make me sally forth. For once, however, & Friday being my only spare evening, I went – it was very cold & wet, so that I almost despaired of my usually good success – nevertheless I bagged 5 brace of trout, & only left off fishing when I could see no longer.

May 23rd

I enjoyed the best sport I ever had in trout fishing, in Mr Girling's stream at Scarning. This was attributable to the late rains and also to the circumstance of the Mill above sending down a large supply of water. I never knew trout so ravenous! They bit so fast & greedily that I almost got tired of catching them, & filled my pannier so full that I was unable to get in another fish.

At a later period of the evening when the water was stopped at the Mill, and had fallen, the fish ceased feeding, and neither artificial fly or worm would tempt them. I consider it a great privilege to have such fishing within a mile of home, & with my success at Bilney the other day, have already killed 28 trout this season, in two afternoon's sport!

May 27th

To my astonishment & annoyance, a letter came from Lady Talfourd[4] to say that her son, who was to have been ordained to this curacy next

Sunday – declines entering the Ministry on the grounds of conscious personal unfitness. One cannot but respect scruples of this kind, but they should have been earlier expressed, as I have, of course, refrained from seeking a curate thinking all was settled. I seem to be doomed in the matter of Curates!

May 29th

Mr Carson, the Rector of Scarning, preached the Sermon to the Clubs, who came to Church as usual & deported themselves with great propriety. I afterwards took the Chair at the Annual Dinner to which about 150 sat down. It was amusing, on this, as on all similar occasions, to observe how each person fell naturally & unconsciously into his own place, the finest grade of superiority being acknowledged in the position of the guests.

June 3rd

Preached a funeral sermon in the morning for poor Long – half the congregation in tears. In the afternoon on the Trinity, & chiefly on the success of the Holy Spirit, was vigorous almost beyond my strength, and half inclined to quite leave my MS. and extemporize. Am sure I could if I had more contempt for my hearers & more reliance on myself. Here I am wanting, but cannot dis-entrammel myself. Alas! We Anglicans are only amateurs. We have never been taught how to preach. And yet, with a little more encouragement, I feel that I could do this, though my sense of taste and horror of twaddle or tautology, absolutely debar my making the attempt.

I almost envy – happy, most happy, as I am, in my dear wife & children – the humble curate, who, untrammelled by 'position', & the calls of Society & of family, can give all his time to his Master's work.

June 4th

As my choristers have long sung at the daily service without further fee than their Christmas contribution, I resolved to take them to Lowestoft for the day's excursion. They were 11 in number, & our town Churchwarden, who voluntarily almost acts as Schoolmaster to them, & who himself, with three other adults, sings in the choir, accompanied us. We all started at 6.13 in a third class carriage, & enjoyed a brilliant day at the sea. As only three of the little fellows had ever seen it, their exclamations of delight were loud & frequent – the most ordinary acquisitions found on the beach were esteemed prizes – they actually revelled in the pleasure. A more beautiful sea I never beheld. There was a high wind causing the waves to fling their high crests in all directions, & as the sun shone brightly & there were some dark clouds, their reflection on the water produced the most beautiful effects. In these lengthened stripes of light green or black many vessels were sailing at great speed, their white sails contrasting favourably with the dark shadows. Having taken a plentiful supply of roast beef & plum pudding, Mr Churchwarden & I set it out for the lads in a 'curing house' the use of which was willingly accorded to us by as veritable a 'Peggoty' as the one immortalised by Dickens. Our friend caught & cured his own fish, & indeed we found him in the act of speculating whether he should be able to sally forth that night or not. He was surrounded by some 'mates' of the roughest features and dress, but civil in their manners, one of whom had had his arm jammed off between the lifeboat he was in & the vessel she went to save. The curing of herrings it seems is simple to a degree. They are salted immediately they are caught – strung upon wooden spits across a beam for two days and nights over a fire of oak logs – packed & sent to all parts of the world. Ash will serve the purpose but not so well as oak. The fires are made on a brick floor, & as there is purposely no chimney, the house is so full of smoke, that during the curing it is hardly possible to enter it. After dinner at the Inn, Parson, Churchwarden, & choir arrived home at 9.00 pm very much pleased with their day.

June 23rd

Discoveries have been made relative to my late curate which have filled me with distress of mind, acting upon my physical health far more than any amount of work could do! I hope my chagrin at scandal thus accruing to the Church is not greater than my regret at the disclosure of his wickedness! God's will be done!

At Sebastopol an attempt of the allies upon some of the principal works has been 'unsuccessful' – it is said that 4,000 of ours are slain! At Hango in the Baltic, the Russians have fired upon a flag of truce carried by a boat's crew & and have destroyed or taken prisoner everyone, except a poor black, who fell wounded in the boat, which drifted out to sea of its own accord while he lay invisible, and saved him. Called yesterday on some people who have taken Haggard's house at Bradenham. They are partly Russian, Gellibrand by name & have resided 22 years at St Petersburg. They say that in winter it is daylight there till 12 at night. The G's speak highly of Nicholas in all respects, giving him credit for sincerity of motive in undertaking the war as a crusade against the Mohammedan power. Whatever politicians may say about 'the balance of European power', and the 'cause of liberty & civilisation', how can we hope for ultimate success if it be the design of Providence that through the influence of Russia, the Crescent should at length succumb to the Cross?

July 3rd

Drove my Churchwarden Mr Drake to the visitation at Attleborough. The choral singing very good, but the sermon one of the most vague & desultory I ever had the misfortune to hear.

Dined with Fowell at Drake's. The former a man, apparently, of earnest mind. May God's blessing be upon his labours here! Said he had a living in which Chobham camp was situated, & that in his ministrations among the soldiers, found that the 'Guards', both officers & men, less open to religious impressions than all the other troops. His experience was that the Presbyterian Scots were the best educated but the most drunken & disorderly, & the Popish Irish, especially the 88th the most devout, but no better than the rest after their religious observances!

July 5th

A day which will long be remembered in Dereham, being the wedding of our young 'Squireen'. I had the church decorated with wreaths of flowers made by the schoolchildren & disposed by myself. The Church was absolutely crammed with people, many of whom had come in from the neighbouring villages on the occasion of the fair. The numerous bridesmaids with pink & white, & others with blue & white, made a goodly show, & the effect was good, when headed by the two officiating priests Mr Dashwood of Stow Bardolph, (the bride's guardian) & myself, the train moved from the Vestry and the organ burst forth. The school children were ranged along the church path, scattering flowers, headed by my darlings, Helen & Louisa, who performed their part very well. The Luncheon & the Speech-making were as usual, and at an early hour the happy pair drove off for Lincolnshire, en route to Scotland. In the afternoon went up again and presided at the banquet to the poor, & came home hoarse with shouting and poisoned with Tobacco smoke. Thus I have lost a charming, interesting and well-disposed parishioner, and one whose happy forte it was, by an unconscious kind of tact to accommodate herself to those inequalities of condition always to be met with in country towns. She has every qualification, I am sure, to make her husband happy.

July 6th

My dearest wife, our five darlings, and two nurses all went to London by the Railway, & arrived comfortably at dinner at Wimpole Street. In the evening looked in at the Princess's Theatre to see Charles Kean[5] play Cardinal Wolsey in Shakespeare's Henry VIII. It was admirably sustained & Wolsey's conduct on the news of his downfall fulfilled all one's expectations.

July 7th

In the evening my dear Father would have me hear a young Baptist preacher, at the Diorama[6] in the Regent's Park, which Sir S. Peto has converted into a Meeting House at vast expense & gives the preacher 700£ a year. He is worth the money, and, barring his Yorkshire dialect, is quite equal to Dr Cumming. The room held an enormous congregation, and Mr Landels[7] preaches from a superb octagonal stone pulpit, lined with Crimson cloth, large enough to contain four or five persons, & fit for a Cardinal. He had no robes, & was purely extempore. The eloquence & force are very remarkable, his action not excessive, and his warmth great, though never degenerating into fanaticism. Speaking of how impossible it was for the worldly to discern spiritual things, he said that Wilberforce took Pitt to hear Cecil[8], and that the great minister declared he did not understand one word which the preacher had been talking about.

In the evening my Father & I strolled into the Spanish Ambassador's Chapel, which is always open for service or Confessions. On this occasion nothing was going on except the latter. Everything was very orderly & still. The Penitents were chiefly females, but the instances to the contrary were a private in the Guards, & a very gentlemanly youth who stepped out of the Confessional just after we entered the Chapel. It looked like a real work was going on, and one in which strangers had no right to intrude. On returning to the back streets, amused at crowds at a corner shop, devouring hot stewed eels & giving them to their children – a horrid production at 2d per basin.

July 8th

Returning in the carriage by Buckingham Palace we were ordered back by the Police in consequence of the rioting which had been going on for some Sundays. The mob stop the carriages, ill treat the servants, &

compel the owners to get out & walk, crying all the while 'Go to Church'![9] Saw the mob coming & the coachman had only just time to turn U and drive back as quickly as possible. The row is caused by an unpopular Bill of Lord R. Grosvenor for the better observance of Sunday, which the mob will have it is levelled at their enjoyments and does not affect the rich. The row is so formidable that the Lords, by an unwise and timid policy, have withdrawn the Bill – a triumph for 'King Mob' & a very dangerous precedent for the future.

July 9th
Walking in the evening with my Father, saw a Penny Exhibition viz the 'Hydro Incubator'. The chickens thus artificially produced appeared equally as strong & healthy as those produced in the ordinary way. Almost next door was another penny exhibition, viz one of those execrable theatres or 'Gaffs' which do so much to demoralise the crowds of dirty, precocious boys & girls we saw coming from them. Being very enquiring, I should have liked to see what was the nature of the performance, but it was so low I could not do it. Next door to this again was a Public Soup Kitchen – so that in one block of houses here was rational amusement, low vice & public benevolence, each at a penny!

July 10th
Having to go to the City to pay my Life Assurance, drove the nurses and children to Vauxhall Bridge for the Boat, in order to show them the great buildings on the route. Fortunately the Queen & the Royal Princes drove by, giving these East Anglians a sight they never expected to behold. The ride on the water refreshing, except for the stench of the water. What a pity this noble river should be made a common sewer! How unfortunate that evils of this kind are seldom cured till they become so intolerable that the very force of circumstances demands it!

July 11th
Hunted through the Registry of Curates at the Society, and took the particulars of four. It is said that the war will cause a dearth of candidates for Holy Orders, the men entering the Army instead.

Dined at the Mansion House 'to meet' as the invitation ran 'The Most Noble The Marquis of Salisbury & the Middlesex Magistrates'. Having before described a Lord Mayor's banquet, I shall say nothing of the luxuries on the table, the music, the lights, the statues, the banners & all the glories of the Egyptian Hall. Certainly nothing could be fairer than the scene, or worse than the speaking. Two members of the House of Lords spoke best – but only moderately. How is it that the aristocracy do not cut a better figure than they do! With all their immense advantages of education, experience, prestige, how very ordinary they look! Here was one looking like a cadaverous Methodist, another like a German Pipeseller, a third so lost in a huge shirt collar that it is hard to say what he *was* like. Even the wretched oratory of the Chief Magistrate – his jumbling cause & effect – his rushing into a metaphorical idea & almost immediately abandoning it – and his ruthless disregard of poor letter 'H' – all this, I say, is more excusable in one risen from the people, than the better but still poor exhibition made by the Grandees. How can we expect the lower orders to feel much sympathy with the nobility or to care to 'keep up' The House of Lords? And yet, the Magistrates seemed to regard them with intense admiration & to hover about them in hopes of a nod or a smile! But the privilege of rank is not restricted to them! We are sad slaves, & the longer I live the more I see how rare is true independence of spirit!

July 16th
The streets full of 'Perambulators', a baby carriage quite new to me, whereby the children are propelled by the nurse pushing instead of pulling a little carriage. Got into a Bus, which contained a Capt. Atcheson – a madman certainly to judge from his vehement conversation on religion. He seems to be well known in London, is said to carry a lighted spirit lamp in the Bus, & to request the passengers to permit him so to hold it, that they may inhale its contents which imparts a new life, he says. They say he has been tried for murder. He is a great preacher in the park & described himself to me as 'lay surrogate of Montreal' whatever that may be!

July 21st
Had a luxurious Bath for 6d being the charge for 'First Class' at the Baths & Washhouses in the New Road. One of the cheap luxuries with which this age & particularly this city, abound.

July 24th
A garden party at Mrs Atkinson's at Ealing, some patients of Dr Challice through whom we were invited. This is the right sort of entertainment in the dog-days, but the English not up to it, & it is therefore rather apt to hang fire. However, though the company was

not aristocratic, & the letter 'H' was generally ignored, there was everything which a kind heart & great wealth could provide.

August 1st

Dr Challice told me the story of Lady Molesworth, whose husband's return for Southwark he had been instrumental in promoting. She was found on the field of battle at Waterloo, no one knowing her parentage – was educated by a benevolent person who afterwards married her and, on her becoming a widow, was subsequently united to Sir W. Molesworth.

Took the children to see the taking of Waterloo at the Surrey Gardens. The scene is partly natural & partly artificial, and the illusion is so good that, when lighted up, it was quite impossible to discern between the two. Of course there was a large amount of firing, but no one feigned to be hurt, & the confusion was so great that the spectators were in doubt whether a heavy mass of pasteboard troops were Russians or Scots Greys. The gardens were crowded & people well conducted.

August 5th

Was sent for to two cases. One, a young man whose Christian name is Nicena, named after that creed. His sister's name is Brittanica – the father being a patriot as well as a churchman, in fact both these sentiments being a sort of hobby with him. The young man, who has led rather a reckless life in Town, dreadfully alarmed at the prospect of death, & earnestly desirous of making his peace with God. The other case, that of a young woman, precisely similar. Both these cases require great care & attention – may God enable me effectually to minister to their comfort & spiritual advantage.

August 9th

This war [in the Crimea] doubles the income tax. This year £100 of tithe is only worth £89, & this, with the expenses of exchanging the Glebes & enlarging the house, has so reduced my income as to cause my expenditure to exceed it: our total nett income being under 600£ a year. On making this discovery I was so alarmed that I discharged my manservant, turned my nag out to graze, & gave away the unprofitable cocks & hens. I know my dear Father would not like this, & would willingly send me some cash, though he has been subject to many calls through the affairs of Dr Challice. But it is far better not to be thus suing for cash, & to have the comfortable and independent feeling that you are living within means. Let my dear boys remember this!

August 10th

Made the curious discovery that a certain Estate in this Parish, belonging to Fountain Wilson Esq., a well known character in Yorkshire, is tythe free, but that the owner thereof is subject to a payment to the Vicar of 'twenty-four shillings and a shoulder of venison'. Now, as I have been Vicar almost or quite five years, the eccentric Mr Wilson owes me 5£ and nearly a whole buck! This matter must be looked into, for the curiosity of the thing as well as the value. I should like the taste of that venison very much! Several visitors among the Parishioners, also the Lee Warners', & the High Sheriff's family, the ladies on horseback, to invite us to dine at Letton next Tuesday.

August 14th

Dined at the Gurdons, surrounded by all that wealth & good taste could suggest. The ladies of the family, as usual, most agreeable, diversifying the evening with music & singing. The Edwardes of Hardingham, The Johnsons of Yaxham were the only people we knew, the party mainly consisting of the visitors staying in the house – one of those charming meetings for which English country life is so remarkable.

August 17th

Drove Fothergill & my dear wife to Watton, to call on Mr Hicks, the Vicar, and his wife - who showed us the restorations in the Church, consisting of a fine organ, a Roodscreen, Altar, painted window, and open benches where he could obtain permission from their occupiers. Among other curiosities brought to light was the 'Leper's Door' through which those unfortunates were able to see Mass performed without the necessity of entering the Church, which was of course forbidden. Also a curious painted wooden figure over the poor chest, so managed that the contributions seem to fall into a bag, whereas they tumble through it into the box. Mr H. said a workman in the Church once stole this figure, which looks like the Idol of the place, & settled afterwards in Liverpool. Failing there, he sold off his stock at auction, among which was the 'idol' aforesaid: this was recognised by a Norfolk man who was present, who purchased it, & sent it back to Watton, where he is perched, as grim as ever, with his nose knocked off & a malevolent scowl on his countenance like a heathen God. The date carved beneath is 1639, & I confess it would have been as well had he been shipped off to America instead of being sent to Watton.

September 1st

During a call on a lady of Church principles staying at Mr Aufrere's, heard that a cottager hard by had fallen from the rick while harvesting. Poor John Wilson! There he was, crushed & dying, & with half his body paralysed – the wife & children weeping around his bed – his life not over good – and the grave staring him in the face.

My dear Father in his weekly note tells the catastrophe of my cousin Ed. Armstrong. It seems he was ordered out to suppress a rebellion on the W. Coast of Africa, & out of 260 men under his command, 80

The Leper's door and the Poore Box in Watton church
By consent of St Mary's Church, Watton

were killed or wounded. His own right arm is so shattered that amputation was considered necessary. He received it under the influence of chloroform, & without pain. He is said to have been a general favourite, was recently appointed Adjutant, & Lord Panmure had been written to by his Col. to confirm the appointment.

September 7th [Wymondham, Norfolk]

There was that miserable Presbyterian arrangement of clerk's desk, writing desk & pulpit one above the other, just before the Altar, in which the Vicar preached the lessons & prayers. There were pews, high & doored, a most haggard & pauper-looking collection of poor, & in the Rails the Bishop & a curate in a black gown, who we may suppose was to be ornamental as he was no use whatever.

September 11th

After eleven months siege Sebastopol, at all events the larger portion of it, with the Malakoff Tower, the key of the whole position, is TAKEN by the Allies. On ascertaining this by the papers, I ordered the bells to ring, & they are pealing merrily while I write at 11.30 p.m. The people have hung out flags, are firing off guns, throwing fireballs in the Market Place – and waking my children by the unwonted row. It is feared that the sacrifice of life is fearful but of this we know nothing as yet. The Russians adhered to their old policy of blowing up their magazines and burning everything, even to their men of war.

September 13th

It seems that at the repulse of the Redan Battery at Sebastopol, shortly before the taking of the Malakoff Tower, the British had 1,500 men killed & wounded, among them nearly 150 Officers. The excitement & enthusiasm are so great that I must make allusion to this great victory in my Sermon on Sunday.

September 17th

Mr Cook of Leicester[10] having planned an excursion to N. Wales & Ireland, & undertaking to convey any individual from my parish to Dublin and back, first class, for 42/-, I thought it a chance not to be thrown away. Started by the 10 o'clock train to Lynn, and as we had to remain there a couple of hours, introduced my father to the pretty town walks. At Peterboro', the delay was just enough to go into the Cathedral. Presently Oakham appeared, the diminutive capital of our smallest county, & where every Peer, on passing through, has to present a silver horseshoe to the town, which are nailed up in the court-house – at least so we were told by an Irish fellow-traveller with a strong lisp, but who seemed quite au fait in this country. He said King John imposed this on the Peerage in return for some favour conferred on himself – a very convenient & cool method of getting rid of an obligation by shifting the payment upon others – a 'dodge' not peculiar to Royalty![11]

September 18th

Mr Cook of Leicester, who plans these excursions, was a great man today. Crowds obeyed his directions implicitly, & evidently regarded him as an infallible authority. Frantic & agitated females such as are always to be seen on Railway Stations, but who on so large a one as this, are worked up into a state of unwonted excitement on account of doubtful suspense – I say even these obey Mr Cook, & their minds relieved by his direction, are at peace. Now we are off, in a train a quarter of a mile long, whistling away through the green pastures of Staffordshire. These sylvan retreats passed, we come to a very different, but deeply interesting, class of scenery. Immense heaps of broken earthenware – piles of iron & of breeze[12] – innumerable kilns and flaming ironworks all betokened that we had arrived at the famous Potteries.

September 18th [en route to Dublin]

We are placed on a huge dirty steamer called The Ocean, with merchandize, horses, & several hundreds of the poorest Irish returning from their English harvest! There was no alternative but to go, or lose a day at Holyhead, which seems a miserable place enough! There was no provision eatable – except half raw mutton chops which were utterly impracticable – but there was superb whiskey, which, with a crust of mouldy bread, and some cigars we had fortunately in our pockets, sustained us through the night. The evening was so starlight, & the water so calm, that we remained on deck, and, on the whole enjoyed the thing much better than we thought. I cannot say much for our companions who joined us somewhat unceremoniously in our snug nook, protected by the 'goods' from the wind. They seemed 'staunch' and rather bitter protestants, one speaking in praise of Orangeism & the other, a low coarse fellow, of 'Irish Presbyterianism' – poor Paddy with his tail coat, felt hat & sickle would have been more a companion to my taste, but the stench arising from so many of them, precluded all communication, though I meditated it more than once.

September 19th, [Dublin]

I have come to the conclusion that Dublin is, after all, a fine city, but its great natural advantages are, in great measure, thrown away, by the delapidated, shabby-genteel appearance of its best parts & principal inhabitants. The lower orders are in dress & appearance almost repulsive while even the best I have seen are not absolutely free from the stigma. We began with a look in at some of the Romish places of worship – the architecture Doric & unecclesiastical – the Altars, confessionals and furniture not only trumpery, but revolting. Filth reigned supreme! Ragged boys with naked feet frolicked on the floor, which was broken, & even the Holy Water was muddy & foul. How crazy & tumble down the confessionals, how bare of ornament (a wondrous thing for a Roman church) the whole affair – had it not been that some, even amid all this wretchedness, were offering the sacrifice of praise, I should have turned from the sight with loathing & disgust. As to the purlieus of the 'Cathedral', they presented an intensity of vileness beyond description; every baker's, every gin shop, every pawnshop were strongly & firmly barred without, – a meet precaution in such a neighbourhood. Yet I have said Dublin is a fine city, and it is. I like Trinity College, though the Chapel has a Presbyterian look, & the student windows were dirty & oftimes broken. A man showed us around in a sort of hunting cap, having an appearance of the Fire Brigade & neither academical or ecclesiastical.

A word about the carmen. The first asked us 6/- to drive to the park (about 2 miles), the next 4/-, the third 2/-. This moderate 'boy' was ragged in the extreme, could not read, was a Catholic – went to Mass on Sundays & 'Holy Days' – had never been beyond the Dublin Mountain.

At one o'clock we went by Rail to Maynooth & spent a very agreeable & interesting afternoon there, the country was fertile, abounding in wood, water, & pasture, with a range of mountains for a background. At Maynooth we found although there is the College as a humanising influence, & the Duke of Leinster as a resident landlord, filth, a half-naked population, whining beggars, stagnant ditches, vile curs, and dejected looking ducks – the dung, straw & offal in the streets are dreadful to behold.

September 20th [in Dublin]

One is better able to judge of people & things by coming in personal contact with them, than by all the description in the world. Thus the neglect & deceitful blarney of this people were well shown in a character I came across this morning. I wanted my hair cut, & was directed to a native artiste in Sackville Street. Could not find him for some time, but was at last directed to his 'rooms', in one of which he was following the occupation of watchmaker which he united to that of hairdresser, though it is not easy to trace the connexion. The rooms were large & dirty – the quicksilver in the looking glass half-gone, the table broken – the paper torn. All barbers seem to consider talking as part of their craft & mystery, so, in reply to his question what I thought of Dublin, I owned its beauty, but regretted the rags of many of its inhabitants. To all this he agreed, & even seconded with warmth my arguments in favour of neatness, when lo! on his turning round the man himself had three absolute tatters in his coat, & an unmistakeable rent in his trousers! He charged me the sum of 5d – and these rags & dirt were in the heart of the fashionable quarter, & indulged in by a member of a trade usually natty, & that almost of necessity in the proper carrying out of the art.

September 21st

While posting our letters another of those extraordinary Irish funerals passed. A hearse drawn by six horses, & ornamented with white feathers & carved at the sides with scriptural & allegorical figures – went first: next followed no less than 47 cars, loaded with men, women & children, some smoking, others chatting, & not one in any kind of mourning. As a cemetery is always interesting the idea struck me of following this motley group, to see the proceedings at the funeral. The priest, without any robe whatever but a soiled stole of velvet & silver, read some prayers in Latin, the responses being made by a boy in rags, whose Latin was with the true Hibernian brogue. At a certain part, he ceased, and solemn & impressive silence was maintained, the Priest standing by, while the earth was filled into the grave, & the corpse buried – then resuming the prayers, sprinkling holy water with the 'asperges', & giving the benediction, he departed. Another odd scene occurred. Two boys (in rags, & without shoes of course) held the ends of a stick, from which something was suspended by a string. As they were accompanied by a woman with an infant, I thought the lads were bringing dinners to their fathers, who were perhaps working at the column. It was, however, their little dead brother or sister, in a box of the roughest possible make. The sexton – a villainous looking fellow – placed it in a grave very little below the surface: no Priest was there, & while the mother sobbed, the sexton shovelled away, & smoked his pipe. I stood under a tree till all was completed & the mother moved away. 'Have you no Priest' said I. 'No, yer honour' 'Was the child unbaptized?' 'Oh sure, no; it is a year and a half old, & the priest baptized him.' But the mystery was cleared up by a notice at the gate informing the public that if corpses were not brought before 12 o'clock, they must remain in the dead-house until the next day; but the poor mother being unable to arrive in time, or perhaps to come again on the following morning, had her child buried without benefit of clergy. Yet, touching as is this, how differently would English parents have behaved, in making the proper enquiries beforehand! In the afternoon we were astonished to see our funeral performing Priest jaunting to the city in a covered car with three or four fat girls, whose hilarious laughter showed that the previous ceremony had been soon forgotten!

September 22nd [returning via Wales]

One always feels thankful at having safely crossed the sea, & the feeling was enhanced today, by seeing a Government steamer with her mast carried away, & side smashed, by being run into last night by an outward bound ship. The sailors said that if the sea had not been calm, she would have gone down instantly.

In the evening we arrived at Bangor, & being recommended to 'Miss Roberts' Hotel', drove there in the bus. It turned out, to our dismay, that Miss R. lived by the Menai Bridge in a private hotel, with gardens tricked out in spruce & cockney fashion. As the Table d'Hôte was just commencing, we joined it, & had an inferior dinner but with lots of Electroplate and a German Band in the garden. The gardens over-looked the Straits and the opposite shore looked like so many glow worms in the moonlight. Miss R. was a specimen of 'the strong-minded woman' – a regular 'Campaigner' and as the whole affair was petit & artificial, we were not sorry to take up our abode in the town.

In the British Hotel we witnessed a singular scene. A company of Welshmen, consisting of the Editor of the Bangor paper, a Doctor & some others were discussing the success or failure of the last national Eisteddfod or Bardic Festival. The argument ran so high that I almost feared the consequence, when a member of the company volunteered a song. He knocked the ashes out of his pipe, & apologising for a cold (which always attacks men vocalists immediately before commencing) he gave us a capital song, with a Welsh chorus in which all (except the doctor, who, having had the worst of the argument, was sulky) joined with good effect.

September 23rd

Providing ourselves with a guide, a bottle of brandy & an Alpen-stock – a long pole with an iron prong, we commenced the ascent of Snowdon. The mountain is 5 miles to the summit, at an elevation of 3,571 feet. At last the summit was gained, laughing & joking were the order of the day on the summit. Excursionists & tourists often adopt odd costumes, but the climbers of Snowdon, partly from necessity, were the oddest group I ever beheld. They devoured bad bread & butter at 2/- per head – smoked pipes – & the huge pile of empty porter bottles showed what had been done in that way.

September 30th
We have now been two months without rain, & an old labourer at Hoe told me that certainly we had not had so propitious a harvest for 60 years. The farmers, however, who are proverbially never satisfied, now complain that the turnips are rotting in the fields.

October 2nd
To Dereham Schools. Children below the average, supposed by the master to be in consequence of my not having a School Feast, which the parents have come to regard more as a right than a favour. On this account, glad I did not give one.

October 26th
Received a letter from my old servant Ray dated 'Camp, near Kadikoi'. Among other remarks, he says, 'I cannot describe the siege when they opened firing; the whole Crimea seemed to shake for three days & nights, and at night the whole place looked on fire with the flashes from the guns. I am sorry to have to tell you, Sir, that we have not had Divine Service in this division but twice since we left England! [This was in April.] I attended, and it was over so fast as they could to go to other divisions. It was at 5 a.m.! I return you many thanks for the Prayer Book you gave me when I left, for I am quite alone, except one Turk that grooms the horses, and we have a tent to ourselves a little distance from the Camp'.

November 9th
Dined yesterday at Hon & Rev. Wodehouse's at Hingham. He is uncle to the present & brother to the late Lord Wodehouse; was introduced to Gurney, the Banker. He and his wife are said to be worth a million of money. He was travelling with four horses, his manner & appearance frank, good-humoured, honest & independent.

November 17th
To Norwich to luncheon with Kingsford at the Royal Hotel, & other matters. He has passed the exam & was just returned from the Palace with his 'choker' on, for the first time.

March 19th

An important law respecting Church & Education has come into operation by which the Board of Guardians compels the persons to whom they are giving regular relief, to send their children to school. The option is given as to whether the Parents prefer a Church, or 'British & Foreign' School[3] for their children. The expense of the education of their children is deducted from the relief, & paid quarterly by the Relieving Officer to the Schoolmaster. Twenty children in the Church School and 12 in the British are being thus paid for. This is clearly the first step – the fine end of the wedge – towards a compulsory state education – without something of the kind our peasantry will always be behind other nations in intelligence.

March 24th

After Matins was the Vestry for the Election of Wardens. After a show of hands the parishioners' warden re-elected by 17 to 8 votes, although an attempt was made to oust him, on account of his working so satisfactorily with the Vicar & his warden – some appearing to think it the duty of the town warden to counteract the Vicar in his. This little squabble all forgotten, however, at the Town dinner when complimentary speeches & songs were the order of the evening. 'Suaviter in modo, fortiter in re' is, I am convinced, the only rule by which to govern a Town Parish.

March 30th

While I was preaching in the morning the Tower guns must have been proclaiming the welcome news that the treaty was signed by the Plenipotentiaries at Paris, whereby the war is happily terminated, and PEACE returned to the Nations! God grant it may be lasting.

March 31st

At evensong we used the Thanksgiving for peace, & were probably the first church in the neighbourhood that did so. I set the bells going immediately.

April 5th

Mrs Wollaston met Kingsford, my curate, at dinner. When the former had left, the latter informed us he had, that morning, made an offer to Miss Long, & obtained her mother's consent. A curate engaged is better than a flirting curate; and the Longs are a most respectable family, but Kinsgford might have done better as regards wealth & position.

April 8th

Met Capt. Bulwer at dinner at Carthew's. The Capt. more communicative than he, or others, generally are about their campaigns. He told a story of a Norfolk Squire who, when a boy, was expelled from Eton. Young scapegrace wrote to the Headmaster challenging him to mortal combat. The Master replied that he declined, & begged that, in future, Scapegrace would not spell 'apology' with two p's!

April 14th

What a thing is love! My poor curate's happiness is, for the time, gone! The fair Emily first accepted him, to his great joy – then retracted to his great grief! In two days she bound herself to him again, when, lo! this morning she again refused him! The excellent, honest & generous fellow could stand this no longer, so this morning he wrote & resigned all his claims, and a few hours saw him in the Rail to London. I fear she is a heartless coquette, & not good enough for so excellent & affectionate a heart as his.

April 29th

To Norwich with Mary Hales, who remains here a few days, to approve my Photograph Portrait before it is finished. Very much disgusted with it, & forbad its completion. Her own not more flattering. Photography a good cure for vanity.

May 4th

Day appointed for General Thanksgiving for Peace. Attendance less than usual on National occasions, there being very little enthusiasm on the subject, & many openly expressing regret, that as we are now in a better condition than we were at the commencement of the Campaign, it is a pity we have not another year's war. Such persons can hardly be aware what miseries attend this 'scourge' both at the scene of action & also at home. It seems now, that at Sebastopol, at one period 3,000 Russians were dying daily, from sickness and the direct effects of the siege. Another year's war would have thousands & tens of thousands of wives, widows, & children fatherless – & all for what? – to prop up an infidel, imbecile, & used up Empire!

May 5th

My dear wife, Mary Hales & myself went to spend the day at Hillborough Hall[4], near Swaffham, the seat of the H.B. Caldwells, who are great friends of Mary. The village & park at Hillborough are well wooded, & the cottages in good order. It looks like an oasis in a desert. The Hall is a nice place, & has all the characteristics of an English gentleman's residence. There is the superannuated servant at the lodge, the long & well-kept drive – the Church at the corner of the Park – the ancestral elms – the sheet of water, with its bridge & the boat under cover – & the pheasant-preserve beyond. Once you have seen one such place, you have seen them all, & yet how excellent & wholesome is the status of these families! What a powerful influence for good they exercise around! It is a great thing for a remote country place to have the advantage of refinement finding a place among its people, while, on the other hand, one almost wonders how Pianos, Harps, drawings & all the elegances of a London drawing room, live & flourish, as it were, so far from congenial things.

May 7th

Our darling Gertrude's monument put up. It is a stone Gothic Cross, at head & foot the inscription reads

In Memory of Gertrude Mary, the beloved child
of the Rev. B.J.Armstrong M.A. Vicar of this
Parish. She joined the Holy Innocents on the day
of that festival (Dec 28) 1855.
Aged XI months.

As this is the first catholic monument erected in Dereham Churchyard, I almost fear some sacrilege. For the sake of my dear wife's feeling however, I trust it may not be so.

May 11th

Preached to the Odd Fellows, & this year the Foresters also, who serenaded us afterwards, as usual, in the garden. We all turn out on the lawn on these occasions, but this year my dear wife had too bad a cold.

May 14th

Visitation of the Clergy at Litcham. The sermon, by a Mr Buck, so very long & uninteresting, that having answered my name I could stand it no longer, so escaping the 'charge', got into my dog cart, arrived in time for the family roast beef & did a good afternoon's writing & evening's sermonizing.

May 19th

Mrs Norton of Hoe brought 14 children of that parish to the National School – engaged a woman to collect them every morning – became a subscriber – & paid for them all, for a month. This is the more encouraging when done in the sneers of the farmers there, who oppose education.

May 20th

The Rev. H. Collison is never so well pleased as in getting his friends around him & affording them pleasure. Today he took a party of 25 to Holkham, gave them luncheon in the Park, & dinner at Bilney Rectory, after breakfasting them before starting. There were seven carriages full, producing quite a sensation as they drove through the quiet villages. I was in Mrs Rearsby's barouche with Mr & Mrs R. and Mrs Lee Warner. Holkham is a princely estate, befitting the late prince of agriculturalists the late Ld Leicester, better known as Mr Coke. The approach is of immense length, with the blue sea for a background, & full of game. The mansion I was disappointed with. It is a huge low building, very dull in appearance, which is akin to an Asylum or Infirmary. There are no very grand rooms, & very few pictures, none of which are of note. The Hall is desperately cold in aspect which may be accounted for by being built of marble, after the pattern of a Roman bath. The profuse gilding of the apartments suggests rather the taste of a parvenu millionaire. The chapel cold & undevotional, but the Terrace & Italian Gardens are very fine. The Countess drove away just as we arrived & seemed amused at our dusty cavalcade. The family seem to live in a homely way even among so much splendour. The children, very plainly dressed, went out with their pony, & in one room were their slates & lesson-books just as they had left them. In the kitchen was the Bill of Fare for the day, from which it appeared that the Earl & Countess were about to regale on Roast Beef & sago pudding & that the youngsters were to have mutton stew & Rhubarb fool. I enjoyed the whole thing immensely, my only drawback being that my dear wife was ill at home with a cold, which made my pleasuring seem very selfish.

May 22nd

The whole day employed in going from house to house collecting a Fund for the purpose of giving the children of all the charity schools in Dereham, a Tea-feast, with a band of music on the 29th when the public rejoicings[5] are to take place in London. Collected £30 & there is more to come. Everywhere well received. The Oddfellows are to give a display of fireworks.

May 29th

Public Thanksgiving for Peace. It was agreed that all the public schools in Dereham should have a Grand Tea-drinking in the Market Place & that the day should close with fireworks in the same place. The Church children exceeded 300 & began the day with Matins at 11, at which both my curates assisted. At 2 o'clock the various schools met & paraded the Town with a Band of Music, and Banners, the procession being of great length. About 600 sat down to tea, & afterwards repaired to the moor for games. With some difficulty I got up a country-dance, which went off very well. I consider dancing ought to be encouraged among the lower orders as a polite & humanizing exercise. There was great fun from the private displays of fireworks from the various windows, from fire balloons etc. but the public display was a failure, although our people did not seem to think it so.

June 2nd [London]

On returning from the theatre, found a note from Mrs North, begging me to go to Blackheath to see Mary Hales. Last week she was struck down by a rocket stick while witnessing the fireworks, and rendered insensible for some time. Yesterday her maid administered a liniment of chloroform & opium internally in mistake for a black draught. So near death was the poor girl, that animation & respiration were suspended for five minutes, & it was only by Galvinism that life was restored.

July 20th [in Great Yarmouth]

Preached in the Parish Church, in the morning, to the largest congregation I ever saw in my life, 3,000 persons being said to be present. It was indeed a noble sight, calculated to raise all one's energies & powers. The vast mass was relieved by the numerous clergy in their surplices on the one side – the Mayor & Town Council on the other – & the military in uniform, many of them wearing the Crimean medal, in the background the blue uniform of the artillery, contrasting picturesquely with the scarlet of the line. Was glad to hear from several, later in the day, that my sermon was well approved & that I was distinctly heard. It must be a severe tax on the lungs, however, to always address such a large & imposing concourse.

August 15th

My old servant Ray returned from the Crimea, my little nephew informing me in my dressing room that a soldier in the kitchen had been seen to kiss the cook. It was but a sisterly act, for all the women kissed him when he left, so I suppose he thought he might exact the same favour on his return. He wore his Sebastopol medal, & was quite a lion all day, being a general favourite. He seems much improved by the various scenes of life he has gone through, & says that the army, though glad of the peace, would have liked a finishing tussle with the Russians this summer, as they were, at the close of the war, in the highest order & discipline. Says nothing was worse than the generalship, & that Lord Raglan was no commander.

September 29th

Started with my dear Father from Euston Station on a visit to my old friend, now Dean Bull near Carrickfergus. We travelled at a prodigious rate which was all the more desirable there being nothing to interest one the whole way to Fleetwood, except it be the spiritual condition of the thousands & tens of thousands who work the endless factories we saw. The train stopping an hour at Preston, we walked through the town which is dirty & somewhat coarse in appearance. We dined at Fleetwood, an unfinished sort of watering place, run up, evidently, for the trade with Belfast. It reminded me of Goole, in Yorkshire & is just the sort of place it would delight Dickens to describe.

At 8.30 we went on board the 'Prince of Wales', – tried cigar & whiskey on deck, but it was dark & cold, & the vessel beginning to heave, I betook me to my berth, & after one qualm of seasickness, turned in & slept soundly.

September 30th

On board steamers you are always being disturbed. On deck you have no sooner settled yourself comfortably than a sailor is sure to pull out ropes from under you, or to pull a side boat over you, so ejecting you from your chosen spot. In the Saloon, you are not only disturbed by someone removing your luggage every ten minutes, but woke so early by the passengers who are performing toilets in all directions.

October 2nd [in Carrickfergus]

Mr Martin, a visitor, & a neighbouring young Irish Squire going shooting, we accompanied them to the hills for the prospect, which is very fine. The oats & wheat were still in the fields & also quantities of hay. This last is left for weeks in huge cocks, as in this moist & rainy climate it would fire if put into a large stack without this preparation. Thus there is a new crop of grass before the old one is removed. The wheat sheaves are very small, so are the carts and horses and men, & work seems to be done very leisurely indeed.

October 14th

At 9.30 the 'Semaphore', screw steamship, puffed out of the harbour & then followed 15 hours of actual misery. About midway across channel, probably near the Isle of Man, the pitching of the vessel was frightful – all I could do was to retch & groan & try in vain to sleep. It was near noon on Oct 15th when we espied Liverpool, with the watering place of Birkenhead on one side & the chimneys & huge docks of Liverpool on the other. Steam tugs were taking huge ships in & out, among which were the Stars & bloody Stripes of America, (fit emblem of her disgraceful slavery) were conspicuous.

November 22nd

Reproved the Choir Master for taking some of the boys to a public house.

Kingsford preached in the afternoon, with some difficulty, being the first time after his father's death. Proposed to add the fees, about 20£, to his original stipend, on occasion of his becoming a priest. Although properly, he should serve me for two years, unless preferred, I prefer making this sacrifice to losing him. A fresh curate would cost me £100 a year, & might not serve me so well.

November 27th

There being no 'squire' or 'leading man' at Dereham, the large houses being chiefly occupied by widows, the Vicar is the resource in secular squabbles, & he is, therefore, most unwillingly obliged to 'leave the word of God & serve Tables'. Thus today, just as I was starting on my rounds, a deputation came to the Vicarage begging me to mediate between certain parties & the gas company, whose quarrel resulted in the town being unlighted for two nights past. After remonstrating with several, I succeeded, & the town was lighted as usual.

December 1st

Wrote a long letter to the National Society enquiring with whom rested the legal power of dismissing the Master from Schools.

December 2nd

Dined with the Lee Warners to meet the Bulwers, the Walsingham people & the Dashwoods. Mrs D. is sister to Lord Hastings. Much talk about the love of Norfolk people for their county, also about a scion of the noble house of Howard, late of the Life Guards, and represented as one of the finest & most fascinating men in the army, who has lately become a Romish priest.

December 4th

Evensong so numerously attended by the poor as to make it suspicious that they had an eye to Christmas charities, but the trick will not succeed!

December 5th

Gave away 50 bread tickets at so many cottages and arranged with butchers about meat for gifts & soup making through the winter at the Vicarage. In family matters, there is Mrs Meynell's affair in Chancery – Challice is threatened with a lawsuit – and I am not on good terms with my wife's family for withholding any courteous recognition from mine!

December 8th

Meeting (Special) of the District Visiting Society to discuss the availability of a coal fund, adjourned as the weather has raised 50 degrees in one week, from below freezing to at least temperate warmth. People won't give for coal unless they feel Jack Frost nipping their fingers. Made out a soup list, & distributed bread tickets to the poor at their homes. After Evensong, a dry meeting to audit the Savings Bank's accounts. The Institution is prospering & all satisfactory.

December 10th

The morning, after Church, with Mrs Lee Warner, drawing up Annual Report of the District Visiting Society, and in kindred operations. Afternoon with the Lady Secretary, filling up lists of subscribers & details. Evening at a meeting of Guarantees for paying off the Church debt. An admirable plan proposed but unfortunately stifled in its birth by my Churchwarden, who has discovered a legal difficulty, said to be wholly chimerical, as to paying the interest of the money. Such a determination on his part necessitates his resignation, which I fully expect, and under the circumstances, almost hope for.

December 13th
Administered Holy Communion to an aged person and her daughter, the widow & child of a deceased yeoman, who have lately settled in the Parish. Obliged to suspend the celebration for a while in consequence of the daughter fainting.

December 16th
Met, in my walk, some of those splendid teams for which Norfolk is famed. Eight fine fat horses, two abreast, with a peal of bells chiming as they go along, & the harness decorated with brass & scarlet worsted towels & fringes. Certainly a fine sight in its way.

December 17th
Said Matins while my curate took School for the Master who is still very ill. At 12, took the chair at a public meeting for the extension of the gas lighting. Opened with advising a better attendance at public meetings whereby mistakes would be avoided, & urged the consideration of this and similar matters from motives of public utility apart from differences of opinion, the meeting (unexpectedly) orderly & satisfactory. Kept school in the afternoon. Went round with tickets for Christmas Dinners – supplied my Curate with Soup List etc. In the evening corrected report of the District Visiting & Clothing Clubs.

December 19th
Went to Norwich with my dear wife. In the same carriage were two of the princely yeomen of Norfolk, one, Mr Hudson[6] of Castle Acre. When he left at Wymondham, to go shooting somewhere, the other entertained us with his history. He was a postilion to Mr Hammond, in which capacity he saved £100; married a butcher's widow at Lynn, by whom he had an accession of fortune, became Lord Leicester's (Mr Coke) tenant at Castle Acre and now, though still an ignorant man is worth £100,000!

A selfish day being given to tooth cleaning by the dentist, hair cutting & a bath.

December 22nd
Set the Schoolgirls to make Christmas wreaths, no slight task for so large a Church. Gave out charity clothing. Called on some parishioners & E. Hastings. Finding him in some trouble about his pupils,

proposed my unfailing remedy of a good stout walk which I took with him. After evensong settled their stipends with the School-master & Mistress, and wrote a short homily for Christmas Day.

December 25th

Christmas Day. As happy a one, too, as we could hope for under the circumstances. The anniversary of family trouble, especially when rendered so marked by the customs of the season brings it back with peculiar force – almost with the keenness of the original event. Thus, while the Xmas Bells were ringing, my wife was weeping for little Gertrude though thankful for her bliss. The day, like all the Festivals this year, was appropriately fine, and the Communicants (137) exceeded by a few, those of last year's Festival. Gave a very short sermon in the afternoon, after which our four darlings sat around the festive turkey, and shouted with glee at the pudding all on fire. In the evening, entertained them, together with the choristers and first class girls, with a magic lantern – Carol singing – dancing – and Snap-dragon[7], to their great delight.

December 29th

Took the children to see a Christmas Tree at the Rearsbys'. Mrs R., being a German lady, the thing done in the orthodox way. On the tree were 300 wax lights, besides all sort of knick-knacks. The dining room fitted up with arbours made of evergreens, decorated with orange trees, with rustic seats & lights amongst the boughs, producing a very pretty effect.

1857

January 1st

In the evening dined at Letton Hall, and met some of Lord Suffield's family, an M.P. & other grandees who are staying in the house. Everything refined & beautiful – powdered flunkies – silver plates – rare exotics, and all that sort of thing.

January 2nd

The Corn Hall opened for business today, it was crowded all afternoon, forty merchants stands being let, & 300 season tickets issued. No scene, perhaps, could more adequately display the rising importance of this place, the Hall presenting all the bustle & excitement of change.

January 3rd

Morning employed on School Report. Saw the Master about School bills. Went to Toftwood Common, my curate's district, & called on six poor people I had not seen for some time, owing to my working the other side of the Parish. After Evensong, allotted the £7.16.0d the Choir have collected at Christmas among them – a difficult task; also dismissed five of the choir from incapacity, a very painful one. I did all I could to pacify, & promised to continue my Sunday instructions to them.

January 27th

After School endeavoured to see 'A' the rich shopkeeper, in hopes of making some religious impressions on his mind – but it was a failure – he was very civil, but declined. Called once more on the obdurate shopkeeper. His nephew very anxious that he should see me, but he sent word that he was 'too drowsy'. Left word I should be ready to attend any call at any time, & can do no more.

February 11th

The inaugural Dinner at the Corn Exchange. After Matins came Baptisms, & after that the funeral of the obdurate one! [See entry Jan 27th]. And now he who had died insensible of the blessings of religion was laid in a costly coffin & an expensive vault, with all the excitement such a scene creates among the morbid! Poor 'A' who was a thorough worldling, had given 50£ for the purchase of some old building on the site of the Corn Exchange, & now, on the very day of its opening, they carried him to his grave, so that he never witnessed an occasion on which his whole heart was set.

At the dinner 125 sat down, Lord Sondes was in the chair, and Lords Leicester, Suffield, Hastings & Walsingham were also present. Also Sir J. Barlow, Sir Willoughby Jones, the MPs for the county, the Mayor & Sheriff of Norwich, the Sheriff of the county, & I know not who besides. As vicar of Dereham I had to say Grace & also to return thanks for the 'Bishop & Clergy' in course of which I endeavoured to show the identity of the ecclesiastical and agricultural interests, & made an earnest appeal to the farmers to aid the Clergy in their work of improving the physical, moral, intellectual & spiritual good of the labouring classes. The speaking was below par, neither the Nobles nor the Members being at all up to the mark. I was not pleased with the wholesale soft-sawdering of the farmers which the speeches invariably displayed. I never could see what there is of patriotism, as such speeches at least infer, in men enriching themselves. Philo, our respectable clerk, was offered to be toastmaster but declined & much fun was caused by the blunders of the substitute! One of our MPs told me I had made 'a deuced good speech', I fancy he had an eye to the next election.

February 12th

It had long been promised to my dear boys that when the fox hounds, whose kennel is at Dereham, should meet very near, I would drive them to the meet, & today as they were at Hoe Common & the morning was fine, I fulfilled it. Passionately fond of hunting as I was, it was with no small interest that I saw the field. But how different, then I was among the riders, now in a pony gig with two little fellows by my side. The meet was very picturesque by Chapel Mill, an ancient oratory on the road to Walsingham with the stream & pool by its side. The sun shone brightly on the pink & the clean dogs contrasted with the emerald grass. Most of the Grandees of last night [Dinner for the opening of the Corn Exchange] were there – indeed the Meet had been appointed in the proximity of Dereham on their account – also several carriages, & ladies on horseback. At last they moved off and drew the woods to Gressenhall, we driving along the road & getting a pretty view of them. Now, as this is the first year of the Hunt, & the recently turned out foxes are very young, they bring a 'bag-man'[1] with them who is turned out on the sly & half the field think it is a legitimate 'find' – so off they went, but poor bag-man was killed in ten minutes, and by a short cut down a back lane my boys and I saw as much of it as any. The Hunt moving off to find another, we drove home. The fact is, this being eminently a game county, the keepers kill the foxes.

February 19th

Dined today at the Rearsbys' and sat down 20 to dinner – one of those formal state affairs from which little or no pleasure can be derived.

February 24th

Shrove Tuesday. The 'Pancake Bell' was rung from the tower at midday.

February 25th

Made some good resolutions for Lent which I pray God most earnestly to give me grace to keep. Not to go into public society – to rise earlier –

to smoke less – to drink very little wine – & generally to deny myself in thought word and deed.

March 12th
On the way to visit Mr Wigg met the head huntsman who showed me over the kennels of the Norfolk Foxhounds. They were exquisitely clean, & the oatmeal such as many of the poor would rejoice to have.

March 14th
Correspondence to my dear Father who consults me on the advisability of being Tom Duncombe's[2] Chairman & Proposer at the forthcoming election. Strongly objected, & gave my reasons in full, the chief being my confidence that my dear Father, although a reformer, is very far from subscribing to all Mr D.'s opinions.

March 18th
Rev. Curtis gave a lecture to the Institute on Napoleon 1st & his family to which my wife & I went. It was interesting enough, but too long, occupying 2¾ hours.

March 19th
Gave my Thursday Evening Lecture on the last events – the agony in Gethsemane. The congregation not so good on account of one Mr Drake, said to be an emissary of Government, giving a gratuitous lecture at the Corn Hall on Australia, with the view, it is said, of getting people to emigrate.

March 25th
The choir sang the Benedicite for the first time, with good effect to a Gregorian Tone, to which noble strains we confine ourselves in the daily service. Visited two poor cases, & two of the better sort. Collected School Subscriptions, & began Sunday's sermon. My curate, from my practice on week-days, tried to preach extempore today, & made a sorry affair of it. Said all his ideas vanished immediately the pulpit door closed. My dear Louisa went to school with Helen today for the first time. It is a great thing in a town like this, to obtain the teaching of so clever a person and so excellent a Churchwoman as their governess, Miss Pollard.

March 31st
At school a little boy fell off the form and cut his ear open so badly that I was obliged to take him to the doctor's to be bandaged up, & thence to his mother, who was not a little alarmed. Collecting money

all day for the National Schools, was successful in finding new subscribers, & very gratified at the way in which the old ones paid up their subscriptions.

April 1st

One of those days when you are interrupted from morning to afternoon. Mrs Carthew wanted me to show her the chancel – my curate wanted testimonials for an election – Drewry Woollaston called about the Church restorations and stayed to lunch – the Gellibrands called – also Mr Wilkinson – likewise the Misses Rag – so that it was not till past 4 that I could steal away, in order to visit two or three sick people. Fortunately I am ahead with my lecture. Never leave anything to the last moment is a good motto for all, especially for a Town Parson, whose time is never his own. Among the poor was a widow near death & a married woman terrified at past sin, a mother dying & heartbroken at the seduction of her daughter. Alas, what sorrows to deal with!

April 2nd

The small-pox being in the town, was vaccinated.

April 9th

After Matins, a Vestry. I had put in the notice the matter of the removal of the Bath House, where St Withburga was buried, and where (under a vile modern structure built on the foundation of an ancient chapel, where Mass was once said daily) there is a beautiful spring of water. On making a similar attempt two years back, I was defeated, but this time there was not a dissentient voice – the proposition was carried nem. con., and I got the Churchwardens to get it so far demolished the same afternoon that all hope of restoration is useless.

April 13th

After Matins came the disagreeable ordeal of a Vestry. Was very anxious about this, as it was threatened that the parishioners' Churchwarden would be ejected, to make place for another, who would oppose mine, on account of differences in respect of a previous debt on the Church. A Vestry is a miniature House of Commons, and, as in the latter, we hear that certain new members are going to do wonders & yet, when in the House, do nothing, being brought to their level. So, in Vestry, one often hears of great commotions to be made, and yet in Vestry, the belligerents are quiet as may be – so happily, it was today. After some sparring between rival lawyers, all went off well, and the previous town warden was re-elected instead of the threatened factious individual. This is a great escape. In the afternoon, presided at the town dinner, at which only 20 sat down, owing to the miserable differences prevailing about the Corn Exchange.

April 16th [London]
My dear Mother & Father having gone out to dinner, I went in the evening to hear Gordon Cumming the Lion Hunter[3]. If only half his exploits be true, he is the first Nimrod in the world. The room is surrounded by the horns & skins of every animal inhabiting S. Africa, & the Hunter (who is in Scotch costume & stands between the elephant tusks) explains his sport by means of very good panoramic pictures. Fourteen elephants, a few Lions, & shoals of Buffalo & antelope are an ordinary fortnight's sport, to say nothing of Rhinoceros. He introduced a male & female denizen of the bush, who went through their dance, but more degrading specimens of mortality I never beheld – their guttural noise, shrieks, yells & manic movements becoming painful to behold. How wonderful that God, who 'making all men of one blood' has so diversified their gifts, that some should seem, like Christ, to be little lower than the angels, & others scarcely superior to the beasts that perish. The exhibition was very instructive.

April 17th
Regent Street crowded about 5.00 p.m. Met some old acquaintances and recognised several habitués of that quarter whom I should have thought had been long since in their graves. My Helen delighted by Tom Thumb's Coach – a thing no larger than a wheelbarrow, with ponies no larger than dogs & a coachman and footman in full livery of similar proportions.

April 18th
Sat for my photograph for my dear wife. My father treated us to the theatre to see Kean in Richard II. Jeannie Challice & Helen accompanied us. Was much more interested in watching the surprise & astonishment of my darling than what was going forward on the stage. She was truly delighted, nor, though I weighed it well, do I think there can be any harm in taking the young to see a grand historical representation like this. The scenery, dresses etc were magnificent, & the entry of Bolingbroke & the King into the City is said to exceed anything ever put on the English stage. There was not, however, the scope for acting in this play as in Henry VIII or even The Winter's

Tale. Nevertheless Kean was natural & real as ever, and there is nothing in London to be compared with his acting & Management.

April 19th

In the evening to St Mary Mag. Munster Square, my favourite Church in all London. The preacher was Mr Milman, Vicar of Lambourne Wilts, son of an old friend of mine, Sir W. Milman of Pinner, & nephew to the Dean of St Paul's. Great complaints have been made recently about the low ebb of preaching in the Ch. of England, but I should like the objector who proposes that the Baptist Spurgeon[4] should preach at Westminster – to have heard this discourse. A most powerful (extempore) appeal, full of intense reality, the congregation being sensibly moved thereat. It was a sermon one could never forget, & must ever stand out in one's memory, distinct from the mass. It was a very exciting scene altogether.

April 22nd

Shopping all day for myself, the Parish & others. Since being in London I have obtained a new school-master – enquired about a curate – procured new Gown & choristers' surplices – laid in stock of stationery – been photographed – purchased quantities of books for Parochial Library & for prizes etc.

April 26th

After Evensong, took my dear wife to a concert in the Corn Hall, given by our organist. Mr Blagrove performed wonders on the concertina & a Mr Wilbye Cooper sang very well. The rest poor enough. We went late & returned before it was over.

April 28th

A person came to me in a high state of excitement bordering on insanity, saying he was about to render himself up to justice for a fraud, but was being tracked by the police & had arrived from Holland via Yarmouth & was penniless. Provided him with food and lodging & advised him to give himself up. If this be an imposture, he is a consummate actor.

May 1st

One of our rich farmer's daughters having expressed to my wife her earnest desire to be actively employed in doing good, we invited her to spend the day, & concocted some plans of future usefulness to her. Meeting her father in the market, he gave me a Sovereign as his first subscription to the School. I had been several years trying this in vain.

And here we see how parochial institutions are wont to work. The Parish Library brings my wife into connection with Miss W., by reading Church books she is prompted to work for the Church. She comes to The Vicarage. In consequence Hoe Church (in which Parish she lives) will probably be supplied with music, a new district formed & by this little attention comes a new subscriber to the School!

May 6th

My curate, Mr Kingsford, being a candidate for a Chaplaincy, & the knowledge of a probable vacancy coming to a Mr Dove, he flew over today, by appointment, to talk the matter over and there is no doubt he will do very well.

May 8th

To Hoe to see a favourite parishioner aged 91, notwithstanding he is well looked to by the curate – he is one of the humblest & most pious men I ever knew, & shed tears at seeing me. Ordered him Porter daily & furnished him with tobacco.

May 13th

Having received a favourable testimonial, acknowledged the same to Rev. Fenwick and wrote to Dove offering him the curacy in October.

May 14th

In the evening took my two little girls to see some Ethiopian Serenaders claiming to be the original company; they were however, much younger men. The performance really very good, & the melody beautiful. One played the concertina quite as well as Blagrove did the other night, another did wonders with a violin, playing it with the bow in his teeth, at other times with the instrument over his head, behind his back etc. The dear children much pleased.

May 15th

Among the things I intended to hear during my late visit to London was one of Thackeray's lectures on the Georges, not because I cared for the Georges, but I wanted to hear and see the mastermind who created 'The Newcomers', & wrote the 'Snob papers' & the novel tale 'Esmond'. He was not lecturing while I was in Town, but this week he addressed the people of Norwich, being engaged on a provincial tour by Cramer & Beale of London at 50£ per lecture!!! This was not to be resisted, so with Mary Hales's cob in our dogcart we drove to Norwich after an early dinner with the children & got home at 12 – the weather warm & lovely all the way save that in the last three miles we ran into the 'tail-end' of a tremendous thunder shower. I must confess to be somewhat disappointed with Mr T. and his lecture – a little disenchanted, and most unwillingly so. I'm sure this was the general impression. There was no enthusiasm, and indeed old Sir T. Bignold[5], a local dignitary, was fast asleep close by me, requiring the continual exertions of his daughters to keep him awake. Thackeray looked older and more sad, with less of genial beaming humour than I hoped to see. There was occasional hesitation in his delivery & his intonation, upon which so much depends, is certainly defective. The Lecture would not have been thought much of, if delivered by anyone else, nevertheless it was full of noble feeling, and exceedingly interesting. George IV was the subject, & the lecturer flew at him 'beak & claw' (to use an expression of his own) and pulled him savagely to pieces.

May 20th
Conversation about a Norwich linen draper who had amassed a large fortune & purchased a neighbouring estate. He made a mistake in not getting further off, for the gentry would not visit him, his neighbour went to Law with him, & last Tuesday he suddenly fell down dead in Swaffham Marketplace. So it often is that the 'independence' for which so many strive often proves anything but happiness.

June 2nd
Being Whit Tuesday this was the Saturnalia of the town. At 11 The Oddfellows, Foresters, etc. came to church with the flags & music. Had a surpliced choir & three priests for the occasion. Stone preached a good extempore sermon. After the band & procession had visited the Vicarage in the usual way, we all went down to see the feast laid down in the Corn Hall for about 300 people. At 4 I took the Chair at the dinner, supported by curate, Stone, & Carthew.

June 16th [London]
After an early visit to the 'Baths & Wash-houses' (a cheap luxury of which I always avail myself when possible) we went to the Royal Academy. To attempt description is out of the question, but there seemed a surprising scarcity of landscapes, & I missed any of those surprisingly sweet cattle pieces by Cooper with which I have been so pleased in previous years. A picture of the wreck of a portion of the Spanish Armada at the Giant's Causeway interested me much, not only from the beauty of the painting and my having visited the spot last autumn, but also from the fact that the artist, Stanfield, was taking the picture and was in fact staying at the same hotel. I remember seeing

him start in his boat with his drawing materials, & standing on the heights, to perceive his craft, looking no bigger than a toy, careening over the waves. It is a very faithful & beautiful production. The picture which excites the highest praise from some, & the highest disgust from others is one by the pre-Raphaelite painter Millais representing a knight on horseback conveying a 'ladye-faire' across a stream. It is in the ultra style of this new school, & might pass for the production of a tyro, minute in detail but unable to produce a general & natural effect. Exaggerated as it is, in comparison with the beautiful picture of 'The Release' by the same Master, it has fetched 2,000 guineas from some enthusiast of that School. The great Ruskin, whose divorced wife is married to Millais, has criticised it most severely – very bad taste when the above fact is called to mind, & before I left London I saw in the Print Shops that the production is being lampooned by him in an engraving wherein for the horse an ass is cleverly substituted.

June 17th

A day to be marked with white chalk in the musical world, being the Oratorio of Judas Maccabeus at the Crystal Palace. Imagine a Chorus of 2,000 voices, selected from the best sources! 500 musical instruments!! 17,000 spectators, including the Queen & Royal family, the Arch-Duke Maximilian of Austria, the Prince of Prussia, and a suite conveyed to the palace in nine carriages, glittering with ribbons & diamond stars!!!! When the Royal Party appeared in the balcony, and this mighty mass rose up to salute them with the National Anthem, the effect was impressive & overpowering – the sight of so vast a concourse towering up from the floor to the aerial roof of this magic building, realised one's conceptions of the 'General Assembly & Church of the first born in Heaven'. The piece 'See the Conquering Hero Comes' was absolutely electrifying. In vain the spectators encored. Costa, the conductor, would proceed, till Prince Albert, instructed by the Queen, advanced to the rail of the balcony & gave the sign for the desired encore, which created a deep & palpable sensation throughout the mighty throng. As an instance of the wonder of art, a perfect Photograph of the whole scene was made & presented to the Queen, at the conclusion of the first part! The Oratorio ended, the whole chorus, with the instruments, gave 'The Old Hundredth' at Her Majesty's special desire. The arrangements were so orderly that, vast as was the crowd, no confusion was experienced. Even at dinner, where several tons of Lobster Salads were consumed by the different parties there was no difficulty in getting served.

June 18th

Everything in London this week, pronounced to be the week of the Season, seems to be on a 'monster' scale, the attendance at the Levée being larger than on any previous occasion since Her Majesty's accession, the presentations being about 600 in number. Two o'clock saw my dear father & myself in his carriage in the string of vehicles down St James' Street, he in Deputy Lieutenant's uniform, & I in full canonicals & three-cornered silk hat. Four o'clock saw us struggling through the various apartments in the seemingly hopeless endeavour to reach the Presence Chamber. And what a brilliant crowd it was. The uniforms (their wearers, sometimes with two or three 'Orders', & sometimes covered by them) were of every nation and every colour. There were English, French, Russian, Austrian, Prussian, Turks & Orientals in their gorgeous but effeminate costume. Scarlet was of course the predominating colour, & the Deputy Lieutenants were a decided majority. The Navy, Artillery & some Yeomanry in dark blue. The Indian Cavalry in light hues of the same; by these were the sombre Rifleman, the white Austrian, the green Russian, the picturesque but barbarian-looking Scot. Guardsmen with glittering & plumed helmets & rattling sabres contrasted strangely with the unwarlike but gorgeous diplomatic costumes, & still more with the sombre divines & ugly-looking judges. In they all went, with military bands clanging away, pushing & striving as at the 'Pit Entrance' to a Playhouse, & scarce restrained by the Medieval Beefeater, huge of stature & solid as a rock. At last the Presence Chamber is gained. Arrived in front of Her Majesty, the Chamberlain reads from the Presentation Card in a loud voice 'The Reverend Benjamin John Armstrong, by the Marquis of Salisbury, Vicar of East Dereham'. A little lady holds out a dimpled little hand covered with fine rings – his reverence falls on one knee, gently supports & kisses it, rises, and passes on – a courtier. What a contrast from the National School, the pulpit, the bedside of the sick & dying! Well, it's done, not to please myself, but my father, & I should have resisted his wish, had it not been that having earned his position for himself, it was not for me to deny him the satisfaction of conferring the result on his only son. I did, however, decline the 'Drawing Room', a still more brilliant sight, although considered a proper sequel to a Presentation. Got back to dinner dreadfully tired.

In the evening to a Ball at Capt. Culpepper's on the invitation of Mrs Lubbock, with my dear wife and Mary Hales. Met there my mother's friend the Duc de Roussillon – somewhat of a French adventurer – &

Sir W. Clayton from Norfolk. However so tired with the excitement of the last few days that we returned before supper.

June 23rd

While in London saw the magnificent Reading room at the British Museum, just opened. Observed that many of the students were deep in books which any circulating library would have afforded, one in particular being in a brown study on 'Charles O'Malley, the Irish Dragon'! It is a matter of expressed regret that in the great free libraries starting up all over the Kingdom few works are read but those of fiction & amusement.

July 2nd

Met my daily service choir at the Railway station at 7 a.m. & took them to Yarmouth for the day. It is a great privilege thus to have a day by the sea, & one which would be highly esteemed by the dwellers of the Midland Counties.

July 14th

Large as our population is, we do not often have so gay a wedding as today, when Lieut. Keddle R.N. espoused Miss Wigg. I felt deep interest in this meek & gentle bride from having attended her father, & then her mother in their last sickness, & afterwards her brother, who, though brought to the verge of the grave, recovered & was our host at a really sumptuous breakfast. I was still more touched on finding that the bride had visited her mother's grave very early in the morning, and decorated it with flowers! What a power is there in a few such frail emblems thus employed? Did all in my power to animate the party at breakfast, though it was hard work, for the house was so associated in my mind with sickness & death that it was difficult to realise the festive garb it had for once put on. May God's blessing be upon this pair, & may the Bride find in her husband that protector & sympathiser of which she stands so much in need. Somehow I am always depressed after weddings, & a dread comes over me when I think of my own darlings.

July 16th

Yesterday had a parochial evening of such as could not well be asked to dinner, consisting of tea in the garden – music & a light repast. Very pleasant as such reunions are with people of conversation & intelligence, but rather uphill work, where the men are scarce & when, instead of mingling with the petticoats, they herd about the fireplace & leave the ladies to themselves.

What wonderful things are railways! And how enterprising are Norfolk farmers! Found a parishioner going into Hampshire to spend £300 on sheep and, by the power of steam, thousands of pigs are sent from our market in Dereham to be converted into Hampshire Hogs! Carriage all the way 1s.6d. each!

In a notebook of this sort, it is remarkable how one ignores public events – one cannot help recording however the awful fact that our Indian Empire is, just now, shaken to its centre, 28,000 of the Native Army having deserted, & the Delhi Mission utterly extirpated!

Have been reading some of the sermons of the celebrated Baptist, Spurgeon. They are very clever, & one cannot wonder at the thousands who flock to hear him as a sight. His Calvinism is frightful, and he states constantly the indefectibility of grace, & that some are born to be saved, & others to be damned. The most heretical, however, say a good thing sometimes, & here is one. 'In fact, make it a wonder if you get through a day so easily. If you remain a week without prosecution, think it a remarkable thing, & if you should, perchance get through a month heaving a sigh from your inmost soul, think it a miracle of miracles'.

July 19th
Mr Blunt of Over, Cambs. in the morning preached for the National Society, & myself in the afternoon – collection £12.16.0d. Mr B. stayed with us from Saturday to Monday. He is a very superior man, & carries out true catholic principles to a great extent. Told me that having once had occasion to box a boy's ears, in Church, his mother cried out 'That's right, Sir, catechise (for chastise) him well'. Although Over is a small place, Mr B. has three choral services on a Sunday, and two daily. Begin to entertain the idea of a third Sunday service at Dereham.

July 28th
Was fully occupied in re-organising the Schools under the new Master & Mistress, & in preparing for tomorrow [a confirmation service at Dereham]. Received Telegraph message that the Corn Hall case[6] comes on tomorrow at 9.00a.m. shall not go, though subpoenaed, as duty keeps me at home. The Bishop before the Judge.

July 29th

Having told the Bishop I was subpoenaed, he bid me return to Norwich with him, which I did, & had a long conversation about many things. The Hon. Dr Pelham is a thorough gentleman in feeling & manner, but I fear he has not yet grasped catholic truth. The journey was, I trust, nevertheless for our mutual profit, & I think we shall, at all events, thoroughly understand one another. In court, at Norwich, found the Dereham Corn Hall case over, & learnt to my satisfaction, I had not been called.

August 3rd

Dined at Gressenhall Hall. The curate of Litcham told a funny story or two about a Mrs Mitford, a Dutch lady living at Gately. In Norfolk, donkeys are called dickies. A new footman, a Norfolk man, applying for Mrs Mitford's place, she told him that among other duties he would have to perform was this, viz. that whenever she drove out in the carriage, he would have to ride in the dickey! The man, thinking he was to ride on a donkey declined the place in consequence, till an explanation was afforded. Mrs M. speaks but imperfect English. One day at a dinner party someone joked her about this, upon which she said 'I don't like being squeezed (quizzed) in public, but in private you may squeeze me as much as you like!'

August 7th

The Indian Mutiny continues, & unheard of barbarities are performed by the Sepoys on men, women & children.

August 18th

The evening rather one of excitement. Mary Hales & my curate dined with us, & in addition to the boys coming to practice, Mr Parker, the Churchwarden came – then Mr & Mrs Carthew about the Gibson testimonial, & lastly, Fothergill for a night's lodging en route to Yarmouth. It was not so much the presence of these, as some vexation I felt at the obstructions thrown in the way of a plan I have suggested for a third service on Sundays in Dereham Church. I last night wrote an address to the congregation, intending to have it printed, in which I expressed my desire to do this, on three conditions, viz. (1) That the third service consist of the Litany, Hymns & Sermon, (2) That, pro hac vice [for this occasion] the entire Church be declared FREE & unappropriated. (3) That it be properly lighted with gas. In making this offer I considered it was a boon, as making demands on my time, health & purse – yet here is one warden bringing the opinion of the other that the Litany so used is not legal – Carthew brings forward the old-fashioned objection about servants going out at night (though perhaps they have not been able to attend a service in the day) – & others say that in the present state of feeling about the Corn Exchange, the parishioners will not unite about anything. Gave Carthew my address to read to the Committee, & hereby I commit the issue to God. I believe it will succeed, but if He be willing that the work should be retarded, I am willing that so it should be.

September 2nd

Notwithstanding the rain, the early harvest has so cleared the fields that we heard pop, pop at the partridges all day, some of which found their way into our larder.

Drove my dear wife & mother to a garden déjeuné at Rev Smith's of Brisley, where about 30 people mostly known to us were eating under a tent. We did not arrive till very late, & drove in torrents of rain. The grass was dripping, & the gentlemen sat with waterproofs over their heads. Poor Smith very much annoyed. He seemed to have picked the worst day in the whole year.

September 6th

Went round the Glebe with a contractor, & marked 132 trees for felling, as they are destroying one another by their too close proximity.

September 8th

A soaking wet day. To the School, where announced Mrs Lee Warner's intention of giving a feast to the children, & also took the names of all the truants and renegades with a view to inducing their parents to send them back. Attended the Savings Bank Meeting, Lord Sondes in the Chair, when he, in conjunction with B. Gurdon M.P. & Mr Keppel entered into a joint loan to pay the expenses. It seems that £4,100 has been deposited in three years. The principal farmer's daughter married at Hoe today, to a Dereham farmer, by my curate, Mr Girling, the father thinking it best to pass over the Vicar, on account of our not being on good terms. Had he been a gentleman, he would have acted in just a reverse way. Wrote two letters for parents to send their sons into the army. Visited poor Philo, my Clerk, who is very ill. Interview with curate. Two or three cottage visits, & dined at Mrs Lee Warner's where met Hon. & Rev. Mr Keppel & daughter & the Bulwers, who are all going to the Archery party at Bilney tomorrow. Miss K. promised to give me a Newfoundland dog.

September 9th

Mrs Gooch gave my dear wife & self a 'cast' as they call it here, to Mr Collison's meeting of the East Anglian Archery Club. Three huge marquees were pitched on the picturesque brow on which the Rectory stands, in one of which was a band of music: six targets were set up for the shooting and nearly 200 people were on the ground, including most of the Clergy & gentry in the vicinity. Unfortunately it was very wet till about three o'clock, when the afternoon turned out fine. About 150 sat down to a capital luncheon under a tent, after which the shooting was resumed with renewed vigour. Some of the Ladies' dresses, particularly in the article of hats were very pretty, & the whole scene quite picturesque. In the evening the large tent was lighted up for dancing.

September 10th

After a good day in the Parish lost an evening to one of those wretched tea-parties which we cannot avoid sometimes in country towns. The rooms hot & small – the lamps odiferous and the company shy & stupid. The host was Mr Brooman who served in the Baltic, the Black Sea, & the arctic expedition in search of Sir J. Franklin & he has a medal for each, which I insisted on his wearing all evening. He showed me a facsimile of a series of newspapers, got up by Ackerman, which the sailors wrote while on the 'Floe', but I could see little wit in them beyond the joke that their creditors were not likely to come after them. The evening was altogether 'No Go'! Smith of Brisley was repulsed by Mary Hales, who flirted with E. Hastings to provoke him. E.H. did not know whether to presume on this or not, Mrs Cooper was annoyed because neither of the bachelors attended to her daughter, & so was Mrs Brooman because Mary Hales eclipsed her in singing. Wretched little conclave! How I wished myself away!

September 11th

In the course of my visits encountered a sad case of sin, sorrow, & contrition. It is that of a pretty & interesting young widow, whom I cautioned two years ago, not because I thought she merited reproof, but because I considered her much exposed to temptation. Alas my caution did not suffice to shield her, though she told me it had rung in her ears ever since. Unhappily she came across an old admirer, & fell – since then the young man is dead, & she likely to become a mother. Her tears, and those of a sweet little girl, who cried because her mother did, went to my heart, and I hope that both by temporal & spiritual assistance I have induced in her a firm resolution to arise and amend. Here is a case where one's daily prayer, that God would so order my walk among my people as would best induce His Glory & their salvation, seems to be fully answered; for I was directed to her cottage in ignorance of what had happened, & for a different purpose.

September 16th

On board the 'Lord Warden', Boulogne packet, & so was Lord Cardigan on his way to the camp at Chalons where he and the Duke of Cambridge have been invited by the Emperor to witness the manoeuvres of some 30,000 men.

September 17th [Paris]

Dined at the Restaurant 'Richard', 137 Palais Royal, where had soup, fish, an entrée, a bottle of wine, bread & a glass of brandy for 2fr. each per person – and this in a room decorated with white & gold, brilliantly lighted with gas & a military band & the fountain playing in the court below! Who can wonder at Parisians thinking their capital an Elysium?

September 18th

To the Bois de Boulogne, after changing our quarters to the Hotel Folkestone, Rue de Castellane, a much cleaner domicile, but rather too English, as I like to live & speak (as well as I can) à la France when I am there. On our way to the Bois was more than ever struck with the simplicity, the cleanliness & the order of everything around.

September 29th

At 1 the schoolchildren, 325 in number, with their teachers, marched in procession from the School House, with Banners, & preceded by music, through the Market Place and up to Quebec, the wagon with the children from Etling Green bringing up the rear. Many of the parishioners living on the route hung out flags, in token of good will, which drew forth rounds of applause from the boys. At Quebec, a select company was in the garden, and as the rustic procession wound through the trees, their appearance was very effective. All sorts of games were provided, and a liberal repast of tea, cake, bread & butter etc., to which they did ample justice. They did not depart till moonlight, & the shouting was heard on their arriving in the town, though nearly a mile from the scene of pleasure. This treat is very opportune as coming just as we are attempting a School revival under the management of the new master & mistress.

September 30th

Walked to see some sick people. My companions were my darling Helen, and a most superb Newfoundland, only a year old, given to me by Lord Townshend. She is the admiration of everyone. Took the Chair at the Annual Meeting of the Institute, & made a long speech to the members, on the importance of self culture, the advantages of literature and of having resources of pleasure within ourselves. Was much cheered & complimented, though many of the company were dissenters. An instance of honesty occurred today which it is pleasing to record. Last Saturday I left my Paletot[7] in a cab at Shoreditch Station – the honest driver took it to Wimpole Street, where he took me up.

October 2nd

Consultation about having a manservant indoors instead of three women.

October 7th

Fast day, on account of the dreadful Indian Mutiny – accompanied as it is by atrocities enough to make one's blood run cold.

October 10th

To Norwich, to hire a manservant. Our expenses have been so heavy that since Ray went to the Crimea, we have denied ourselves this luxury. Now, however, our children are so far able to look after themselves that we mean to try the experiment of doing with one maidservant less, & to 'put on' a man in her stead. The office literally crowded, even up the stairs, with women to be hired.

October 16th

Dined at Collisons, and met a party of twenty people. These dinner parties are very unsatisfactory, especially when two come together. They are evenings lost, generally. I never enjoy my dinner so well as at home, & if you have a stupid companion to entertain throughout the long ordeal, things are even worse. As to dinner parties generally, our people require the excitement of continual eating & drinking to keep them at all alive. They are not sufficiently well informed, unrestrained, and vivacious for evening parties – witness the horrors of a drawing room even after a dinner.

October 24th

Rev. Stone called to tell me about his Parochial troubles & consult on a controversy with his Squire. Verily Squires love to have the pre-eminence & I'm thankful there is not one in my Parish.

October 27th

Our crop of apples so abundant that I have sent a huge quantity to the Schools, & gave to each of the 170 children there as many as they could carry.

News came to the town by telegraph, or, as it is now called, telegram that Delhi is taken – 600 men & 40 officers killed. I hope my poor one-armed cousin of the 75th is not one of them.

October 28th [at home in Dereham]

'Richard' the French Restaurateur (on my late trip) sent me a letter[8] hoping for further patronage. How did he discover who I was? And, what industry to take this trouble for one he might never see again!

November 1st

The Corn Hall dispute still going on, & likely to come before Chancery again this month. A dreadfully scurrilous & anonymous poem going about, which brings in all the people connected with No.1 Company in a most offensive way. I escape better than any, having no shares I presume. It is said ...

> 'And even the Vicar, to stand well with all
> Took a stout affidavit to keep up the Hall.'

November 3rd

Mr Press & Mrs Robberds, Rev. Barry Girling & his sister, Kingsford & Mary Hales dined with us, preparatory to going to a concert at the Corn Hall, on behalf of the Indian mutinies. It was got up by the Organist 'under the patronage of Rev. B.J. and Mrs Armstrong'. The room was crowded. As the singers were all amateurs, the 'talent' was not very grand. The Corn Hall – Gas – singers etc. were all given gratuitously.

November 11th

My birthday. My 'patron saint' is St Martin, Bishop of Tours – people say there is always 'St Martin's little summer' – three or four days of parting sunshine, just now, before the winter settles in. In accordance herewith the day was brilliant and we therefore, as a treat, drove over to see Capt. & Mrs Adlington, a Crimean hero, married about a year.

He has just purchased a fine house & park at Hale, which was most fortunately in the midst of his own land, on which there is no mansion. Having 2 horses killed under him in the Crimea – with fine property & a nice wife he is certainly a most fortunate man. After luncheon he showed us over everything – all in perfect order and best taste. His little camp bed still in his dressing room, & his Crimean charger in a most luxurious stable.

November 22nd

My poor cousin of the 75th Regt who lost his right arm in the West Indies[9] has been wounded in the capture of Delhi, but is said to be doing well.

November 26th

Laid up all day from my work, which I prosecuted all yesterday in great pain with an abcess boil. Employed the time in directing copies of a 'Proposal for a third service on Sundays' to those inhabitants who are most likely to take the matter up. Mrs Lee Warner paid a long call, during which I won her over to the plan, which is a great point gained. Mr Dove, my new curate came to dinner – a very priestly-looking man – and so far as I can judge will suit me exactly. Long conversation with him about parochial work.

November 29th

Advent Sunday. My new curate preached an admirable sermon on the Judgement according to works, which I was pleased to see gave great satisfaction. Placed the 'Proposals for a third service' in all the pews, having previously sent one, with a note, to the influential parishioners, to the Bishop & to the local paper, which published it in extenso.

November 30th

Went with Dove to assign him his especial district in Etling Green, calling with him on all the parishioners. In the evening supplied him with a stock of work I had cut out for him in the shape of a sick list – an occasional one also – another, of children who have not been baptised, – and another of those who ought to be sent to school. Also gave him permanent instructions as to his sphere of duty in the three grand compartments of parochial life, viz. the Church, the Schools, and the Cottage.

December 1st

A long morning with the Dist. Vis. Soc. and Clothing Club, being the 'wind up' of the year. The ladies have collected 26£ which will give a bonus of 2/6d to each poor contributor who has saved 3/6d.

Had a good gallop on a hired pony with my Newfoundland galloping alongside, to Hoe, where visited Mrs Norton & Mrs Blomfield who is likely to die, & like too many prefers the ministrations of the Vicar to that of a curate. Explained to her that all priests are equal & she promised to receive the Curate in future.

December 6th

By dint of very hard work daily for some weeks, I have made a new 'Speculum Gregis' visiting nearly 700 families & recording my remarks. On the whole, improvement is visible, & I have every reason to be thankful. A new Schoolmaster, & a new Curate, & this domiciliary work is evoking dissenting activity, but all is for the best. My proposal for a third service has elicited a letter from a very forward & uninfluential parishioner, in the local paper, advising a postpone-ment till the church debt be paid of. How strange that the most disinterested of offers should thus meet with cavil!

December 8th

Any little annoyances which ensue about this proposal, which has only been touched on by avowed malcontents, is compensated for by my good new Schoolmaster, my excellent new curate, & by a donation of 40£ to be dispensed at my discretion among either or all three divisions of parochial work, the Church, the Schools & the Cottage.

December 23rd

The Leviathan steamship[10], which is larger than Noah's Ark & which will hold 10,000 troops, which is to be lighted with gas & which carries two steamers as lifeboats, remains fixed, though a month has been spent in the attempt to launch her, which cost £25,000.

December 30th

Mr Barwell showed me a sham bird of prey, flown as a kite, in fields where partridges are supposed to be. Terrified at the sight the poor birds are completely scared, flying one at a time, & almost in the face of sportsmen.

1858

January 6th

Sad news from India again. General Havelock has closed his heroic & triumphal career in an attack of dysentery – an immense loss to our cause there. General Wyndham has been beaten by the insurgents, who have, however, in turn, been beaten, by Sir C. Campbell.

Our servants had an evening party which they kept up to a late hour.

January 9th

To Norwich with my dear wife on various minor occasions. Lord Hastings was in the same Railway carriage, whose conversation with some friend was exclusively upon horses, dogs, foxes, pheasants & rats. He alluded, with evident chagrin, though trying to pass it off pleasantly, to the eccentricity of one Mr Phillipo in his neighbourhood, who printed and published a handbill against the 'wicked & absurd practice of fox hunting' & gave notice in the same document that he would prosecute all he caught trespassing on his land, in this diversion. This P. is a relation of an old woman of very obscure station in Dereham. She is an inveterate Baptist, & her son in the West Indies, continuing trading with missionary enterprise, has become a great & wealthy man, driving about in his carriage, with nags for his fashionable daughters to ride. The Norfolk P. above mentioned, has a barn near Lord H.'s estate, on the summit of which he has erected statues of Lord H., Mr Morris (whom we have met at Quebec) & of two evangelical parsons in canonicals. They are all highly grotesque & he gave 10£ a piece to a Norwich sculptor for them[1].

At Norwich went to the Hospital to see my chorister, Rogers, laid up with a bad leg from an accident while playing cricket at the Vicarage, or, as others say, while bathing in the river. He reads the Church service morning & night to his fellow patients. Did not like the conduct of the nurse, who hid up some trifles I had brought, with a sly wink.

January 12th

Several clergymen called about the same time. On our way to Church, the following anecdote was given. An Archdeacon visiting a certain church asked the Clerk, while waiting for the parson, whether they had a piscina[2] in the church? No sir, said the Clerk, but there's a pot in the vestry!

January 16th

My schoolmaster & mistress are leaving me for Bradenham. They have not acted well, leading me to believe they were well satisfied, while in fact advertising for another situation.

January 20th

Had a delightful interview with Mrs H. & her husband. She was one of the most abandoned & drunken women in the Parish and now, by God's grace, reformed.

January 23rd

Called on the family of a dissenting Minister who does not 'officiate' in my Parish, & whose daughters come to Church, to condole with them on their father going mad & being removed to Bethlehem Hospital.

January 25th

My darling Helen & I went to London for a 10 day's visit, & were met by my father with the carriage at Shoreditch Station. The Princess Royal being married this morning to the Prince Frederick William of Prussia, considerable excitement was everywhere visible. All kinds of flags were festooned about & among them the funereal black & white of the Bride's adopted country. In the evening had the chariot to see the illuminations, but was speedily blocked up by the dense mass of carriages & people. Our patience at length exhausted, we left it to its fate and took to the pavement. After getting down Regent St and up Bond St with great difficulty, we at length got home. The carriage came back a few minutes afterwards, with the panel marked in attempting to get away from where we had left it & where it stood blocked up for 3 hours!

January 30th

The Prince of Prussia & his bride came to St James's Palace today for a drawing room. My father wished me very much to accompany him there, but for several reasons I declined. Went with him, however, in the carriage as far as Piccadilly, & 'took an observation' of the people who were going to Court & who were patiently waiting in their carriages, evidently not displeased at any amount of scrutiny which the pedestrians chose to exercise. At dinner, it turned out that my father, along with hundreds of others, never got into the Presence Chamber at all, the numbers being so great that the Queen could receive no more.

January 31st

In the evening accompanied my father to the service at Westminster Abbey, conducted in the nave for the benefit of the 'working classes', though as it has been observed, there is no reason to suppose that they want preaching to more than their betters – perhaps, all things considered, not so much. Although we arrived at 6.30 & the service did not commence until 7.00 there was no gaining admittance as the Church was quite full. My father being known to the Inspector on duty, he let us in by the Dean's Yard & Cloisters. The Abbey was very cold arising from the draughts from all sides blowing the gas about as you may see it in a butcher's window on a windy night.

February 2nd

Took the children to some consulting rooms which Dr Challice has, opposite St Thomas's Hospital, to see the Prince of Prussia & his bride pass on the way to embarkation at Gravesend. The city received the Royal Cortège very loyally, Temple Bar was converted into a trophy, & flags were suspended from the houses & across the streets. The poor bride had obviously had a hard struggle in parting from her home, & her face showed unmistakeable signs of tears. Indeed as the snow descended on the cortège, & the carriages being quite open, the occupants looked miserable enough. Prince Albert & the P. of Wales occupied the same carriage as the Prince of Prussia & his wife, who, by the way, looked a mere child. It is said she feels leaving home keenly, & at the wedding, when the Archbishop said he hoped she would be as good and happy as her mother, she replied that her mother had at least been spared the great sorrow which fell to her lot, the misery of parting from her native land.

February 4th

Took my dear mother to Claudets in Regent Street to be photographed for the stereoscope. The result was very successful.[3]

February 28th

In the evening gave my lecture on Ireland & N. Wales at Bradenham School, taking Helen, Miss Pollard [her governess] & my curate in the Fly. Considering the intense cold, & the snowdrifts caused by the high East winds there was an excellent attendance. Knowing Stone's excessive sensitiveness about his country, his aptitude to make a speech & the feud raging between him & Haggard, I felt I was on tender ground & therefore erased from my MS overnight all that could possibly give offence, & in the course of delivery threw in several compliments in order to gratify Stone, but, the lecture concluded, he began a speech including St Patrick, Burke, the Duke of Wellington, & at last read a long extract from a speech by Curran. Manifest impatience was exhibited by the audience. This made Stone work himself into a fury, till at last he absolutely dashed the book he was reading from on the floor, & walked out of the room though repeatedly called upon to come back. I never witnessed a more painful exhibition of temper & regretted very much that it should occur before so many of his own flock. Ireland is the best place for the Irish.

March 10th

Dined at Bradenham Hall, a most unusual thing for us to go to a party in Lent, but a variety of circumstances seemed to render it expedient in this case. The Carsons, Langtons, Gellibrands & others present, 18 in all. Among the curious wines & liqueurs was some 'Extract Vegetal' concocted by the monks of the Grand Chartreuse solely from herbs, & of which they have the sole recipe. It is something like oil of aniseed, & frightfully strong. It is very efficacious for external applications.

March 15th

There were first rate congregations at Church yesterday & 41 persons at Evensong tonight. I question whether the solar eclipse had not something to do with it. Notwithstanding the advancement of science, the generality know as little as ever. Fear may have been heightened by the information supplied in the newspapers by Astronomers, according to whom something like total darkness was to prevail, nature was to assume a purple tinge, and the stars were to be visible. However, nothing of the sort occurred, the chink of the sun at the height of the obscuration did not even reduce us to twilight.

On Saturday, Mary Hales had asked me to accompany her to a cottage in her district where some new people had come to reside, & to which she could never gain admittance. Eventually a dirty little girl came & said that her mother was not at home. 'Well, let me come in' I said & in we went. There was the mother, ragged & dirty, but of a nice countenance, the children to correspond in both respects & the cottage also, in respect of dirt. A heap of potato peelings was in one corner - & everything wretched in the extreme. The reason she had denied us was that she was ashamed of her poverty. Her husband was a stonemason's journeyman, now in work here. They had come from Liverpool, & knew no one. All the clothes etc. were pawned & she showed us the tickets with tears in her eyes. I persuaded her to send 3 of the children to school, & promised to call to take them, & did all I could to make her regard me as a friend. Mary induced her to save a trifle for the clothing club & promised her a cotton gown. There is nothing more to record in this, than in hundreds of similar cases, but for the improvement in so short a time. When we went for the children, they were beautifully neat & clean, so was the cottage, & though the woman was in the same ragged gown, she looked hopeful & cheerful.

April 1st
After Matins to an aged woman to write a letter at her dictation to her grandson in Australia. When she had finished the usual formula 'I hope you are well, as it leaves me at present, thank God for it' the poor dame had nothing more to say though she had not seen her correspondent for many years. An instance of the undemonstrative stolidity of our poor.

April 2nd [Good Friday]
Dissent is very inconsistent. The Puritans of old turned Christmas Day into a Fast, & their successors in Dereham have turned Good Friday into a Festival by means of a monster tea-drinking at 9d a head, the profits to be given to the dissenting churches in Dereham. What profit can be got out of 9d a head when the Corn Hall is paid for, I know not.

April 5th
Having given my warden his congé for declining any longer to devote the Church Fund to the liquidation of a debt of 600£ still on the Church, the dissenters determined to re-elect him as the Parish warden. This would have been most serious for me, for apart from the triumph Mr Drake would have had over me, my new warden, Mr Carthew, said he would not qualify for the office if Mr Drake were elected. As there is no other person eligible in all respects, it was with some anxiety that I awaited the result. Mr Hyde being preferred by the guarantee party, & Mr Drake by the dissenters, I was obliged to call for a show of hands, when there were for Hyde, 35, & for Drake, 29. A great deal of noise followed, Mr D. justifying his refusal to pay the debt, & certainly doing all he could to render the office as distasteful as possible to his successors, in fact threatening them with all if they paid the money, & charging Carthew with obtaining a signature to what he knew was untrue. All this proceeds from animosity on account of the Corn Hall litigation.

April 18th

Visited a man of Shipdham aged 80, who smashed his arm so frightfully between two railway carriages that one of our surgeons was forced to amputate it. He lies at a small Inn. He is very resigned, wonderfully well, & complains that his hand feels the cold – the hand which is no longer his!

To Litcham to dine with the Rector, & afterwards attend an SPG meeting. Dr Caswall was among the company, & gave an interesting account of his connections with America, where he was sent by the Archbishop of Canterbury to represent the Church of England at the convention at New York. Having made a visit to Utah, the Mormon settlement, he'd visited Joseph Smith, the Prophet, whom he described as a 'coarse & repulsive looking man'. With a view to testing his acquirements, he presented him with a Greek Testament, saying 'Mr Smith, can you tell me what this is? Smith, who examined the book upside down, said 'Yes, I can. It is a dictionary of Egyptian hieroglyphics!

April 26th

Gave both the wardens notice of my intention to commence a third service next Sunday.

April 29th

For a year and a half I have been without a horse. My dear father gave me 25£ some time back to buy one, but the money is spent, besides I have had no one to look after a horse. Now this is not the case, so I gave 30£ for a 5 yr old thoroughbred today, & am again mounted. She is very handsome & a beautiful goer.

May 4th

Though our Dereham newspaper is conducted by a Dissenter, they speak in great praise of my having instituted the third service, & call on the people to back the 'respected vicar'.

May 6th

Drove Mary Hales & my darling Helen in the dog-cart to Hillborough Hall to dine and stay all night. It looked more beautiful than ever – the grass so green – the lake so blue & a perpetual chorus going on of cuckoos, young rooks, & young lambs. There are vast numbers of nightingales here, which were 'juggling' & screaming at the top of their throats when I went to bed. Mr Buskworth dined at the Hall, who has recently had one eye shot away, or the sight completely destroyed, by a friend in a 'battue'.[4] It is feared he may lose the other eye as well. This was rather a melancholy visit, not only on this account, but because the Duke of Wellington has purchased the estate, for its splendid shooting, & the Caldwells are dreading their farewell to their former home.

May 7th

After breakfast the young ladies took to archery, & riding about the park; finding the young squire's fishing tackle in the Billiard Room, I went down to the stream. It does not contain many trout, but I succeeded in landing one with a May-fly.

May 17th

Opened the School at 9.00, addressed the children on the subject of the new master, set them to work. Began to think an afternoon's trout fishing would be agreeable. Found the river, as usual, so dry & low that fishing was no use. Nevertheless enjoyed the walk through Long's woods which were carpeted with primrose, dog-violet, wood-anemone & hyacinth. Hard by was a steam engine, by which trees which had been felled were sawn up into the required lengths, on the spot. Norfolk agriculturalists certainly do the thing well.

June 2nd

As we drove down the street the Bells were ringing a merry peal on account of the fiat of the Attorney General that the Corn Hall is NOT to come down. Not wishing to make the bells a triumph for either party, I stopped them, making the ringers very angry & rebellious.

June 7th [London]

In the evening to an Italian Opera at Drury Lane, to which my father had a free admission. This seems to be an attempt to bring the opera to 'the million' as the prices are remarkably low. I thought it gratifying that such a vast assemblage should go to the Opera at all, & still more that they behaved so well.

June 8th

As usual on my first morning in London I went to the Bath, & afterwards my father and I took the boys to see 'The American Horseriders' at the Alhambra Palace, Leicester Square. I have witnessed feats of this kind in London, Paris & various places, but these Yankees 'take the shine out of all'. Never seen were such feats! One balanced himself on the summit of 100 glass decanters, another balanced a pole on his chest, on the summit of which a man stood on his head & danced a huge globe on his feet. The smallest babies performed as equestrians, double somersaults were thrown – leaps over 6 horses – riding on naked horses & a variety of pieces, 16 in number, of the most marvellous kind. The performers were clearly all Yankees & their performance, which is causing a great sensation, certainly the most extraordinary ever witnessed.

June 9th

All the morning shopping – an expensive & tedious progress. In the evening to the opera, to hear Trovatore. We took the girls & occupied Miss Burdett Coutts' private box, which the lessee had placed at the disposal of my father.

June 10th

We met our friends in the afternoon at the Exhibition of Paintings, & in consequence could not give that attention to the works of art which we would otherwise have done. One picture though must be noticed – 'The Derby Day' by Frith. It is a marvellous picture painted with immense care, & containing an extraordinary number of figures, the several groups of which were a study of themselves & each had a history of its own. It was evidently the pet of the Exhibition.

June 14th [Norwich]

The Bishop of Oxford & Rajah Brooke[5] attended the annual meeting of the S.P.G. presided over by the Bishop of the Diocese. Curate & I drove in the dog-cart & Mary Hales took Miss Abbot in her carriage. St Andrew's Hall was crowded to excess. The Rajah a more feeble speaker than I had anticipated – our own Bishop very indefinite as usual & all 'nowhere' in comparison with the Bishop of Oxford who positively electrified the vast audience. Certainly I never heard anything so magnificent in the way of oratory in my life. After the meeting our party joined about 100 ladies & gentlemen at lunch at the Norfolk Hotel.

June 22nd

Took tea & smoked a pipe with the doctor. There are very few parishioners I admit to smoking terms, viz. my Churchwarden, the doctor, & old Mr Cooper.

June 26th

After usual work with my gardener, I set the flower beds to rights at St Withburga's Well. While there a young girl, daughter of one of our best tradesmen, brought a chaplet of white roses for her sister's grave

& a piece of paper attached thereto 'You are earnestly requested not to touch these flowers'.

Sitting up over a book unusually late, I was startled by a powerful ring at 1 a.m. It was my late gardener's wife in a state of great agony on account of her husband leaving home in the morning & not being heard of since. As his father had committed suicide & his mind is not over powerful, she feared he might have done the same, in which fear I fully participated, though kept it to myself.

June 27th
Clements heard of at Ovington, about 9 miles off, whence he had driven some sheep from the market. So far, well – but the mystery not explained as he departed without letting them know.

June 30th [London]
In the afternoon we took the children to a juvenile fête in Cremorne Gardens[6], the proprietor having sent my father a free admission in order that he, as a Magistrate, might have ocular proof that it was 'all right'. No doubt it is so, till 12 at night, but there are sundry indications that after that hour the reverse is the case. My father told me that the other evening when another magistrate went at a late, or rather early hour to ascertain this point when lo! he saw his son figuring away on the 'platform'! There were horseriders & marionettes & what delighted the children most a Balloon ascended just over our heads & hung over the Thames in the clear atmosphere.

July 16th
After service, & taking the Manager's place at the Bank (where an old fellow, who could neither read nor write, put in 10£ apiece for 7 children) escorted Lady Maria Keppel round the church, & afterwards took luncheon with them at the Hydes, during which a terrible storm of thunder lightning & rain came on, so as to imperil Mary Hales's Fête in the evening – the garden swimming in water, with pipes and banks overflowing & water coming through the ceiling. Though it cleared for an hour or so in the afternoon, it was a thoroughly soaking night, the rain rattling over the tent in which dancing went on, & the house not half large enough to hold the 80 people who were present, being uncomfortably crowded. The archery, cricket etc. had all to be abandoned.

August 2nd

Rode over to Hoe to persuade the farmers to unite in giving a Parochial Harvest Home, as an improvement upon 'largesse' & the suppers which the Masters give at public houses, at which (as they do not go themselves) scenes of riot often occur. One of the three willing, but both reluctant unless the third consent. They are entirely independent of him & have no love for him, but it is simply the weight of his purse. My tenant at the Glebe opposite the Vicarage had two horses valued at 70£, die in the field, from cropping a yew tree growing in the plantations.

Tried to get Mrs Lee Warner, as our 'grand lady' to give a School Fête, but she declines, fearing it might be considered an annual thing! What if it were? Neither Squires or Farmers are very liberal!

August 4th

In the evening we all dined at the heath, and had a game of cricket. Took the opportunity of calling on Mrs Long to congratulate her on Emily having obtained an Indian chaplaincy which will enable Kingsford to marry her.

August 10th

Took my dear wife & mother (who arrived last evening) to an 'al fresco party in the Orangery' (so the invitation ran) at Col. Mason's. It was a very pleasant day & we used the Brougham for the first time. It looks like getting on in life to use a close carriage. The Colonel's grounds were in perfection & the view from the Italian terrace with the fountain playing, the trees in full foliage, the ladies playing at archery, the harvest wains in the distance & the church like the eye of the landscape presented a charming coup d'oeil. We had a beautiful repast, a visit to the beautiful Parish Church, a little concert by the Choir – altogether a charming summer party.

August 15th

People are getting anxious that the evening service should not be stopped, but I see no alternative as the church debt (now being reduced) prevented any collection for lighting it with gas.

September 2nd

Received a letter from an influential parishioner petitioning that the third service may not be discontinued & saying he would subscribe for candles etc. After much deliberation, however, I have come to the conclusion that if I agree to make shift with candles, it will be made the excuse for not lighting the church with gas.

September 4th

Mrs Lee Warner died, after an illness of only 3 or 4 days. She caught cold while working in the garden, sore throat set in & terminated fatally. She will not be very much missed as a supporter of local charities, but she was always a lady, behaving kindly to all & regularly attending Sunday services in all weathers.

September 5th

There was an immense congregation, & general regret is felt at the discontinuance of the (third) services – many offers to light it with candles. Feeling sure that to do so would be the very means of defeating my plan to get it well lighted by gas, I gave my reasons in full, and left it in the hands of the congregation.

September 6th

Inauguration of a statue on the Corn Hall, to Lord Leicester as the great patron of agriculture in this county. Anyone who tries to improve the local taste, & travels out of the usual humdrum course is worthy of sympathy, though he seldom gets it from lesser & less courageous minds. The figure is not a bad one, but the arrangements for the inauguration were very imperfect, & the oratory of Lord Sondes & the dons within the hall, painfully below par. The bag which enveloped the old gentleman in hessian was suddenly pulled over his head – one man fired a gun – & six more got up a cheer. The meeting in the Hall was not very numerous. Dined at Letton Hall & met Lord & Lady Bayning & several first rate people. A very agreeable, refined, & intellectual evening.

September 14th

My cousin, E. Armstrong[7] who lost his right arm in action in the West Indies, & was wounded in the leg at Delhi, has been promoted without purchase to the rank of Capt. in the 23rd Regiment by the Commander in Chief, who, at an interview, shook him cordially by the hand, called him good-humouredly an 'unlucky beggar', & said he must do something for him.

September 15th

The School Feast is a day of more anxiety than any other parochial gathering. Fancy 320 children, with a host of teachers & subscribers at an al fresco tea, under a pouring rain! Today, however, all was

127

propitious, the day was fine, the band of music good & the procession with flags & banners through the Town reached its destination without a contretemps. Old & young, rich & poor joined in Sir Roger de Coverly – there were various sports & games – after Tea the teachers & subscribers had refreshment in the Vicarage – the whole was wound up by a discharge of rockets, the band playing 'God save the Queen' & being accompanied by 500 lusty voices.

September 21st
Started for my annual holiday. By the kindness of my dear father I have, of late, made two trips to France and two to Ireland. As we have never seen Scotland we proposed, this year, to wend our way thither, especially as one of Cook's excursions was advertised for this day.

September 22nd [Edinburgh]
Among odds & ends we find the precincts of Holyrood are a sanctuary for debtors, where they may set their creditors at defiance. Butchers are 'Fleshers' & smoke their pipes unrebuked among the meat. Grocers sell spirits. The houses are lofty, & occupied as 'flats' as in Paris, but like only so far, being roughly put together without any attempt at ornament.

September 26th (Sunday)
Being desirous of seeing the Presbyterian worship we selected St Giles Church, as it is the resort of the civic dignitaries. Arrived before the commencement, & were issued into a most miserable pew, which, like the rest, was of deal panelling, very dirty, had never been painted & constructed in a curve, looking towards the pulpit, in the manner of a Lecture Room. The church was not a third full & the congregation consisted chiefly in persons of advanced age, & of an inferior class of life. They made no prayer or reverence on entering, but commenced chatting & laughing with their acquaintance. The Minister was intensely secular-looking, a stout young man with a bushy mop of hair & whiskers to correspond. The sermon was a composition of a vague & desultory character, lasting just an hour. Then followed other prayers, then a 'dismissal' was sung & finally they all turned out as they had behaved throughout, viz. with no more reverence than they would show at a Mechanics' Institute.

September 27th
The coach ride from Callendar to Trossachs is, to my mind, superior to Snowdon, to anything we saw in Ireland, or to the Rhine itself. One

feels, on such occasions, the desire to keep silence in order to enjoy the great luxury of contemplating the wonderful works of God. However, silence was out of the question, for first, the driver, a handsome young Scot, would quote The Lady of the Lake perpetually, then from some cause known only to himself, fall into fits of laughter. Then there was a Yankee with us, a most original character, to whom travelling is a passion, and who talked of a run of 3,000 miles much as a Londoner would of a journey to York. After we had dined at the Table d'Hôte at the Trossachs Hotel, he proposed a walk to the head of the lake, & though the evening was drawing in, with an occasional mist from the mountains, my dear Father accompanied him. As we hesitated a little, 'Look now' said he, 'we people in the new country like to go ahead, & that's a fact, so if you won't go with me, I'll go alone, that I will. See, I am provided.' Upon this, to our astonishment, he pulled out a Colt revolver, loaded & capped. 'Now then', he said, 'you are safe with this, surely?' Well, said I, perhaps we shall be safer without it.[8]

September 29th [Glasgow]

Here, as in Edinburgh, we have the Old Town, & the New. The latter is remarkable for a fine square, very fine houses & public buildings, and streets well paved & rectangular, designed on a uniform plan. The bridges are also very fine, & the shipping on the Clyde shows what a vast emporium of trade Glasgow must be. The Old town is a scene of the vilest filth, misery & depravity imaginable, the 'closes' teem with human life in its very lowest condition, they are the scenes of the vilest drunkenness, the chosen spots for fever & contagious disease, where existence is allowed to be far below the usual average. It is well known from the Government reports that drunkeness, a prevalent vice in Scotland generally, prevails to an unprecedented extent in Glasgow – many thousands remaining in the state from every Saturday to Monday. Accordingly the number of liquor shops is truly wonderful - to the right – to the left, two or even three being in a series without any other sort of shop intervening. A Temperance Hotel, significantly enough, was closed, but we have been assured by many that by an egregious Phariseeism, they vend beer & spirits the same as the rest, though the articles are called by different names. When to this is added the return of the Registrar General, showing that the illegitimate births, small as the whole population is, exceed those of England three to one, we are compelled to set down the vaunted morality of the Scotch nation.

October 5th [Edinburgh]
The last day of our holiday. My dear father, who, as a visiting Justice of Hanwell & Colney Hatch Asylums, takes great interest in the treatment of the insane, wished to view the Edinburgh one, at Morningside. We found it much as such places usually are. It has often struck me as remarkable how very few cases of eccentricity occur among the insane. One would think that madness almost pre-supposed it, but such cases are very rare. The Physician surprised me by saying that the generality of patients come from the Orkney & Shetland Isles, rather than from the towns & that most of these people suffer from monomania – doubtless resulting from their isolated state.

October 7th
The marriage of my çi-devant curate, Kingsford, with Miss Long. The Church was crowded, & darling Helen had decorated the Chancel very prettily with flowers. Went to the Luncheon & proposed the health of the young people. If marriages are made in heaven, this was no exception to the rule. They met accidentally, being perfect strangers, in the Cambridge Senate House, & the first person he saw in the congregation of his new curacy was Miss Long. Money being a barrier to their marriage, they were waiting for 'something to turn up'. Miss Long goes to Dr Gully's[9] Hydropathic Establishment, and, hearing of the case, he gives Kingsford an Indian Chaplaincy, on the strength of which they are married. The affair went off much as these things always do – smiles, flowers, speeches, eatables, tears – and an old shoe thrown after the coach, as the 'happy pair' whirl away on the road of life.

November 20th
Adminstered H. Communion to the wife of an influential tradesman. Her husband also partook, & promised more seriousness in future. Since he has 30 men under him, it is important to win him to good things on account of his influence.

November 24th
Relieved the monotony of pastoral work by accepting Capt. Haggard's invitation to luncheon in Bradenham Wood where a Battue was going on. It was a pleasing & exhilarating sight, & rabbits, hares, pheasants & woodcocks were knocked over. When the gamekeeper laid them out in rows on the green grass, & the bright sunshine shone down on the plumage of the birds, & the sportsmen stood around, it was very picturesque to see. We counted 50 rabbits, 40 hares, 36 pheasants & 6

woodcocks – not a bad bag for one wood. Trotted home with a brace over my saddle.

December 25th
Began with 5 weddings, my curate having a sixth at Hoe. One of these was a case of concubinage which my curate prevailed on the parties to abandon, & a second was a similar case in which I had been equally successful.

December 29th
In the paper I put out a year ago about a third service, I expressed the hope that God would put it in the head of someone to move in a matter which was for them & not for me. Today I administered Holy Communion to a retired builder & his wife, who, from age, and in her case, infirmities, could not come to church. He had been a guarantor of the church debt, & had withheld all subscriptions until an effort was made to repay it. With a reserve belonging to these Norfolk people & an honesty which is intensely real, he had warded off receiving H. Comm. because he did not feel quite right with me, on account of (as he thought) my not having set about the liquidation so quickly as I ought to have done. However, a Committee being formed & 300£ raised, he now felt that he could comfortably receive the Sacrament. At its conclusion, we drew round the fire for some profitable talk. 'Sir, I made my will a little time ago, & left 100£ for paving the streets, but now they are nearly all paved, & you say 100£ will fit the church for gas, I'd thought of leaving it for that.' I replied 'An excellent idea, but would it not be more satisfactory to you, & be productive of more good to do it now, rather than defer it to a period which I hope may be distant?' 'I'll do it at once, & as soon as you can attend to me, we will set about it!'

Coming home, a poor woman told me that Baxter would like to see me. I know him well, but she added 'a wooden-legged man, Sir, with mortification begun in his toe!'

December 31st
In the evening, the united choirs of Hoe & Dereham, the Curate, Organist & Parish Clerks & Choirmaster, 25 in number, were entertained at the Vicarage. The evening was spent in dividing the collection, speeches & singing, & the company did not separate until our beautiful peal rang the old year out, and the new year in.

1859

January 8th

Mr Harvey called to expedite the lighting of the Church. Agreed to drive him to Swaffham to see the gas-standards there. He also said he had made a will in which he has left 100£ to the Church School & something to the poor.

January 11th

Mr Lane of Harvey's Branch Bank in Dereham gave a gratuitous concert to the town & neighbourhood in the Corn Hall, his object being a patriotic desire to improve the public taste. The performers were a section of the Norwich Harmonic Society. An uglier set of used up looking musical hacks I never saw, but they performed a selection from Mendelssohn's Elijah, & some secular music very nicely – the latter being much better appreciated by the vast room-full than the former.

January 20th [London]

In the evening heard Dickens read Little Dorrit & the trial from Pickwick. St Martin's Hall was crowded, the public feeling a natural desire to hear and see one who had catered so pre-eminently for their amusement for 20 years. On the whole I do not think I realised these portions of his works more keenly than I have done over my evening pipe at home, though the imitation that accompanied the reading was admirable, but I was disappointed with the appearance of the man. Not only did he remind me of a hairdresser, but there is an unmistakable look of ill-temper about him, contrasting very unfavourably with Thackeray's genial face. I should not have thought such a man capable of the keen pathos Dickens is, & there is, no doubt, fault on both sides in the separation between him & his wife, on this score of temper. On the whole a great treat.

January 22nd

To Albert Smith's 'China', which we could only accomplish by being in the Egyptian Hall an hour before time, the places being taken for a fortnight to come. Very inferior to his 'Mont Blanc' – indeed it might be called 'The Overland Route', or anything else, so little is there about China, & so much twaddle about men & other things. Indeed with all his wit and humour, Mr Smith evidently found it hard line to make any lecture out of it, for he was only a fortnight there, & found Hong Kong a complete English settlement. His only piece of Chinese life was a dinner at Howqua's[1] who had 14 wives, whose 'grace' lasted 20 minutes & his dinner 4 hours, consisting of filthy dishes of birds-nest soup, rats, frogs, ducks' tongues & I know not what else. It seems that, in China everything is the reverse of what it is with us, e.g. here boys fly kites, there it is the pastime of old men: here we wear black for mourning, there, white or yellow. The word 'pigeon' which the Hong Kong Anglicised Chinese put to everything Mr Smith says is a corruption of 'business'. He represents them as supremely indifferent to life, & that if at all annoyed or depressed they go home & hang themselves.

January 26th
In the evening my father took us to the famous Pantomime at Drury Lane having procured a Private Box for us. Three of the scenes were very lovely, with floating fairies in the air, and a cascade of real water from the top to the bottom of the stage. The children were highly delighted.

Saw an exhibition of Canary Birds in the street, who danced the tight-rope, climbed up ladders, sat in a little Phaeton which others harnessed themselves to, and dragged it. Wonderful dogs seem also to be a novel street amusement.

March 1st
Capt. & Mrs Haggard, Rev. Hicks, Mary Hales, Mrs Lawford, & Rev. Barry dined with us on the sensible principle enunciated by some letter-writers to The Times, & called 'a la Russe'. It consists in having fruit & flowers on the table, & the abolition of side dishes & only one dish at a time placed opposite the host. The plan worked very well, and the cook said it was much easier for her.

Took the boys to Wombwell's Menagerie[2] yesterday, where a pair of elephants went through a variety of manoeuvres, standing on their heads etc. & the keeper was fool enough literally to put his head in the lion's mouth. The most interesting part of the exhibition were two Zulu Kaffirs – very fine men, of intelligent aspect & in the best physical condition. Their delight & astonishment were great in discovering among the company a Mr Edwards, who had formerly seen them in their own country, & could speak a little of their gibberish. My boys shook hands with them.

March 2nd
Entertained my Curate, the Churchwardens & Mr Cooper to dinner, & previously to an experimental illumination of the church. It is very beautiful & catholic in appearance. The Chancel is in a flood of light so that you might pick up a pin from the floor. The two standard Corona by the altar have a splendid appearance, & the tout ensemble more resembles some grand effect in a cathedral abroad than the ordinary appearance of an Anglican Church. Provision must, however be made for better lighting the pulpit and organ loft.

March 6th
The resumption of the Sunday evening 7 o'clock service at which about 1,200 persons were present. The church looked very brilliant, chancel & all being lighted fully up. The junior members of the choir were surpliced & sat with the clergy. The service was Keble's Evening Hymn, the Litany, the Old 100th, a Chapter from the pulpit by way of a text, & a sermon for ¾ of an hour. People very attentive & deeply interested at the explanations about the service, & the principle that I laid down as forcibly as I could, that for this service, the whole Church was FREE[3] for any & for all. A collection for lighting was made at the close, amounting to exactly 10 guineas, which will cover the expense for a year to come. Again, I desire to return thanks to God!

March 20th
It was observed to me that, at the evening service, vast numbers were present who had never been seen at any place of worship. Only two families persisted in occupying their regular seats, so falling in with my idea of a free church.

28th March
In the evening Mr Penrice gave a lecture in the Assembly Room, entitled 'The Dark side of London', which drew a large crowd of the working classes.

April 11th
Mr & Mrs Hicks dined with us, & H. afterwards gave a lecture at the Institute on 'Old Customs' etc. Though I say, dined, he only indulged in smelts & asparagus, & eats no meat in Lent, nor smokes except on Sunday nights.

April 17th

Buried Percy Tollady at Hoe. He was nearly 100 years old, & one of those righteous peasant patriarchs, the last illness of no less than four of whom I am now attending. After the funeral all his relatives came into the Church & thanked me for my kindness to him. The last of his days were spent in saying the Creed & the Lord's Prayer, always ending with the exclamation 'Lord, I'm willing'. He could not read, and had worked hard all through life until he lost an arm, amputation being necessary from a thorn prick from which mortification ensued.

April 26th

Notwithstanding the annual growlings & threatenings, the Vestry passed off amicably. I re-elected Carthew as Warden, & the Parish Mr Hyde. My father accompanied me to the Town Dinner at the King's Head where the Church & Parish officers & several tradesmen & professionals assembled, some 40 in number. As usual I was in the Chair.

May 11th

Drove Dove to Barry's to dinner & have some rook-shooting afterwards. Killed three dozen.

May 31st

Drove my dear wife, Helen & Mary Hales to Watton. Dined with the Hicks' who had prepared a tent accommodating upwards of 30 persons; the dinner, though cold, was a luxurious one, with plenty of Claret & Champagne. At 8.00 the whole party went to a Conversazione got up by Hicks in connection with the Institute, the object being to show goodwill to the lower classes by mingling with them, & providing them an agreeable evening in which amusement & instruction could go hand in hand. Certainly the object was abundantly achieved. The room was crowded & all enjoyed themselves supremely. The Hall was fitted up like a Crystal Palace, & contained festoons of flags taken in the Russian & Chinese wars – also pictures, porcelain, MS's, rare books, curiosities, ancient plate, medieval embroidery, photographs, stereoscopes, Roman antiques, statues, microscopes, a printing press, galvanic batteries & I know not what else besides. At intervals as a part of a concert the owners of some of the fine things were so good as to give short lectures about them, prize poems & recitations were recited, & there was tea or coffee at 6d per cup. On the whole the experiment was thoroughly successful.

On our return we had a most providential escape from accident. The night was dark, & mist was rising from the earth after the late heats. The carriage lights threw a glare upon a poor donkey who was lying in the middle of the road, & no doubt magnified him into spectral dimensions. The horse turned sharply round in fright, and to prevent an upset – the carriage being very low – I got out, reins in hand. Unfortunately my foot got entangled in the wrapper, & I fell in the road, firmly retaining the reins and being dragged along by the frightened horse. My weight, however, induced him to stop & I escaped with a badly cut hand & bruised arm. Nell & Helen had descended, but Mary was still in the carriage, & had I let go of the reins there is no knowing what might have happened to her, the horse or the carriage.

June 2nd

Returning, we met with another accident, and again providentially escaped. My mare shied & turned around with the dog cart, tried to jump the fence, cleared it, fell head-foremost into a deep ditch, leaving the cart embedded in the bank. Neither Nell, Johnnie or myself were hurt, but the mare was so injured that she had to be bled etc. & after trespassing on the hospitality of the Rev. Gurdon, we were driven home by the Veterinary Surgeon amid sheets of lightning, which was succeeded by rain. The mare will not be removed for some days, if ever. This is the second accident in one week!

June 6th

Attended public meeting in the Corn Hall for the formation of a Dereham Rifle Volunteer Corps[4], & made a speech urging the people to join.

June 14th

Took all my dear children yesterday over the Union Workhouse[5], which they had long been desirous of seeing. Everything in famous order, but the 'House' itself being much older than such places usually are. It seems it was a Union before the last poor Law, & was built 80 or 90 years ago. The children much interested with a poor wooden-legged boy who pets a tame owl, and with a poor old idiot, who had been found in the roads, dresses in Theatrical costume, supposed to have been ejected from some show when he became useless, having been exhibited as a wild man, or something of that kind.

Mrs Collison & Miss Barwell. It was given 'a la Russe', with plateau & dessert on the table. In the evening there was plenty of music, as all the ladies did something that way, our darling girls playing duets. Miss Barwell is certainly the best amateur I have heard. The whole thing went off admirably.

December 16th

The snow so deep & the weather so piercing cold, I drove in a sleigh to the Evening Service in the School House at Etling Green, which had not a single track across it. When preaching to these rustics in their working dresses I thought how different my company & occupation to that of last evening! What a contrast between the well got-up military guests at the dinner table, & these fellows ingrained with toil – between the silk & lace & crinoline of the ladies & the cotton gown & shawl of the resident of the hamlet! Much as I enjoyed last evening, I derived much greater satisfaction from this, though the cold was 20 degrees below freezing & the water in the bedroom ewers was thickly frozen the next morning.

December 20th

This week my busiest in the year – we have to decorate the church, distribute 400 loaves, also the clothing Charities, to give our soup to 40 families, to send out Xmas dinners, to send Turkeys to London, to start the choir in their collection, to send out reports of the Dist. Vis. Soc., to give shoe club tickets etc. – add to this a couple of weddings – the regular daily service, sermons to prepare & sick to tend, & it is clear that the office of Vicar of Dereham, even with two curates, is no sinecure. In short to multiply curates is, in one sense to multiply work.

December 26th

The children who wove the Church wreaths had tea and snapdragon, & we all had some dancing with them, & the servants in the kitchen.

December 29th

Two fearful occurrences have taken place in Norfolk. Lord Hastings, a man of dissolute habits died suddenly in London of apoplexy, & Mrs Gurney, wife of the celebrated Norfolk Banker & M.P.[11] has run off with her footman. She has an independent income of 15,000 a year.

1860

January 2nd

Dined at the Collisons & met 18 or 20 people there. We have had so much of this lately that we would gladly have excused ourselves, but it is one drawback of a clergyman's going into Society that he cannot say 'nay' without some good excuse, or will give offence.

January 10th

Gave an evening party on our dear children's account, to which upward of 50 came, & kept up dancing until 2 o'clock. These sorts of parties always go somewhat against my ecclesiastical conscience.

February 15th

Conversation turned on poor Stone's [Vicar of West Bradenham] want of judgement in taking a pair of scissors to the school, and cutting the children's hair *nolens volens*. The wrath of the British matrons is kindled to the uttermost, and the next day a placard was fixed near the Vicarage, 'Hair cutting gratis, in the Irish fashion, by G. Stone'. He might have known that nothing irritates mothers more than meddling with children's hair: they seem to associate a closely cropped head with the prison or the penitentiary.

17th February

Had a sheep killed and cut into 20 portions for the very poor, putting it under the dog-cart & leaving it at their homes – the boys delighted at this calling it 'playing at being butchers'.

23rd February

The trials of a Town vicar are not a few. My excellent curate, Mr Dove, is a candidate for the chaplaincy of Colney Hatch Lunatic Asylum, & as my father has kindly taken him up & is active & influential among the Committee of Visiting Justices, I fancy Dove will succeed, & leave me suddenly. Then Mr Hillyard comes & can't make pupils & Hoe curacy pay, especially since his improvident marriage.

April 9th

A distressing event occurred to a promising young parishioner, apprentice to a stationer in the town, & who had been educated in the National School since my vicariate. Without any assignable cause, he wandered from home and drowned himself in Lowestoft Harbour. Did all I could to console his afflicted parents, & read them a most kind &

Christian letter I received from a stranger staying at Lowestoft & who followed the corpse, & offered 1£ to set up a memorial to the poor boy, suggesting an appropriate epitaph.

April 11th

In the afternoon, after visiting my sick people, took 5 choristers who had regularly attended the services in Holy Week, to Mr W. Freeman's of Swanton. His pretty farmhouse is on the banks of the river & he lent us his boat for a row. We pulled to Elsing Mills, the fingering of the oars, of which I was so fond at Cambridge, being almost like a new sensation. The scenery very pretty with fine views of Bylaugh Hall & the picturesque church – the wild ducks rising from the sedge & the noble swans affording the boys great delight.

May 18th

Dove & I dined at Tuddenham Rectory and spent the evening in the rather unclerical pastime of shooting rooks. The two lads were with us & were delighted with securing the fallen birds.

June 20th

To London with Nell for a dinner party at my dear parents. Dinner carved on the sideboard & served in French fashion, and the evening very agreeable for a London dinner, where you know nothing of the people and the whole is rather formal & stately.

July 8th

As we have none of us seen or heard anything for a long while of an old friend, Rodwell,[1] my father accompanied Helen & myself to St Ethelburga, Bishopsgate, where we found him reading the second lesson. There was a very nice surpliced choir, candles on the altar, preaching in surplice but, alas, little or no congregation. It seems a detachment of rioters from St George's East, in which church disturbances have been going on for a year, paid Rodwell a visit; but informing them from the pulpit that he would personally take into custody anyone who created a disturbance they have not paid a second visit to a clergyman who was likely to prove so awkward a customer.

July 29th

Published the Banns of Marriage between Geo. Dove of this parish & Caroline Octavia Roy of Skirbeck, Lincolnshire! I am thus to lose my dear Curate & friend in 3 weeks, he having accepted an S.P.G chaplaincy in Adelaide, Australia.

August 6th

Annual summer treat to the choir. Started at 7 in pouring rain, 20 in number, including the Clerk & Choirmaster, with a pair-horse van, a chaise cart and my carriage, in which were my dear boys who, in sight of being choristers claimed to be of the party. Showed the boys round the Cathedral [Norwich]. We next visited the Museum, Castle etc, and, at 1, sat down to an excellent cold dinner at a tavern, the landlord of which is a Dereham man. In the afternoon took two boats and pulled down to Whitlingham to see the woods and the cave where Kett and his followers secreted themselves in the Rebellion which goes by his name. The lads highly pleased, as they had never seen a cave before, and some of them had never been in a boat. I never saw so many anglers! Several hundreds were all along the banks, a few bream being apparently their only sport.

August 8th

I have at this time eleven cases of sickness, six of which will end in death. Two of them are wives of our principal tradesmen, whom I must have attended myself even had I any number of curates. People in that class of life regard the curate coming much as they would the surgeon sending his assistant.

August 15th

One of those few occasions after 40, when one laughs till the tears run down one's face. It was in giving some impromptu Charades at the Vicarage, for which Helen is very famous. Mr, Mrs & Miss Boswell, Mr & Mrs Carthew, & Mr Hastings dined with us à la Russe & the Misses Carthew, Cooper, Hastings etc. joined us in the evening. The scene in particular which caused roars of laughter was in 'Plaintiff', in which the dining room was the courthouse. Carthew sat on a raised seat as the judge, books, papers, writing materials before him, with the tongs and shovel to represent the Great Mace. The girls had made him a judge's wig of wood shavings, & having naturally a most comical face, and putting on a judicial look, it really was too much for our gravity. I was Counsel for Plaintiff, & Barwell for defendant, with wigs made of cotton wool & legal bands of foolscap paper. The waiter stood by the judge with a poker over his shoulder as Clerk of the Court. The action was for Breach of promise of marriage, & made much fun.

September 22nd

I took Helen & her friend Edith Stutfield to hear the Messiah at the Norwich Festival. By 11.30 St Andrew's Hall was crowded from one end to the other, including, among the patrons, in a special gallery, all the aristocracy of the county. There was one noticeable exception, however – the Bishop declines having anything to do with the Festival, on the grounds of the questionable character of some of the singers engaged. The dissenters, who never go to these festivals, are delighted at this instance of piety, but the Church people think it very narrow, & talk of the objectionable character of some of the Cathedral singers. There, however, were Lords Stafford, Hastings, Walsingham, Bayning & Sondes. In the centre sat the Mayor, in his official capacity of course, and I could not help thinking what a value are our municipal institutions which should bring such men, actually side by side as Mr Tillet,[2] Radical, dissenter & newspaper editor with Lord Stafford, Tory & great landed proprietor. The music was, of course, very grand.

September 29th

An aged clergyman called, to introduce a curate, but it turned out he was lame & had an impediment of speech.

October 18th

Dined at the King's Arms with Major-General Sir W. Clayton, Bt[3], his son-in-law Capt. Culpepper, & his nephew Capt. Clayton-East. Sir W., who owns large estates hereabouts, but has no mansion on them, comes down every year with a retinue of servants etc. & puts up at our chief hotel for a fortnight. He attends Church regularly & expresses himself much gratified at my sermons & the way the service is performed. Hence an annual present of game, & the present invitation. Sir W. is upwards of 70, but still lively after the partridges. In the course of conversation over the excellent dinner he told me that he had now shot regularly for 50 seasons, but this is the worst of them – he has been in 10 pitched battles in the Peninsula & ended with Waterloo – has sat 14 years in Parliament, and spent 30,000£ for the privilege. Was at Cambridge & Eton, & has great estates in Berks. The old gentleman, who is very courteous & entertaining, invited me to both his London & country residences.

October 20th

Mr Skeat,[4] Fellow of Christ College, & 12th Wrangler, came down as a candidate for the curacy. What an anxious thing is the choice of a curate! One forms a beau ideal and, of course, finds that no-one comes up to it. His advantages are that he is well off, clever, & will marry & settle – but he seems to lack physical health & zeal.

October 21st

Mr Skeat, though not yet ordained, read the lessons but was quite unable to adapt his voice to the Church.

October 22nd

Experimentalised on Skeat in church, & found his voice capable if properly managed. Offered him the curacy as I am getting fagged, and curates are very scarce.

October 24th

To a gentleman's party at Tuddenham Rectory, present the Revs Jessop [Headmaster of Norwich Grammar School], Anderson, Paddon, Johnson, Lawrence etc. A great deal of 'shop' talked. To which, in the entire absence of laymen, one did not object.

October 27th

There followed a host of callers, among them a priest I had observed at daily prayers. He is in the neighbourhood to arrange an exchange of livings, with a neighbouring incumbent, and with excellent catholic feeling, offered in my present unassisted state to help me tomorrow & next Sunday also. This is something like – & very different from the Oxford man (he is a tutor in Dereham) who regretted he could not save a drowning man from want of an introduction.

November 23rd

A gentleman's party at Capt. Haggard's, after his battue. Capt. Adlington, Mr Laurence, Rev. Carson & some officers of the 10th at Norwich. Rather stupid, the conversation all about shooting. It was noted that artillery practice at Languard Fort,[5] was distinctly heard by them during the morning, causing the pheasants to crow, which the military men said was an ordinary effect. The fort is more than 50 miles distant, as the bird flies, but I distinctly heard the firing myself, though ignorant whence it came.

November 27th

One of our Dereham Subscription Concerts. Ella Haggard & her governess Miss Moberly came to dinner, and joined our party. The Hall was very full. An additional attraction was presented in the Dereham Amateur Sax-Horn Band who had never before exhibited in public. They played admirably, although two years ago not one of them knew a note of music. The Dereham Fifes & Drums were another attraction, they brought out a famous roll in the concluding

'God Save The Queen' & gave a military character to the scene as they passed about offering books of the songs for sale. Many of them are choristers, wearing surplices on Sundays & uniform in the week.

November 28th
Wrote the Annual Report of the District Visiting Society, also an analysis of Church institutions in progress, and his future share of the work for my new curate, who comes this week. Mrs Skeat, his mother, has completely furnished his residence, and exhibited 150£ worth of wedding presents which she was putting in order. Some thieves today took Mary Hales's clock off the mantelpiece, but it was found on the doorstep by Philo, with whom she lodges.

December 2nd
After service, to Quebec to be introduced to the wife of Capt. Caldwell, of the 'Mersey'. This vessel in which my nephew & godson is a 'middy' has been ordered to the W. Indies for 3 years, as his parents feared, but I now learn it is only for as many months. My object in seeing Mrs C. was to further the boy's interests. He is so deaf that it is feared by the Captain that he must leave the service, but I hope to have secured that such shall not be done without positive necessity.

December 19th
A very agreeable dinner party at the Carthew's, where I congratulated myself on the amicable state of my parish, seeing that the Squire, Vicar, Curate & 2 Churchwardens, met on the most friendly terms. This week employed as usual in distributing public & private gifts of 400 loaves, men & women's clothing, Soup, meat etc.

December 25th
Mr & Mrs Skeat, and Mary Hales dined after second service, all our children being of the party, to partake of the Beef, Turkey & plum pudding. We spent a very happy evening during which Philo the Clerk & some of the choristers came in & sang some ancient Xmas Carols. Last night they serenaded us with these from the garden & to our astonishment, Mary was among them. She it was who had conceived the idea, and taught the rustic choir, & very kind it was of her. Escorting her home my breath actually froze to my nose, and the moon being full, it was as light as day.

December 28th
Concerning the frost on Christmas Day, I find it stated in the paper that it exceeded in severity every thing that has been thought possible

in this country, being but 3 degrees above zero. Several bad accidents have occurred from falls, among them our unfortunate friend, Mary Hales, who fell on the pavement in the Market Place, was brought here in a fly, and is now in bed upstairs, under the doctor's hands, who fears it will be a long affair.

1861

January 8th [London]
During a morning walk with my dear children, went to 'Mudie's'[1] for his catalogue of surplus books for our school library, and saw his new library. Very wonderful was it to see thousands of copies of a single work in heaps on the floor, & no less to observe them on the shelves, the showy cases of pink, mauve, magenta etc. having a very different appearance form the musty tome of an ordinary library.

Looked in at Spurgeon's tabernacle, upon which about 50 men were employed. It is made for 5,000 people, being constructed with double galleries having a light open iron balustrade in front, & open seats. There is a 'balcon' for the preacher, under which is a platform for the 'deacons'.

January 9th
After luncheon to Southwell's the Photographers, but he will take no one till March or April on account of the atmosphere. While writing there is dense pea-soup fog, & the gas burning in the dining room.

To the Serpentine with my mother & the children, which we crossed on the ice. There were thousands of skaters, among whom might, here and there, be seen a female. The whole place had the appearance of a fair, & carriages lined the roads. At night they have fireworks, torch-lit processions & bands of music.

January 12th
In the evening, Challice obtained a ticket for me to hear Mr Spurgeon at his 'Monster' Tabernacle near the Elephant & Castle. It holds 5,000 people and every seat was full, the majority men, and all of the shop-keeper class, or lower. I saw no exception to this except 2 High Church clergy who sat near me, & who had evidently come, like myself, as spectators & to discover, if possible, the secret of Spurgeon's power. He preaches from a huge 'balcon' up & down which he

continually walks, addressing first one portion & then another of the vast congregation. The preacher is exactly like the pictures of him, viz. a pudding sort of overgrown-boy face without intellectual or spiritual expression. His voice is powerful but without sweetness or modulation of tone, there was really nothing extraordinary in the address, and the only clue I could discover to the unbounded popularity of the man was his wonderful assurance.

January 17th
In the evening dined with the Middlesex Magistrates at the Quarter Sessions at the Sessions house in Clerkenwell. 34 sat down to a splendid repast provided by Staples of the London Tavern. Observed that the company were almost all beyond the prime of life, & that there were not 6 heads at the table which were not bald or grey.

January 22nd
Our dear children had an evening party & kept it up till 2 o'clock. This annual reunion enables us to invite many who we could not ask to dinner, and is so far useful in a Parochial as well as a social way.

January 29th
The Southern American States have revolted against the Northern & a fierce civil war is said to be imminent.

February 10th
Preached for the Gas Fund for lighting the Church & obtained 12£, an increase of about 30/- on last year.

February 26th
Had the boys photographed in one picture, very successfully & Helen in another for my Photograph Album. Also some 'Cartes de visite' of myself. It is a wonderful art to give you 24 perfect & full-length portraits of yourself for 1£. Cottages in the remotest part of this Parish are adorned with 6d likenesses of sons who have enlisted, or daughters who have gone to service. What a solace to the parents! And how utterly out of the question before the discovery of this interesting & beautiful art.

149

February 27th

Investigated a case (one often gets them) of which I was informed by letter, by a person living in London, urging me to prevail with a father to receive his fallen child, who was this lady's servant. Alas, I found the parent had no home, but was living in the house of another daughter, who is kept by a merchant in this town! The old man seemed insensible to the arguments I brought to bear on him, whether grounded on natural affection or religion. A very sad case.

March 3rd

A poor woman, whose family (a large one) I have known since I came here, called at the Vicarage in a perfect paroxysm of grief because her favourite son had 'listed'. She had looked up a few poor things, upon which she implored & entreated that I would advance the Guinea to pay to set him free. I was on the point of handing her the money, without her pledge, but thought I would first see the youth. He was a handsome lad, only 17, but ill fed & clothed, with no money & no work, & it occurred to me he could not, in soberness, have done a wiser thing than he had done in rashness. He assented. I then went to the Recruiting Sergeant to enlist him in favour of the lad, gave him some money, & saw him off to Norwich. Then to the poor mother, whom I comforted & supplied with necessaries, & left her much more composed. I hope I did right in not buying him off, and really think that he will do better as a soldier than as a poor shoemaker without clothing, food or work.'

March 18th

I have always considered that a clergyman compromises his principles by meeting with dissenters for religious purposes, but no reason seems to exist why we should not do in secular ones, e.g. a Mechanics Institute or a Savings Bank. Therefore I went purposely to a lecture on Garibaldi tonight, because it was to be given by a dissenting minister of Yarmouth, Mr Dunning. It was very ludicrous that he should begin by observing that the best speaking was that which exhibited an entire freedom from provincialism, & then gave his lecture in the broadest Yorkshire I ever heard out of that famous county. Moreover he was one of that coarse physical strength class with much assurance, that one sees among dissenters – men capable of achieving much, & who lose nothing for want of pushing – a sort of being eminently qualified to jostle through life & to put everyone aside.

April 21st

Some Sundays are certainly more joyous & bright than others – the weather and our stomachs being great influences to exhilarate or depress. Today, owing perhaps to the East winds so long prevailing, people were cranky – the senior members of the choir would not attend Church because they had quarrelled with the deputy organist, & the needlework teacher would not attend the Sunday School, & means to resign her post because she has quarrelled with the Master's wife. Such is our love of self that God's service & teaching may take care of themselves while we enjoy our pique.

April 24th

Hearing it was the first day of cartridge shooting with our rifles on their ground at Swanton, Helen & I rode there. The ground, a very picturesque & broken piece, near the church, on which was a tent for the ladies, & where groups of lasses & volunteers, were diversifying the scene. Our horses stood the sharp crack of the rifles better than I expected, but we were eventually compelled to dismount. A watch-man, near the 'Butt' but securely protected, indicated by differently coloured flags whether the shot was 'Bull's Eye' (Red & White), 'Centre' (Blue), 'Outer' (White), 'Ricochet' (Red), 'Miss' (Red). As the men came forward & gave us cards with these instructions, it became very interesting to watch the shooting, which appeared to me to be very good. After a while the Volunteers crossed over the river in a punt for the long range, when we departed with Capt. Haggard & his son Andrew. What a new feature is all this! But sure I am that it will do a vast deal of good in many ways to the men themselves, though they never be called into action.

April 30th

Am now employed every day in calling on the middling classes to obtain candidates for confirmation. By the middling class I mean that between the lowest & the shop-keeping little proprietor who lives in rows of little private houses – & to whom the subject of confirmation affords a good excuse for a visit. I found next to no candidates however, all being either too old or too young.

We were all posed, at the wish of Mary Hales, in a view to be taken of the house & grounds, Helen & I on horseback in the drive, Nell on the garden seat, the boys fishing in the pond, Lilly reading on the stump of a tree. The Photograph proved a failure, which was of little consequence. Dined at Capt. Haggard's – a party of 20. Had a bad dinner, the inevitable consequence of such large parties.

May 1st
Capt. Bulwer walked down in the evening to survey our park-like glebe where the volunteers might occasionally drill. Received a letter from my nephew J. Challice dated 'H.M.S. Mercury, Portsmouth Harbour' (He has just returned from the West Indies) and answered it with some good advice and ½ a Sovereign.

May 3rd
Visiting the middle classes for Candidates & found some new inhabitants, such family of which would make a study for Dickens. The pride, the grief, the eccentricities of this particular class are very wonderful.

May 4th
In my visits today met with a case which would make the basis of a good tale. A girl in humble life seems to have possessed the fascination of a Lola Montès[2]. According to her mother's account she 'always carried herself superior to the rest of us' – studied music – & somehow got noticed by her betters. Being on a visit to a sick relation, the doctor, a superior man, became so enamoured that he proposed to & married her. In about the same time he died, & also the only child she ever had. She then went on a long visit to the Isle of Man & on board a gentleman of large property was so struck by her, that he also married her, & they now reside in that island. She is far from forgetting her parents & insisted on her father being present at her wedding & writes to them every week. She was always discreet & judicious & (to judge from her portrait) beautiful. Clearly she had that mysterious innate attractiveness which is purely a gift of nature.

May 14th
A grand day for Dereham, as our Volunteers made their first out-of-door display in the Vicarage grounds which I had placed at their disposal & which are admirably suited for the purpose. We invited several neighbouring families & the better parishioners, others to the amount of some hundreds being admitted, they conducted themselves admirably. There were four tents on the ground for the ladies & which had actually been used in The Crimea, but the day was so fine that no one used them except the one in which I had a barrel of ale for the men & another in which was wine for the officers. Being perfectly at a

152

loss to describe military movements I shall only say that there was the usual bugling, running, kneeling, combining & firing, & the two bands played at intervals. Among the company was Mr Lombe of Bylaugh Hall[3] who has recently succeeded to his estate (19,000£) a year. He introduced himself to me as one who took a deep interest in rifle corps. Certainly he looked anything but a fitting inhabitant for so superb a residence, but I am told he has been ordained, though he has long since renounced his orders.

May 26th

The 15th Norfolk Rifles attended morning service in full uniform, with their Officers, & the Fifes & Drums. The pew-holders very kindly yielded their sittings for that service. Chose for the subject of my address 'Military Life not incompatible with religious duties'. Heard in the evening that the sermon gave great satisfaction, with hopes that it might be printed. The men behaved very well but two or three of the dissenting members were so bigoted that they would not come to the church.

May 28th

Made up a riding party, viz. my father on my horse, Helen on her pony, Johnnie on Mrs Long's and myself on a hired nag. In our ride we took Mr Grounds of Hoe, and got him to consent to remit a quarter's rent of some poor people if I paid another quarter. Then to Bylaugh Mansion to leave a card on Mr Lombe, & home via Elsing. The children rode admirably, and all enjoyed it very much.

June 15th

Took the children to an admirable travelling circus (Bell's) whereat were exhibited acrobats, a dwarf, performing lions, and an elephant trained to do the most wonderful things – among others, carrying the keeper around the arena, aloft, in the coils of his trunk. The 'fools' too were not the types of the vulgar, thieving, grimacing old Drury Lane clown but a refined sort of Frenchified philosophising fellow who may do a good deal of good (or harm) to the ignorant rustics by his remarks.

June 18th

Started for London by 8 o'clock excursion train, returning on Saturday, for 1£ First Class. Walked from Shoreditch station to Wimpole St for the sake of the exercise, through the city. Drank a tumbler of delicious claret at a restaurant in Cheapside, & paid 4d for it – a thing which could not be done until Mr Gladstone's restrictions were removed, or rather, until he removed them.[4]

June 24th
Two very awful events in today's Times – a fire among the wharves in Tooley St[5] to which London has seen nothing like since the Great Fire. Two million of property is said to be lost & many lives, among others that of Mr Braidwood of the fire brigade. The other event is that Lord Campbell, the Chancellor, after attending Parliament & a Cabinet Council, was found dead, sitting in his library chair.

June 26th [Norwich]
In the Town Hall saw the 'snap-dragon' a monster which headed the medieval civic processions, & was made to draw his neck out & 'snap' at the boys in the crowd.

July 2nd
Began hay-making. A comet is visible with a huge tail. I only hope it may not be followed by such fearfully hot weather as was the last comet.

July 19th
Dined at the Bulwer's & met Mr Hyde, Mrs Knatchbull & Rev. & Mrs Eyre. The latter said that at Bungay is the tomb of a musician on which is recorded that his harmonies could only be equalled by those of Heaven. Next to it is the tomb of a firework manufacturer, whose friends have recorded that his fireworks could only be excelled by those in hell!

August 8th
Started at 7.00 o'clock from Victoria Station for Paris, via Newhaven. Morning wet & cloudy & on arriving at Newhaven found to our surprise, the wind blowing a perfect hurricane. Off we went, the steamer plunging violently, and within 10 minutes of starting, all, including men, were sick. The spray flew over the vessel, & every now & then she staggered under the violent strike of a wave. Seven hours misery over, we were in harbour, as wretched a set of beings as ever disembarked from a steamboat. It was new to see Queen Victoria's medal on the breasts of the French Soldiers & to be allowed to journey on without Passports, as British subjects – two outward signs of unity between England & France, which we hope may long continue.

August 29th

To Highbury Park, Islington, to see my old friend Rodwell, & to ask him to be a Trustee under a marriage settlement now being effected in consequence of Mrs Duncombe paying 5,000£ as my wife's dowry. I am glad to say he consented, as it is very difficult to find a fit & proper person for so responsible an office. He is married a second time, looks considerably older, & was employed in smoking a cigar & translating the Koran, which he intends to publish.

September 2nd

The inhabitants of the Eastern Counties have few opportunities of witnessing military displays & consequently the whole county is in a state of great excitement consequent upon the review of 2,000 volunteers at Holkham today. The shops are closed in all the towns, not even excepting Norwich, & 6,000 left Dereham alone for the scene of action. Lord Leicester dined the whole force & 500 private guests besides.

October 5th

Yesterday I attended the Magistrate's Court. The mother of a favourite pupil had pleaded guilty to a charge of theft, a Sunday School teacher became implicated apparently by having been seen in company with the mother at the time, but I brought a companion of the teacher to prove that they were taking a walk at the time & that the meeting with the mother at such an unfortunate time was purely accidental. Fortunately she had gone on with her companion & accounted for all the time & could have had no hand in it. The poor girl is daily hysterical & Mary Hales has shown her the greatest sympathy & kindness.

October 14th

Dined with Sir W. Clayton at the King's Arms. Capt. Culpepper & Capt. Clayton-East were also there. The old General as usual got into his military reminiscences, & said that when he entered Paris in the Allied Army it was with the utmost difficulty Wellington prevented Blücher from sacking it, & that its preservation was entirely owing to its not being fortified, so there was no excuse for the sack. The Prussian officers, however, walked into shops & ordered what they liked to be sent home to them without the least intention of paying.

October 21st

Drove Skeat to dine at Winter's and attend an S.P.G. meeting at Bradenham. Capt. Haggard was in the chair & the speakers were Winter, Morgan, Bell & myself. The meeting was well attended, as they always are in these villages. I suppose this is owing to the people having fewer attractions than they have in towns.

October 25th

In the afternoon & evening the Haggards were with us. Having let their house for 2 years we wanted to show them a little hospitality before they went. They came to lunch & to dine. In the afternoon we went, a large party, to Swanton Church by Bylaugh, to Elsing Hall which Mr Haggard had never seen. We were all disgusted at Swanton Church to find a mouse, or rather a rat, trap on 'The Table', baited with a piece of bread, into which a sparrow had inserted his unfortunate little neck & was instantly sacrificed. Took the liberty of displacing so painful an object from the altar.

October 26th

Sent for to see Gregson Grant, a notorious drunkard who has hardly been sober for years. On my return found the Caldwells, late of Hillborough Hall, & Mr Knatchbull & presently Mr Wollaston called, adding to the large number of visitors this week. Nevertheless got on for some hours with visitation with my curate, & found several children unbaptized, showing the District Visitor to be at fault!

November 2nd

Jumped from summer to winter, the snow two inches thick & great boughs twisted off the trees & lying on the ground with all their leaves as green as at midsummer. Went on, however, with my visitation & caught a bad cold thereby. Since my last visitation I find cleanliness on the increase, but no diminution in illegitimacy – the girls seeing nothing sinful in it, and the mothers apparently conniving.

November 8th

Having long promised Johnnie to take him to the first Meet of the Foxhounds at Gressenhall Mill, he claimed the performance of that promise today. The morning was lovely, the scarlet coats & the green fields having a beautiful effect in the sunshine. A fox was found & showed good sport to those who, like ourselves, were only lookers on, as we had a good view of them as far as Bittering, where we lost them in the wood.

January 31st

After visiting a sick case on the road, rode over to Letton Hall to call on our M.P. His charming wife at home, with whom I had a long chat, during which agreed to an exchange of photographs. My album now contains a list of about 40 relatives & friends, & is very much prized by me.

March 4th (Shrove Tuesday)

The 'Pancake Bell' was rung out from the steeple as it has been since time immemorial on this day – an announcement I presume that Lent-tide was about to commence & that shriving[3] should not be neglected. I don't suppose now that 10 people in the parish know (though it is loud enough) that it is anything particular......it is some testimony to Lent, however, that an amateur concert on behalf of the Rifle Corps was hastened on for today.

March 16th

While at Crowle accompanied Mr Duncombe to the 'Bench' at Epworth, he having qualified as a magistrate. Being a magistrate appears to me incompatible with the efficient discharge of the Priestly office. Who would, e.g. confess a crime to an administrator of the Laws? However, people in our Church very seldom do confess to the Clergy, & lay gentry are so rare in these parts that there was no alternative. As it was, the Bench was composed of three 'Black Squires', the other two being the Hon. & Revd Dundas, & Revd J. Lister. The cases were numerous and exciting – a murderous assault – an ordinary one – a female Irish row – and a Bastardy case.

Had a long & satisfactory conference with a tradesman in this town, who, from an improper connection, is fast going to ruin in spiritual & temporal matters. Argued the matter on religious & also worldly grounds. He seemed much touched by this pastoral & friendly interest in his affairs, & promised to marry at once.

April 7th

A sea fight which has taken place between the Federals & the Confederates in America is likely to revolutionise naval architecture, & everything belonging to the service. An iron-cased frigate dashed her prow into the side of a wooden man-of-war, split her & sunk her at once. In turn, a floating battery with turret & guns silenced the ironsides.[4] Nothing can be more hideous that the appearance of these iron rivals as compared with the majestic ships to which we have been accustomed. It is a wholesale & diabolical style of warfare totally extinctive of chivalry.

April 10th
Drove my dear wife & Helen to Norwich. Shopping & business matters all day, in the evening took Helen (Nell returning by train) to hear Jenny Lind[5], who is a great favourite at Norwich. The Swedish Nightingale's powers of song are marvellous! The sustained note on the highest key, the shakes, and, above all, the 'echo' in the Swedish song are astonishing & partake of the character of ventriloquism. Her favourite 'Bird Song' was also given so that it was a rich musical treat for her admirers.

April 18th (Good Friday)
Several dissenters in church & people not seen there but on this day – the fact is some Masters pay their men all the same on condition of their going to Church – hence a lot of rough fellows came tramping in late, & looking scared and bewildered.

April 20th (Easter Day)
I married a tradesman to a person whom I had induced him to marry.

April 23rd
By way of Easter treat took all the children & my dear wife to see a Rifle match at Swanton between the Dereham & Wymondham Corps, which ended in our defeat. The day was so windy that the shooting was almost chance work. Johnny rode his pony by the side of the carriage. I thought of the days when I used to do the same thing with my parents, and how happy we ought to be to have our children yet around us.

May 8th [London]
Took dear Helen to the International Exhibition where we remained the whole day till late in the evening. Marvellous as is the combination of wonders it contains it is not equal to the effect produced in 1851. That millennium of peace & goodwill which it was said that 1859 would produce has not been realised – we have been fighting ever since & all kinds of weapons & destructive ordnance are a more prominent feature in this than in the first Exhibition.

May 30th
On account of the breaking of a sluice gate in the Fens, near Lynn, the sea has re-asserted its sway over 50,000 acres, & steamers are plying

over homesteads, roads & luxuriant crops. This is a sad disaster, & coupled with the Hartley Colliery accident whereby hundreds were killed, railway accident, Lancashire & Irish distress etc mark the last year as fertile in great disasters.

June 4th

A day in Norwich. Took Emily Plumer to the cathedral but was ashamed of the service. Neither Bishop, Dean, Canon or Minor Canon were there & the prayers were read by a strange clergyman, producing a most depressing effect. The anthem was 'Unto us a child is born' – why a subject appropriate enough for Christmas should be selected for Ascensiontide I know not. This, with the behaviour of the boys, & the fact of the communion being only monthly, notwithstanding the express rubric that it should be weekly in Cathedrals, shows to what a low ebb things have got in Norwich. Met the Minor Canon afterwards in the Reading Room who had been to a flower-show, & saw the Chaplain just starting for a ride at Cathedral service time! Who can wonder that people ask what is the use of Cathedrals when this sort of thing is in vogue!

June 12th

To Norwich to attend the first meeting of the Pastoral Work Association, on which committee I am, & was invited to read a paper, but declined, not being sufficiently interested in the subject, Sunday Schools.

I no sooner congratulate myself on getting up a petition in favour of Church rates, than I am impelled to get up another against Sir M. Peto's Burial Bill[6], which enacts that any dissenter may officiate at funerals in Churchyards – which is, of course, only a prelude to their officiating in our Churches. Impudence can go no further!

July 8th

This is a gay week for Dereham being the first of the two days of the Agricultural Show[7]. The town have subscribed nearly 60£ to be spent on decorating it, and on prizes, & 20£ more for fun & fireworks. There are 6 triumphal arches in various parts of the town, and literally several thousand flags flying. Indeed every house has put up something of a decoration, & the 'oldest inhabitants' declare to have seen nothing like it. Among the various mottoes, a pork butcher set up a farmer with a Latin quotation from Seneca!!! It was to the effect that 'Land, however fertile, required farming to be profitable.' The thing to be seen today

163

was the steam plough at work – and a most wonderful machine it is, laying over 4 furrows at a time & going at the speed of 4 miles an hour.

July 9th

I took dear Helen to the show-yard, consisting of two fields, one for implements & the other for stock. There were the usual huge rams, bulls & pigs, which to the uninitiated always look the same. The streets were one dense mass of people from morning to night. At the dinner (the main thing, after all, on these occasions) I had a seat on the dais, as Vicar of the Parish, in which capacity I said grace, and returned thanks for the Bishop & Clergy. As this was an important occasion & presented an opening for good, I had prepared my ideas beforehand. Taking the steam plough as the foundation, I argued for the improvement of the labouring man – the conversion of the ignorant & coarse rustic into the skilled and intelligent workman. After showing that farming had been raised to an organised science, and undertaken by men second to none in wealth & enterprise, I pointed to some results e.g. the Toftwood Common & Badley Moor enclosures waving with crops of grain, & I then entreated them, with warmth, that the children of the labourer might partake of that advancement which a Christian & liberal education could alone impart. The Chairman was Mr Bagge M.P. There were also present Lords Sondes, Hastings & Walsingham, Howes M.P., Bentinck M.P., Sir W. Jones, the Hon. Mr Coke, Gurdon M.P. & I know not who besides. The whole rounded up with a display of fireworks in the market place, which, with the Volunteer Band, the shouting etc. ended a day of the greatest pleasure & excitement.

July 28th

Returned to Dereham by the 3 o'clock train, Nelly meeting me at the station, called on a Mr & Mrs Metcalfe who has lately become an assistant to Dr Vincent. Now the Doctor (or rather his wife) being an opponent (chiefly, I believe, because we chose a different medical man) my dear wife, who – like all good wives is very jealous for her husband, was very much against calling, but kindly gave in.

August 3rd

About two years ago, I noticed the falling away of a man who had hitherto been a constant attendant not only at all three of the Sunday services, but also of the daily ones. Today he returned to the Church & received Holy Communion.

On the other hand I shall in future miss the estimable ladies from Gressenhall, the family leaving suddenly &, I fear through losses on the turf by the 'author of Guy Livingstone'.[8]

August 22nd [at Great Yarmouth]

Met several people whom we knew viz. Hall Plumer, who is with his family, four horses & three carriages at Lowestoft (the result of marrying a rich wife), Mrs Martin, Mr Aufrere and the Rev. & Mrs Dunlop, née du Pré, a cousin of my wife. Mr D. has a living in Suffolk. I have not seen his wife for many years. When young, a deaf & dumb person was so unfortunate as to become attached to her, and, as proof of his affection left her 800£ a year at his death!

September 12th

Helen & I went by excursion train, which also conveyed our Volunteers, & walked to the beautiful grounds of Crown Point. The Sheriff had erected an admirable Grandstand for his friends, with the Royal Standard in front. General Sir A. Wilson reviewed the troops & Lord Leicester, on a superb charger and in full uniform represented Royalty as Lord Lieutenant. I thought the review itself, with the exception of the marching past at the close, a very tame affair. It was said to be a sham fight, but the movements were only those of an ordinary drill – except when Mr Hay Gurney swept past with his scarlet company of Mounted Volunteers. These were supposed to represent the cavalry, but no one knew whether it was a gallant charge or an ignominious defeat. At the conclusion of the review a Balloon was brought in front of the stand, in which an aeronaut ascended, & the day being lovely, the machine, which was of a bright yellow, soon assumed the appearance of a very ripe pear against the sky. Then came the dinner under one vast marquee at which all the volunteers & all the invited guests, being several thousand, dined at one time. The French giant, M. Breze, 8½ feet high, preceded by a dwarf, made the tour of the tables. The tallest of the volunteers looked mere pygmies beside him. The dinner & wine were excellent, after which the rest of the day was spent in sport – horse racing by the officers, Aunt Sally, the Post Office (for chaff letter writing) & even Punch & Judy were there. Meanwhile the various bands continued playing, & the whole ended with a display of fireworks. It is needless to say that all the rank & fashion of Norfolk were present. People now wonder why Mr Harvey[9] gave such an entertainment, some say he has so much money he does not know what to do with it – that his ambition is to cut out Lord

Leicester's fête of last year – that he wishes thus to pave the way for being M.P. for Norfolk. His liberality is great indeed.

September 17th [London]
A terribly trying day – one which every affectionate father never forgets, i.e. took my boys to school at Finchley College. They cried much before I left & made me promise to see them again before returning to Norfolk. The worst of it was that, ruminating over what I had done, I began to suspect that I had made a mistake. The boys were, to my mind, too delicate to rough it, as would there be necessary & perhaps too young. Then why send them 120 miles away from home?

September 18th
In the evening a note came by Post & written in pencil from the boys begging me to come and take them home as they were so 'very very unhappy'. Of course this did not help to dispel my doubts as to placing them at Finchley, or promote the best night's rest.

September 19th
Off to Finchley by a most wretched Bus which took nearly 2 hours to get there. The boys in terrible grief – had eaten nothing. They looked ill & let down & when I saw their spare frames my previous doubts became certainties. They were not fit for that school. Actuated by the best intentions, I had made a wrong move & determined to rectify it by taking the boys home & sending them elsewhere. Did so. Doubtless those boys themselves if they should read this when they become men, will suspect that my sympathy usurped the place of my judgement. But, in all conscience, I think not.

September 24th
Arranged with Rev. Thompson for my boys to go to school there after Michaelmas. He has not always been the best friend to me, but his school is a good one. As Finchley was too far off, so this is too near, but the advantages are that we are close in case of illness, & they will attend Dereham Church.

September 25th
My wife & I called to ask after Mr Lombe who is much hurt by his horses dashing through a shopfront in Dereham & completely destroying it, & irreparably damaging themselves.

October 6th

The town much shocked by hearing that Mr Lombe is dead! Since we were there a few days ago, gout has flown to the stomach & killed him! The worst is, they say he has not made a will, but while our grand friends, the Lombes, are come to grief on one side of us, our other grand friends, the Gurdons are in the very height of festivity, on the other. Their son has brought his bride on a visit – met by the tenantry – & their carriage dragged in by the labourers. We called there today & missed on the road their equestrian party, who had been sent to our house with an invite for dinner.

October 26th

Preached in morning & afternoon – the second on the occasion of a military funeral of one of the Volunteers being the first since the formation of the Corps. The officers & men attended in full uniform, drums muffled, & the band playing the Dead March. At the conclusion three volleys were fired over the grave. There were many thousands to see so novel a sight hereabouts. The Oddfellows also attended, so that Anthony Dye, Plumber & Glazier of Dereham was more honoured in death, than ever he was in life.

December 1st

In the evening took the Chair at a public meeting on behalf of the distressed operatives in Lancashire mills, being at a standstill in consequence of the supply of cotton being cut off through the blockade of the American ports. A Committee was formed, of which I am Chairman, and people of parties in Religion & Politics entered with zeal into the scheme.

December 4th

Took my wife and daughter to the Assembly, which was not so brilliant or so numerically attended as usual. Helen having got into the ruck, & finding plenty of partners & my wife some friends, I stole away & was much more interested in reading the Bishop of London's Charge over my study fire till 2 o'clock, when they returned.

December 22nd

Took the boys to Norwich, which was alive in anticipation of Xmas. One man there has 9,000 live geese, which he will kill and consign to all parts!

December 23rd

Though this is the busiest week of the year, performed my promise of taking Bertie to meet Lord Hastings' hounds at Elsing Hall. It was a very pretty sight, the huntsmen and dogs in front of the picturesque & ancient mansion, his Lordship driving to the meet with four-in-hand, & the pinks clustered about on the greensward under the ancestral trees. The hounds being thrown into a small wood, found instantly, & Reynard bolting off at one end almost as they went in at the other. As this was at the edge of a large heath & being open country, we were enable to join the run for 20 minutes at a tremendous pace, reminding one of the old days with 'The Queen's' & warming up one's blood. It 'fared' as they say hereabouts, to do me good.

December 25th

Xmas Day. It was a hard day in so large a Church without help, weddings, morning service & 100 communicants, afternoon service and christenings, ending with a funeral.

1863

January 15th

Our children had an evening party of about 40 young people, who kept up dancing with great spirit till 2 o'clock. Among the company was Mr Everington who has purchased the Dillington Estate of the Long's. Before leaving he asked me to give a letter to Laura Long, who is staying a few days with us for the Xmas parties. It contained an offer of marriage. He is the son of the great India shawl dealer on Ludgate Hill, a kind-hearted worthy young fellow. I am sorry he has done this, as Laura, though a good girl, is not calculated either by position or intelligence, to raise him in Society, which is what he wants.

The Prince of Wales is a Norfolk squire, having come to Sandringham which he has purchased. He met the foxhounds yesterday – had a good run, and killed in the open.

January 30th

To Cranworth Rectory to see some representations of Tableaux Vivant, Helen & myself accompanying Mrs Bulwer in her carriage & Nell taking Mr Hyde in ours. It was a numerous & very elite assembly. Lady Wodehouse, Lord & Lady Walsingham, Sir G. & Lady Nugent etc. being of the company. The Tableaux were very beautiful & the dresses splendid, but the whole very tedious & dull. At much less expense, private theatricals & acted charades would have been infinitely more amusing. Tableaux are but dummies after all, and can be performed by those who have neither talent or wit.

February 4th
A meeting was held to promote festivities on the approaching marriage of the P. of Wales, but did not attend it. I could not promote 'Festivities' during Lent, & yet did not like to throw a wet blanket on the proceedings – so stayed away.

February 15th
Preached in the morning on 'The sojourn of Noah in the Ark, a type of Lent' & took the occasion to deprecate 'festivities' on the occasion of the coming marriage, drawing lines between food given to the poor, and the Balls, Public Dinners & Fireworks which are to go on all over the Kingdom.

February 17th (Shrove Tuesday)
The town have adopted my suggestion on Sunday as regards the marriage.

February 18th
On looking over the curates' register of the Additional Curate's Society, out of 90 curates there are scarcely any that will suit. Almost all want a sole charge, or else a house, or the stipend is too high or the views don't suit, or locality is defined. What is to be done? It is very convenient not to have to pay a cheque for £25 on the next month, & my health is good now, but my time is fully occupied – I visit 6 or 7 cases of sickness in a day – it is hard work to get the sermons ready, I live for the third sermon on the charity of neighbouring incumbents, but how is it to end?

February 28th
To Norwich to procure help for tomorrow. Everybody engaged but one, & took such a dislike to his appearance that I would undertake any amount of work, rather than employ him for a day. Have advertised again for a curate in the 'Guardian'.

March 5th
The day after tomorrow the Princess Alexandra of Denmark will arrive at Gravesend to be met by her fiancé, the P. of Wales, and be conducted in State through the City to Paddington, en route to

Windsor, where they are to be married on Tuesday next. Such a sight has not been seen in London for many a year – vast preparations are being made, and enormous prices being given for seats along the line of the procession. My father, being for many years a Director of the Amicable Assurance in Fleet Street has a window allotted for him & his friends, & wrote today inviting us to occupy it. After many 'pros & cons' it was decided for my dear wife & Helen to go.

March 10th

The Wedding day of the P. of Wales with Princess Alexandra of Denmark. Of course every town in the Kingdom followed in the wake of the Metropolis. At Dereham the Volunteers fired a Feu de Joie[1] in the marketplace, and 2,080 poor were fed with roast beef & plum pudding in the Corn Hall & the marketplace. I said grace in the former place & Capt. Bulwer briefly gave two loyal toasts. Fortunately the morning was fine, but the afternoon was the most winterly, by far, of the season: down came the snow, & put an effectual stop to certain 'rustic sports' which were announced to take place. The public houses became filled, & the more respectable families wended their way home as soon as possible.

I would not countenance anything beyond feeding the poor & was not therefore on the Committee, my objection being to 'festivities' in Lent. Carthew, my Churchwarden, though an old Tory, joined very un-willingly on the same grounds, & Hyde, the other Warden, a Radical, refused even to subscribe. There was no good leader, then, among the Committee of Tradesmen, & the consequences (as one of them told me) were such endless disagreements that the only wonder is that the thing went off so well.

March 23rd

Case of a married woman living in concubinage – providentially settled. Wrote to clergyman of Caistor to ascertain whether her husband was alive, & whether she was as cruelly driven from his house as she said. Both replies in the affirmative. She is now truly penitent & consulted me on the difficult point – how to break away from her present state? How to support herself? Told her if she were sincere in the wish, God would provide a way. In the course of the next 24 hours a way was most unexpectedly provided – a quarrel taking place (a most unusual thing, as they lived in harmony) – she has left him & has promised never to return. I have provided lodging & necessaries until something can be done.

March 24th

To Peterborough by train to meet Mr Bellingham Swann, a candidate for the curacy. He seems every way qualified the drawback – there always is one – being that he is Irish. Engaged with him to begin on the first Sunday in May. May this be to the advantage of my people, but the Irish are so vain, and so apt to take offence that they are unsafe. Beggars cannot be choosers, as the difficulty of getting curates is extreme.

April 7th

The Rural Sports came off which were originally intended for the P.'s wedding, but deferred till today on account of the weather. There was some excellent, and ludicrous, donkey racing, climbing greasy poles for hats & joints of meat – racing etc. Any attempt at 'Old English Sports' are generally dreary failures in these modern & railway days, but this was more successful than any I have ever seen, & the whole was terminated by a very brilliant display of fireworks, the Rifle band playing all the while.

April 9th

Having been placed on the Committee of the Church Defence Association[2], attended the meeting in Norwich. Felt a painful conviction that if all the Provincial Committees were as slow as this, the movement would stand no more chance with the 'Liberation Society'[3] than an old stage coach would in racing with an express train. Lord Bayning – amiable, timid & irresolute – was in the Chair – the Hon. Dr Pellew, the Dean, who is obstructive, – the Archdeacon etc. were present, but none seemed qualified to cope with the state of things. An extreme of kindly, gentlemanly & Christian feeling produced results so mild as will certainly be mistaken for apathy by our opponents. Mr H. Hoare, M.P. was there – I had heard of him as a great Church advocate. A very plain man, with hair unbrushed, old-fashioned stock, tail coat, small fishy eyes, no voice & a bad manner, he was yet listened to with great attention.

April 15th

Met my father at the Amicable Life Office having gone there by the Metropolitan (Underground) Railway. It seemed very odd to go to earth in Marylebone, and to emerge in Saffron Hill or, as it is now called, Farringdon Street. What aqueducts of old Rome or wonders of any ancient city equal this? The carriages are lighted by gas, manufactured in the train itself, and the engine consumes its own smoke. Such things but a few years ago would have been regarded as utterly fabulous![4]

May 4th

Mr & Mrs Du Port spent the day with us, together with their cousin from Guernsey, like themselves. Since the nightingale is unknown in the Channel Islands they had never heard one, and as one sings every night in our wood, here was a fine opportunity. We sat in the hut among the Spring leaves with a full moon overhead & listened to Philomel, whose song was exhaustless. To complete the scene, I had the choir secreted among the trees, and at a pre-concerted signal they burst into song, the bird supplying the accompaniment.

June 2nd

Drove Carthew to the visitation at Hingham. The only point for notice was the after dinner debate as to the proposed Bill for closing the Public House for the whole of Sunday. Made a strong speech against it, showing the tendency of legislation to be against the poor man, e.g. stopping Excursion trains on Sundays and that the poor man went to the public house as the rich man went to his club, more that he might enjoy 'society' than drink. No division took place.

August 24th

Called on Mr Anthony Trollope, (author of Barchester Towers, & second only in my mind to Dickens & Thackeray) who is staying at the King's Arms having a Post Office appointment in East Anglia. He is very like the late Albert Smith, but I could not get a rise out of him.

September 3rd

Laura Long's wedding [see entry for 15th January 1863]. As it was known to be done in great style, the Church was crammed with people. The Bride and an array of Bridesmaids all wore veils and wreaths and looked quite imposing as they walked in procession to the altar. A splendid breakfast (supplied from Norwich) was given in the Assembly Room, to which 40 friends & relatives sat down.

September 9th

Our gardener, while digging up potatoes, while I was talking to him, dug up a gold coin, very thin, but larger than a shilling. It is pronounced to be a 'noble' of Edward III's reign and is in excellent preservation. The gardener says he has heard there is a great deal of money in the Vicarage kitchen garden, but if so, I only wish he would find it, as it is a somewhat scarce article with the Vicar.

September 16th

My curate being suddenly summoned to Ireland, naturally led to the subject of his return. He said he could not live on 100£ a year & felt incompetent for so important a curacy – an opinion with which I could not do other than coincide, so he leaves tomorrow & I am again alone, yet with a certain sensation of relief. He may not be able to live on 100 a year, but he is not worth that, as a matter of value.

September 20th

Great excitement on account of Hubbard's premises being fired by an incendiary[5] for the third time. They were burnt down this summer & are now rebuilt, but seem to be the object of a determined attack.

September 22nd

A grand entertainment to the Dereham & Wymondham Volunteers, at Letton Hall. On arrival we found a large party in the Italian Garden consisting of the gentry & clergy of the district, most of whom were known to us. The band was playing & the Volunteers were performing their usual exercises in the park, where a vast crown was assembled. An elegant repast was provided for the guests in the dining room, and the volunteers, about 150 in number, sat down to an excellent dinner under a tent. I acted as Chaplain, saying grace, before and after. The speeches were unusually good, especially that of Lord Wodehouse, and Robert Gurdon, who is Captain of the Wymondham Corps. Capt. Bulwer replied for the Derehamites. The afternoon was occupied by promenading the grounds, the Band playing at intervals. What a wonderful change all this is! Here is a new source of interest – a new bond of fellowship – and appliances for pleasure and festivity which were not in existence 10 years ago.

October 5th

My father treated the boys (who came home for the holidays on Oct 3rd) & myself to Norwich, where they performed feats of mastication peculiar to boys just home from School!

November 29th

Advent Sunday. Took the morning and afternoon services myself. In the evening had quite a 'function', Revs Moxon & Martin besides myself. Moxon preached an excellent Advent sermon. His uncle, he told us, is the Rector of Sandringham, where the P. of Wales is building good cottages & schools. In carrying out his plan, the P. was anxious to consult the Rector; he being one of the old school recommended the P. to consult his nephew, to whom such matters were a hobby. The result was an invite to dine with the Prince & Princess. He describes the character of the house to be one of perfect ease & familiarity – the only state being that the guests & household assemble in a separate room from the Royal Family, special introductions to whom take place after dinner. The P. very like Geo. III (no compliment) with eyes too protruding, & receding forehead and chin. The Princess not pretty, her face being too long. The P. played whist with the Duke of St Albans, Lord Granville & Mr Fisher, one of his household. Asked Moxon if he objected to cards, in which case there would be none. Moxon played a favourite round game of cards with the Princess called Chow Chow. They played for fish at a penny a dozen! Princess Dagmar very zealous at it. They talk English, but often break into Danish – a guttural & harsh sounding dialect.

December 30th
Made a day's holiday with my dear boys. Having an excellent mount from a horse dealer both for myself & John, & Bertie riding his little grey – we went to Elsing Hall for a day's coursing & had very good sport, killing 12 hares & having several runs besides. The gallop over the stubble & turnips – the fine prospect as seen from the hills – the sudden rush of the wing as we put up partridges, pheasants, wild duck, and also a fine fox, was quite a new & exhilarating sensation.

1864

January 6th
Our children's evening party, consisting of 40 young parishioners – too large a number for a small house, but as to omit any, in a small place like this, would do more harm than good there was no alternative. Having now entertained all our dining & young friends, and the choir, our 'season' closes – & must needs do so for economy's sake, though I hope the interests of the Church are served, which is my main object in view.

January 11th [London]
Took the boys to see the palatial wonders at Westminster & in the evening to see the grand horse-riding in the Agricultural Hall at Islington, where 10,000 people were assembled, reminding one of what the concourses were at the Coliseum at Rome. It was a significant feature of the day that this vast concourse were almost all

most sensible & intelligent old fellow he is, with a white beard to his waist & he is a Waterloo man. We saw Hougoumont, defended by the Hanoverians, when it was discovered that the cartridges would not fit the bore of the muskets & they were slaughtered to a man. He also told us of Picton's heroism – I never knew that the brave old fellow went into battle with a broken rib & a wound in his thigh, which he received at Quatre Bras, a few days before Waterloo.

August 6th

Bruges is a dull place, the grass being occasionally seen in the streets. It is full of Priests, Monks & Nuns. Indeed the long black Spanish cloaks universally worn by the women make them all look like nuns.

October 10th

The Dissenters, who are terribly at sixes & sevens, have inaugurated a series of 'Religious Services' on Wednesday evenings in the Corn Exchange. Rev. Mr Haslam, a clergyman of Irish Revival calibre having been announced as a Preacher, I wrote him a letter of expostulation. I brought the subject before the Ruri-decanal Chapter, when they unanimously signed a letter of protest to Mr Haslam, of which he took no notice. Then the Norfolk News, notwithstanding its favourable notice of me in the spring, wrote an article concluding that they 'preferred Mr Haslam's irregularity to Mr Armstrong's Orthodoxy'. The Argos gives an article only too highly in my praise, & in a jocular description of the illuminations at Norwich for the visit of the P. of Wales, they said one would be a transparency of 'Haslam destroyed by an Armstrong gun.'[2]

October 21st

Preached at the parish church of Great Yarmouth for the restoration. The papers said there were 4,000 people there – the largest congregation since the Bp of Oxford preached there.

October 30th

Marched with our Volunteers as their Chaplain, forming a Guard of Honour to the Railway Station to receive the Prince & Princess of Wales & the Queen of Denmark on their way to Cossy Hall, where they remain during the Norwich Festival. The Duke of Edinburgh & Lords Leicester, Stafford & Newry were there, and a very numerous suite. The Princess looked very thin, but very pretty, The Q. of Denmark is a fine woman, but much rouged.

December 6th

This being St Nicholas day, our patron saint, a few of us in the vestry before Evensong, instituted the 'Guild of St Nicholas', a proposed institution for young men, having for its object religious instruction and also Church work. This must really be my last institution, as our Parochial machinery is now quite complete. At the Vicarage, a few days ago we also inaugurated a 'West Norfolk Branch' of the E.C.U. of which Scott Chad Esq. of Thursford Hall is President & myself V. President.

December 25th

Married a young parishioner, by name Mahershallalashbaz Tuck He accounted for the possession of so extraordinary a name thus: his father wished to call him by the shortest name in the Bible, and for that purpose selected 'Uz', but the clergyman making some demur the father said, in pique, if he can't have the shortest name, he shall have the longest.

1867

January 10th

The gayest week perhaps ever known in Dereham. The Volunteers gave two theatrical representations, the bachelors gave a Ball, & there was the annual distribution of prizes to the Volunteers, at which, at the request of the Captain, I addressed the men. I have now the proper braided uniform coat, kepi, cross-belt & cartouche box. Our new Adjutant, as well as our Captain & Drill Sergeant are all Crimea men. I offered a prize to be shot for during the coming season.

I was but a very few minutes at the Bachelors' Ball, during which I had some conversation with Mr S. Reade M.P. the Conservative Tenant farmer who ousted Lord Leicester's brother, a Whig, at the last election. He modestly attributed his success more to the unpopularity of his opponent than to any merits of his own.

January 15th

Took my dear boys to London for a week's visit to my parents, during which we went to the Colney Hatch Festival & to the pantomime at Covent Garden. A dreadful accident happened on the ice at Regent's Park[1]. The ice was very thick, but the water had somehow been drained beneath it, consequently it suddenly broke up in all directions and 200 people 'went down quick' into the waters of whom 50 perished! This dreadful catastrophe produced a profound sensation, & greatly diminished the ardour for skating.

Tragic accident in Regent's Park
(*Illustrated London News*)

March 8th

A Tradesman sent me his unpaid Bill, receipted amounting to 3£ to say he was sure I had so many expenses that he would take no money from me. Called & told him I would apply the money to the Daily Service Fund.

March 26th

As our penny readings were to be closed this evening for the present season, we met in the Corn Hall rather than the Assembly Room, & added, as an extra treat, the Rifle Band, the Church Choir & some amateur singing. Owing to these novel attractions I was astonished, on taking the Chair, to find 600 people before me, & they not of the 'Reading' class, but of the lowest including some 'roughs'. The conduct of these last showed me that it was an occasion demanding great tact & firmness on the part of a chairman, so when their cat calls & noises began I went to the front & said that if they 'did not put a stop to their discord, we would stop our music'. This had the desired effect. I read, but it was a case of pearls before swine with that class. They had come for the music & were impatient of anything else.

May 10th
Met a gentleman's dinner party at Walker's (always an odious affair) there were General Carthew, Captain Haggard, Colonel Blomfield & several clergy, making 15 in number, but it was rather a heavy affair, & I got no tea.

May 25th
The opening of the Rifle Butts for the season, celebrated by farmer's races & rural sports. Put on my uniform & drove Miss Nelson there, the girls going in another party. The cold wind was piercing & if old Mr Collison had not gone about with a bottle of punch, offering it right & left, some of us would have suffered seriously!

May 28th [London]
Took Lilly to the Royal Academy which always looks as if you had never left it since the last visit. Sir E. Landseer's portrait of the Queen, all in black, on a black horse, attendant in black etc is clearly the freak of a disordered mind.

May 29th
My dear father went to the Levée in his Deputy Lieutenant's uniform – a dress I never contemplated, at one period, he would have worn again. Even as things are, he was very feeble, & I wonder at his going, but the humour seized him & a brother D.L. offering to take him in his carriage, the opportunity was not to be wasted.

Took Lilly to the Horticultural Show in the Regent's Park, at which the chief features were the dresses of the ladies – their enormous chignons and dresses trailing along the ground and apology for bonnets, making them look like so many Bedlamites!

June 3rd
Took Lilly in a steamboat to point out the wonders of London & to obtain a view of the Thames Embankment which reminds me of the Paris Quays. Then to see the House of Lords where the Lord Chancellor was engaged with appeals. Then to the glorious Abbey to see the reredos, only unveiled on Easter Day. Saw, for the first time in my life a soldier in uniform, prayer book in hand, seating himself for the service. On the continent it is common enough to see soldiers kneeling in the churches, but I never before saw one on a weekday & voluntarily in England.

Saw another un-English group in Portland Place. Two of the 'Little Sisters of the Poor'[2] driving a picturesque tilted cart & calling at the houses for the crumbs from rich men's tables. They wore the full habit of their order. The cart was provided with large tin cans for the food, & had an alms box at the tail of it. One sister drove the stout pony & the other managed the cans, lugging them with all her strength from the house doors & ranging them in the cart.

June 8th
Returned to Dereham by the Express Train, doing the 115 miles from Shoreditch to Wymondham in 3 hours.

June 12th
Dined with Sweet of Colkirk on my return, meeting several people in wagons etc. returning from grand races at Dereham, & in which (as usual here) one of the running horses broke his leg & was killed on the spot.

June 24th
The 15th Norfolk Rifle Volunteers went into camp at Hunstanton Park. I had promised to accompany them on condition they attended a short Morning Service before parade, to which the Officers & men willingly consented. But alas! News came that my father was so dangerously ill that, hourly expecting a summons to London, I was obliged to countermand my tent.

June 26th
News arriving that my father was decidedly better, resolved to have a day at the camp & started by rail at 8 with Mr Hastings, the surgeon of the Corps. On arriving at the ground we at once reported to the Adjutant. Drill was going on, after which joined my own regiment & went through the tents. Each officer has a tent to himself & the men are 6 in each tent, their feet meeting in the centre, like the spokes of a wheel. Some tents are more smart & complete than others – that of a Capt. Scott of Aylsham was quite a lion having carpet, looking glass, flowers etc. The two objections to camping were the noise & the earwigs which infested the beds as soon as the damp began to rise. There were 2 other chaplains besides myself & the number of men about 500.

At 1.30 had lunch in the dining room at the Hall which Mr L'Estrange placed at the disposal of the officers for a Mess. Ladies were admitted & the band played on the lawn.

July 3rd

Dined with Mr Eden, the vicar of Wymondham, to meet the Bishop of Massachusetts. I cannot say that I consider him a favourable specimen of an American Bishop. He is decidedly & vulgarly low Church & I suspect, judging from his vanity (especially in the dress of his hair) & also from his manners, that he is of Irish extraction.

July 18th

First meeting of the Guild of St Nicholas. About 20 became members – they all engage in some sort of Church work, much or little, & we shall give lectures on Church principles, Church History etc. I hope by this means to reach the young men in shops, offices & banks. May God bless this design.

August 10th

Administered private communion to three persons whose combined age amounted to 244 years!

August 23rd

Rode to call on Mr Lane, the new Rector of Whissonsett. The Church & Rectory were formerly in the most miserable condition, now both are restored, & to my surprise we found not only a surpliced choir, six huge candles, and two more on the altar, but the full Eucharistic vestments to be followed in a Sunday or two, by incense. A few years ago, people could not be got to Church, but Mr Lane says they now come in crowds – that no complaints have been made & the farmers are wanting the few high pews which yet remain, to be forthwith removed!

September 10th

By permission of Lord Sondes the show of the Dereham Horticultural Society was held in Elmham Park. The gardens were delightful & Lord & Lady Sondes were very hospitable, inviting us into the House, where various grandees were assembled, & giving us refreshments.

September 19th

Drove to Holt, calling on Lord Hastings by the way, & returned the same night by 12 o'clock. My good horse, King Rufus, did the journey very well. The occasion was to preach a Thanksgiving Sermon after a special Harvest Service at the Parish Church. Among the company at the Rectory was a Miss Armstrong who enquired whether I belonged, like her, to the Irish, or the Borders Armstrongs – I told her the latter, but finding our motto was the same, and the arms only differing slightly, came to the amicable conclusion that we were a sort of relative.

October 2nd

As there is just a week before the boys come home, we spent the interval in Yarmouth. The weather was very indifferent and during a storm a vessel was driven ashore & 4 of the crew of 8 perished. One poor fellow was picked up two days afterwards 17 miles out to sea in the ship's boat, quite alone.

October 17th

The Bishop & Mrs Pelham invited my dear wife and self to luncheon previous to the Cathedral service. It was in fact, early dinner, as the hot soup, haunch of venison etc. fully testify. About 40 people sat down, including the Bishop of Ontario, the Bishop of Illinois, the Archdeacons of Norfolk & Suffolk & many clergymen of note. It was my wife's first introduction to the Palace. The Bishop of Illinois preached an orthodox but somewhat dry discourse nearly an hour in length. The service was of its usual florid description. The Dean was to have been present at the dinner but met with an accident to his knee which it is feared will lame him for life. This seems to be the fate of Deans of Norwich, the last being very lame.

November 22nd

Being Chaplain of the Rifle Corps, I mix and chat with the men after Parade. There is a new volunteer, a Frenchman, M. Moy, a journey-man leather-dresser. He fought against the Austrians at Solferino & was taken prisoner & detained for 2 years, but treated with every consideration. His father was an Army surgeon in France. He can speak English, German, Italian & some Hebrew – a very remarkable person, but a mauvais sujet, I suspect, nevertheless.

November 28th

M. Moy came to see me 'by night' to say that his father was a Jew & his mother a Lutheran, & that the latter had secretly brought him up in the Christian faith, but that he has never been baptised, as the very idea of it made his father furious. My morning among the privates had emboldened him to make the request & after he had given me assurance of his repentance & faith I agreed to baptize him. May God grant he is sincere.

November 29th
Baptised M. Moy in the presence of Capt. Bulwer, Mr Minns my curate & the Clerk.

December 10th
On the Friday, all London panic stricken by the Fenians blowing down the wall of the House of Detention at Clerkenwell[3] with a barrel of nitro-glycerine at mid-day, under the hope that two of their leaders, who were in the prison, might escape amid the general confusion, but through an anonymous letter to the Governor the prisoners had been 'aired' at an earlier hour. It reminds one of Gunpowder, Treason & Guy Fawkes. The Opera was burnt to the ground a few weeks ago & believed to be the work of Fenians out of retaliation for three of their leaders being hung at Manchester.

1868

January 1st
Today met an old gentleman of 74, who last week married a lady of 84. Though moving in the lower-middle class, he seems well off & had visited Rome, Naples, Jerusalem and Cairo, and 'had a particular mind' to see the Land of Goshen. He can't tell how he came to marry – supposed it was a providence! But the old lady is said to have 800£ a year!

January 17th
On arrival at Rokeles [the new home of his brother-in-law] my good horse, King Rufus, escaped from the stable & going into the moat at the back of the house, to drink, got into a deep hole & got out with difficulty.

January 19th
Took the service at Elmham in the afternoon. Lord & Lady Sondes & their family present, & though he is a very unassuming person, it was curious to see the deference paid by all: no one presumes to leave the Church at the conclusion of the service till 'the family' have departed in State. There was a very large congregation, with few of the middle class – all cottagers or aristocrats.

February 17th

Went to London for a week, chiefly to watch the state of my dear Parent's health. I very much fear my dearest mother has incipient cancer. Another object I had was to consult on Herbert's future career. I thought of the Royal Artillery but a Capt. McMahon, whose niece I escorted back into Norfolk, gave such an indifferent account of the Corps, especially in the matter of pay, that I abandoned the idea in favour of the Civil Service or a merchant's Counting House.

February 28th

Preached the first of a series of Mission Services at Whissonsett. Under the former Rector this used to be the most wretched Church & service imaginable – now all was orderly & beautiful. During my sermon I was so often interrupted by a member of the congregation that I began to think he must be one of the wretched beings sent by the 'Church Association' to interrupt the service in 'Ritualist' churches. Indeed I had to expostulate with him from the pulpit, but it soon became evident he was drunk & was prudently ushered out of the church by his friends.

My Annual Church Report came out. There is an increase in the offertory in all our various religious & charitable institutions. Deo Gratias. I suggested no further advance in ritual, for the experience of the previous year convinces me that this congregation are now brought to the extent of Ritual of which they are capable.

March 3rd

A very large & excited Vestry on the subject of the new Burial Ground, at which every rate-paying dissenter in the Parish was present. The dissenters were all for a cemetery & their burial grounds being closed. This was the cheapest way of obtaining a new one, besides which it levels the Church (in outward appearance) with the sects. The Church people were mainly for an extension of the existing Churchyard, but this was found to be impracticable. There was only one piece of land suitable for the purpose, & two dissenters having premises within 100 yards, objected. I frankly conceded this point, thus allaying the irritation of the dissenters, & they in turn conceded our point, viz. that out of the 9 members of the Burial Board, five should be Churchmen. The whole affair took 3 hours, & passed off harmoniously. The Vestry took place in the Assembly Room, & so saved our beautiful chancel from the profanation of puritans & freethinkers with their hats on &

that peculiar & irreverent class who never miss a Vestry, but are never seen in Church at any other time.

March 10th
Mr Lane, Rector of Whissonsett handed me a paper of apology signed by the man who interrupted the sermon the other night. He readily acknowledged the offence to God etc.

March 25th
Mr Gladstone, the Leader of the Opposition, is going in for the complete disestablishment & disendowment of the Irish Church. Upon this would follow, in time, they say, the 'established' kirk in Scotland, & the Church of England. Startling as this proposition is, I see so many evils arising from establishment that I would willingly relinquish it if endowment could be secured as an equivalent for the commuted rentcharge. If we were paid according to population, the present anomaly would cease, viz. the village livings being better provided for than the towns. The evil of establishment is (a) inducement to take Holy Orders for position (b) the temptation to rest authority on state influence rather than priestly functions, (c) subservience on the part of the Episcopate to the powers that be, paralysing their action & involving their deliberations with all sorts of legal difficulties.

March 29th
At Hoe Church the largest congregation I ever saw there, except on the occasion of the Bishop preaching last year. Three gypsies there, in regular costume, & one a beautiful brunette aged 12, dressed in scarlet & white, with a string of coins about her neck. They were sisters & the family are 'camping' in the Parish. They were baptised (so they said) & attended Church, but neither read nor write. Their names are Eva Angela, Gloria & Leanabel, the latter being a favourite name among them.

April 3rd
The great case which has excited so much interest at St Alban's Holborn[1] has been concluded by a most elaborative, exhaustive & catholic-minded judgement of Sir R. Phillimore. The three points of ritualism are Vestments, Lights & Incense. The first of these do not even form a count in the indictment, the second are declared lawful in day time during celebration of Holy Communion; the third is unlawful as a ceremony but may be used before & after service. On the whole, therefore, the promoters of this suit have taken little by their motion,

and (as a writer in The Saturday Review remarks) a visitor to St Alban's must be very keen-sighted to perceive any difference in the service. Mr Machonochie has written to his Bishop to say he will abide by the judgement.

Archbishop Tait wielding the crook of the Public Worship Regulation Bill to manage the ritualist sheep heading on the road to Rome
(Punch 18th December 1869)

April 11th

After a happy ride on horseback with my eldest boy, found a letter from Dr Peregrine by second post, to say that my mother had undergone a consultation, & that there was no doubt as to the nature of the disease. The most painful part is that the doctors consider it highly inexpedient at my parents' age & state of health that they should be informed of the real state of the case.

April 27th [London]

My dear wife, the girls & myself went to Wimpole St & Lagley for our annual visit, the boys having returned to school. It was a day of exciting news, political & domestic. Read in the papers in the train that the Queen's son (Duke of Edinburgh)[2] had been shot in the back by a Fenian at Sydney! He is not dead, but is in a precarious state.

King Theodore of Abyssinia has been killed by our troops in the attack on his stronghold of Magdala.[3] He had previously surrendered the English prisoners, 60 in number, but refused to surrender himself. Mad, fanatic – not unlike King Saul – he died a more noble death, fighting sword in hand.

The domestic excitement was that a few minutes before our arrival at Wimpole Street, a sort of tornado, accompanied by lightning struck the adjoining houses, causing 700£ damage to one, & injuring 6 or 7. The parapet of my father's house was knocked into the street.

May 1st
Took Helen to the service at St Ethelburga's. My old friend Rodwell said the communion service in a crimson chasuble, and with lights, but since the recent judgement [see entry for April 3rd] he has discontinued incense as a part of the service, tho' the Church had been 'censed' heavily beforehand.

May 5th
Attended the great meeting at St James's Hall in deprecation of the proposed disestablishment of the Irish Church. The Archbishop was in the Chair & the Archbishops of York & Armagh & a host of other Bishops, Dukes & Lords were present – the recital of whose names occupied a third of a column in the Times. The Hall & galleries were densely crowded & all seemed unanimous except two individuals on opposite sides of the Hall who interrupted the Bishop of Oxford with cuckoo cries of 'No Popery'. This caused so much confusion that at one time I thought the meeting would not proceed, but two stalwart country parsons tackled the malcontents & summarily ejected them. The cool way in which they resumed their seats after this feat was worth seeing.

May 7th
Went with my dear father to Highgate Cemetery where he chose his burial place!

May 9th
Visited my old friend Martin at Thatcham. The town contains about 2,000 people. It is on the old Bath road but has an unprosperous appearance on account of the coaching being superseded by the rail. Martin has difficulty in instituting his mode of Ritual, and it is curious to observe how exactly the same kind of opponents are to be found in every place & how they resort to precisely the same tactics in order to

September 26th

Harvest Thanksgiving. The collection amounted to £23.0.0, for the Norfolk & Norwich Hospital – just double what we usually get. The causes, I imagine, are that the subject was (1) local, (2) physical, (3) unsectarian and (4) there is a quid pro quo (which is sought for in all modern charity) in the shape of recommendations to the Hospital.

October 3rd

A new curate, Rev.W.H.Sandon, began work today. He is B.A. of Oxford, a younger man, single, than I have lately had as my coadjutors. Today was a sort of break up of old connections. My neighbour, Rev. J. Thompson, has sold all his property & the good will of his school, & this is his last Sunday. Two other families also leave. They are none of them any loss – the former family, especially in past years, being very antagonistic. Indeed the little band of opponents, with the exception of one couple, are all dispersed by removal or death. I paid them a call & made my wife subscribe to a little testimonial got up by the low church people for Mr Thompson.

October 5th

Took my dear wife & girls & Herbert to Lowestoft for a week. Lowestoft decidedly the best East Anglian watering place, & now very animated with the herring fishery. The Bathursts, Hydes etc. are all here. Had a fishing excursion with Capt. Bathurst on the famed Broads, but it was too late to catch many. Sea fishing, & excursions to sea answered better.

October 14th

By invitation of the Bishop met my old friend the Bishop of British Columbia, the Bishop of Labuan & Borneo, and several others at a luncheon-dinner at the Palace.

October 19th

Today took my eldest son to be entered at Caius College, Cambridge. Had a bedroom in College at Mr Day's, a Fellow, & was amused that after an absence of exactly 29 years I was at once recognised by some of the college servants, as I subsequently was by several tradesmen in the town.

November 15th

Went to London, having in view the following subjects – to claim my father's promise to give me 300£, chiefly to start John at Cambridge –

to determine upon a monument for my dear mother's grave – to get Herbert's name down at the Horse Guards for a commission – and to induce my father to employ a regular agent. These matters took up the whole time so that I had not an hour for myself.

December 18th

The whole of this quarter has been of a very busy character. As Christmas approaches the work increases. This week I have visited every cottage in Hoe & supplied them with coals, & most of them with meat.

December 21st

In Vestry after the service & usual distribution of clothing, the Master of a Reformatory School in Suffolk, brought a lad who had been convicted of a trifling offence & been afterwards sent there. The Master left £2 with me for the boy to receive in instalments, 5/- for a Christmas Dinner & promised him an outfit for Canada, if he behaved well. The boy – about 18 – actually cried because he was not going to return to the Reformatory.

1870

January 4th

Dined at Mr Lane's, Whissonsett Rectory. They bear the Royal Arms impaled with the motto 'Garde le Roi' from Charles II having ridden in disguise with their ancestors on a pillion & so escaped the Roundheads.

January 18th

Our new neighbours, the Pillings, are very much more like neighbours than their predecessors to whose house my wife & self were never invited, whereas this was the second occasion of our accepting their hospitality. The invite was to a friendly dinner & all the young people came to dance in the evening while the old fellows (myself among them) had a pipe in the study. Pilling is much better informed than his friends, a good musician, fond of literature, a scholar, & a man of general information & yet he wants the finish of a perfect gentleman. But the exchange of neighbours is a very advantageous one.

January 28th

News came that a parishioner had fallen down dead. He had been telling me only two day's before of the probability of this, as he suffered from a heart complaint. Unfortunately, I fear it has been expedited by his daughter, a pupil teacher in a school, having formed an imprudent acquaintance with a young man in Cambs where she now is, a correspondence having taken place between me & the clergyman on that subject. What must be the feelings of this poor girl, who may thus almost charge herself with being the cause of her father's death!

February 7th

Our old Brougham literally came in two, on crossing the railway lines, cutting Miss Plumer with the broken glass & hurling the Coachman & Curate, who was on the box, to the ground. The horse bruised by the carriage falling on his hocks & the carriage done for.

February 15th

Mrs Gooch died at the age of 98 years! She never had a day's illness, or knew what pain was. Correspondents to the 'Times' are fond of sending 'remarkable instances of longevity', in which they often cite 85 as a great age, but in Norfolk, nonogenarians are common. Widow Mayes, now living, is 90, Mr Harvey 91, Lord Hannent 98, Lord Cocker, recently deceased, was 98 & I have conversed with a person in Dereham 110 years old!

February 16th

Drove to a penny reading at Elmham, the first they have had. The schoolroom was literally crammed, & the choir sang some things in the interim. I read 'Sir Rupert the Fearless', Legge some Tennyson, Mr Eaton some Mary Howitt, & Lane of Whissonsett some Christmas Carol. To sup at the Vicarage & a drive home on a road hard & white with snow, with a moon shining as light as day.

Febr 25th

Took Lilly & Emily to see Adams's Circus, a temporary wooden structure at Norwich, the performance being under the patronage of Lord & Lady Stafford, who were present, as well as a large number of the aristocracy. The performance very good, though equestrian entertainments, still so called, are fast giving way to 'acrobats'. The great attraction was a celebrated 'artist' on the flying trapeze but, truly wonderful as he was, he is not to be compared with the famous

'Leotard'. Lady riders seem now to be getting rare & the only two who exhibited were of the most modest character.

Mr Harvey died suddenly, aged 91. About 10 years ago he lighted the Church at his own expense, and being minded to warm it also was about to carry it out, instead of leaving money in his will for that purpose, but, alas, the second time I visited him he was speechless, & not having given the definite order I fear that between two stools we shall fall to the ground. If so, it is very unfortunate as our Church is terribly cold in the winter.

March 14th
Attended the funeral of P.N.Aufrere Esq, by invitation, at Scarning Church, where his father was formerly Rector. He has lived in Dereham about 20 years & though deformed in body & weak in mind is descended from a very high French family who, having been Huguenots, fled their country at the revocation of the Edict of Nantes. He was well off, always a gentleman notwithstanding his sad drawbacks, a regular & devout attendant at Church & a supporter of Church projects.

March 19th
Drove the girls & Sandon to Great Cressingham to bid adieu to Henrietta Taylor who is going into a London sisterhood. I rather doubt her vocation, but this seems to be the recourse nowadays for girls who do not marry. This is the complaint of the young men, who, nevertheless, do not marry them. Mr Taylor has recently married his third wife – a very nice person about the age of his daughter.

May 12th
I desire to record my heartfelt gratitude to Almighty God for preserving my darling Helen & myself from destruction yesterday. Our horse (always in some trouble or other) ran away with the Phaeton. I lost all control over him for a mile, & passed between a huge waggon of straw & some cottages, where it would seem impossible to pass in safety. Fortunately I succeeded, at a certain turn in the road, in getting the horse's head away from home. From that moment hope revived, & some men being in the road had the effect of stopping our mad career, and we descended in safety. I need scarcely say that we walked home & that the horse must be sold. Our work is not enough for him.

June 2nd

Surprised by a notice in the Times that all candidates for direct Commissions must go up on July 25th. This is so much earlier than my dear Herbert expected that I fear he will not pass. Nevertheless wrote to his 'coach' to give him a second evening in the week. The fact is the Army is being put on a different footing altogether.

June 18th

Everington introduced me to the Farmer's dinner at the Norfolk Hotel. I was surprised at the expansiveness of the viands & the intelligence of the men. They seemed pleased to get a parson among them.

June 23rd

Baptized Capt. & Mrs Bathhurst's child, by name Launcelot Villebois, & afterwards took early dinner with them, accompanied by my wife. Rev. Onslow, Rector of Sandringham there. It seems the Princess of Wales saves her husband from much unpopularity. He is hissed at the theatre – I fear he is a degenerate son of his good (but cold) father.

July 9th

A day of panic in our town! A Radical & dissenter returned for Norwich, Sir R. Harvey, found shot in his garden, supposed to be by his own hand! The Bank stopped payment![1] His superb entertainments have been more than once recorded in these pages, he has built a palatial bank at Norwich & a magnificent mansion. But the heir to the baronetcy had recently formed a disgraceful marriage. To complete all, war has been declared between France & Prussia about a Prussian prince being nominated to the throne of Spain.

August 3rd

The new (H.M.) School Inspector Rev. Mr Synge came. Alas! What a difference from his predecessor Mr Meyrick. This man is one of the most objectionable style of clergy, in comparison with which one could embrace the evangelicals. He was full of self-importance & conceit.

August 8th

Seldom as this diary chronicles public events, the victory which the Prussians have just achieved over the French cannot be passed over. They took (at Wörth) 30 cannon, 6 Mitralleuses (a murderous engine said to kill 500 at a discharge & of which the Prussians are provided), 2 Eagles, 4,000 prisoners & the Camp & Baggage. Nothing like this has occurred to the French Army since Waterloo. Paris is in a state of siege & the position of the Emperor is most critical. English sympathy seems with Prussia.

August 13th
Proved the debt of the Clothing Club at Harvey's broken Bank (80£)[1] & transferred it to Gurney's.

August 17th
A day to be marked with white chalk. Telegram from Herbert to say he had successfully passed his exam for a direct commission. This is the more creditable because his time & attention had been taken up with other work. His getting a commission will now be a matter of time – perhaps a long time, but having youth on his side & employment in the interim he can afford to wait.

August 23rd
Took Helen on an excursion to Cromer, via Aylsham. Visited Cawston Church & Blickling Hall en route, but could not see the interior of the latter on account of the recent death of the owner, the estimable but afflicted Marquis of Lothian. The quaint & picturesque Hall & beautiful park & surroundings struck me as being in the most perfect order imaginable.

August 24th
Drove Helen to an Archery Fête at Gunton Park (Lord Suffield's) about 5 miles from Cromer, through the picturesque village of Thorpe. The park seemed tame and wanting in variety of timber. The house seems commonplace after Blickling. As to the fête, it was like all others. We were invited by the Bulwers, they being members of the club & in consequence had good places at the luncheon-dinner in the Marquee. Lord & Lady S., though in the house, did not come near the guests, a piece of snobbery which is all the worse in a 'Liberal' & 'friend of the people', especially as this was the last & prize day.

September 6th
Dr Russell, the Times 'special' at the seat of the war, has a most affecting description of the Emperor Napoleon giving up his sword to the King of Prussia & surrendering himself prisoner. He is to be sent to Germany, where, Revolution having taken place in Paris, the Empress

will join him. It remains to be seen if the 'Republic' will defend Paris, which is open to the march of the invaders.

September 7th
The Bishop requests me to be on the Committee for the Norwich Centre for the Diocesan Conference, the more gratifying because at our public meetings I have expressed opposite views to his own.

September 13th
My old friend Sister Mary, who is staying at Whinborough, has done some good works here. In conjunction with my wife & Mr Carthew, she has sent three huge bales of bandages, shirts, pillows etc. for the sick & wounded in the war, and has sent to me for special Confession & Absolution an erring Sister in whom she has taken great interest in London & for whom she has found a situation in Dereham.

October 6th
The Officers of the Volunteer Battalion & the Sgts & some men from each corps had a 'rope-drill' at the Vicarage, being at it from 11 to 4. Provided an 18 gallon cask of ale for them, which they drank up, & also lots of sherry for the officers. It would not do to have them too often!

The Prussians have cleared everything before them up to the walls of Paris. The French government removed to Tours, the only communication between it & Paris being by balloons. A German & French aeronaut fired at each other's balloons when at immense height. Anything more desperately horrible it is hard to conceive.

October 27th
The unfortunate French, now shut up in Paris, had another terrible reverse. The almost impregnable fortress of Metz is taken by the Germans, with 173,000 men, 6,000 officers & 3 Marshalls taken prisoner. It has been a remarkable feature throughout this war, that whole armies have surrendered without apparently striking a blow.

November 7th
To London. The Branch from Tottenham to St Pancras just established is an enormous improvement on the Shoreditch terminus, bringing one to a better part of town & causing a saving of time & cab fare. The Station is a magnificent Gothic building & without any doubt the finest in London.

November 11th

Attended a short sevice at St Ethelburga, Bishopgate & accompanied Mr Rodwell to his residence at Highgate. His daughter is sub-Prioress of a convent at Metz, where she has been all through the late seige. They have been terribly anxious about her, & only heard of her safety this morning.

December 27th

Buried two inmates at the Union for the chaplain & addressed the sick in the wards, & said prayers with them. A sad & half-demented lot. Drove through the deep snow in a sledge.

December 28th

Found out a child whose mother in London had lost sight of him, & wrote to her. Visited a sick woman who was formerly married to a gentleman, now to a stoker on the Rail! A sad tale of sin & misery!!

1871

January 12th

Hard frost & deep snow. The sufferings of beseigers & beseiged before Paris must be awful. 6,000 of the German Army have been frostbitten & the Parisians are eating horses, dogs, cats & rats!

February 3rd

There is an Armistice between Germany & France for three weeks to enable the latter to elect a Constitutional Assembly to determine its future form of government. The Emperor is still a prisoner, his wife & son residing at Chislehurst, Kent. King of Prussia declared Emperor of Germany. He claims as indemnity from the French 400 millions in money, 20 ships of war, cession of Alsace & Lorraine, & Pondicherry in the East Indies!!!!!

Seeing Everington's name announced as Chairman to the 'Farmers' Tea' at the King's Arms, I supported him, in order to do away with the imputation under which the clergy lie, that they will not consort with Farmers. The 'Tea' was in fact a good dinner & dessert at which 50 sat down, among them our M.P. Mr Reade. They seemed highly pleased at my coming & drank my health. It may do some good.

May 5th

A most respectable old man & his wife, retired farmers, have lately taken a little place in Hoe. Now it appears that they have done so as a refuge from their son's wife, who is a fearful drunkard, smashes their windows & is frequently in prison. This is on the plea of recovering their two little children whom the old people have placed in safety elsewehere. The husband is obliged to leave her. The old lady came to say that this woman had discovered their whereabouts, & that they were living in daily dread of a visit from her – a troubled termination to a long life, during which they sacrificed themselves to this son. Whether any fault is with him did not appear, but it looks suspicious as he was divorced from a previous wife by whom he had two boys, who are maintained by the self-denial of these good old people.

Completed a visitation of the rows of new houses in Norwich Rd, & found them to be tenanted by strangers, exactly one half of whom are dissenters, including 3 Preachers!!

May 17th

Dined with the Officers of the Volunteers at the King's Arms. Sat next to Col. Duff who said that when he was taken prisoner by the Russians in the Crimea, he was marched – with other officers, nearly 1,000 miles inland. Sometimes they slept at a gentleman's house & sometimes in the jail. On one of these latter occasions the fare etc. was very bad, & Col. Duff asked if there were any Englishmen there? There was one – a poor fellow earning about £30 a year. He came & offered to be surety for the Colonel if he might be allowed to sleep at the Inn on parole. Granted. On leaving, the poor Englishman asked if he could do anything for the Colonel in England, where he longed to return. 'Yes' said the Colonel, 'tell my family I am safe & take this letter to my brother-in-law who is an M.P.: he may be able to do something for you'. The M.P. finding that the man could speak Russian perfectly, sent him to the Prime Minister, Palmerston, who sent him back to Russia in the employ of the British Government at a £1,000 a year & his expenses paid. When his chief died the fortunate man was promoted to his place and has now £3,000 a year, whereas when the Colonel first met him in the Russian village he was a poor tutor at 30! A very genial fellow, Colonel Duff.[1]

June 15th [at Bradford on Avon]

The greatest curiosity here is an old lady, a Mrs Jones, who is a spiritualist. In her garden is a stone coffin (circa 1300) with a skeleton

entire which is covered with a movable flap. She told us some extraordinary stories of manifestations which happened to herself: how she
played two games of chess with a spirit who wrote the moves on a slate
on the lap of a medium, & beat him!! How glasses of wine had been
presented by unknown means to her lips, and after tasting were
incontinently and suddenly removed & how baskets of flowers and
fruit had come through the solid walls – to all of which we listened
with great politeness & considerateness, but returned to dinner under
the conviction that Mrs Jones is a monomaniac.

June 21st

Accompanied William Duncombe to the sale by auction of the celebrated Merton flock of Downs for which the late Lord Walsingham
was famous. Luncheon was prepared for 400 at which the prizes won
in former years were exhibited on a buffet. I counted no less than 40
gold & silver cups, & the medals were by the dozen. Nothing could be
more picturesque and orderly than the 'pens' & attendant shepherds,
who were almost theatrical in their get up. The animals fetched
enormous prices e.g. one ram £65, another £84 and a third £185! The
principal purchasers were the Prince of Wales, the Duke of Richmond
& Lord Portsmouth. The animals were to go on to Denmark, Prussia,
Canada, Australia & Peru!

July 16th

A poor man who has been confined to his house 5 years was dragged
in a chair, two miles, by his wife to receive the sacrament. As the chair
could only stand at the West End of the Church, I went there to
administer.

August 1st

Took Lilly, as bridesmaid, to Miss Paddon's wedding at Mattishall &
went to the breakfast. As the only child of the late Vicar the sympathy
was great on her behalf, but it rather detracted from the pleasure that
the match was not approved by her mother, chiefly on the ground of
the Bridegroom's position – a yeoman – though he seems a careful and
presentable young man. The 'settlements' not having arrived at 10
minutes to 12 we drew up a paper for the contracting parties to sign,
but it is doubtful whether it is of legal value!

August 17th

It must be, I think, from my people having some confidence in me,
that this morning I have been consulted in my study by a Parishioner

with a relative who is a curse to her, by another on the advisability of separating from her husband for his frantic malice, by a third to make confession & by a clergyman in the choices between two little pieces of preferment.

October 10th

Was awoke at 6.30 to go to Mrs Andrew's, who had just discovered her son dead in his bed. From my first coming here have taken much interest in this family whom I had rescued from dissent. Aged people, who had raised themselves by years of industry, this son, aged 20, was their sole joy. But Thomas was an old man's child, and always sickly. I got him a clerkship at Gurney's, but he was obliged to relinquish it for ill health. Remained with the mother all the day nearly, ordering everything & writing to all her friends etc.

October 18th

Our eldest boy is of age this day. Sent him £5 and his Grandfather did the same. He is a very steady, good, boy though somewhat lacking in that energy which is necessary for success in life.

Went to my Mission at Toftwood. Baptized two children there & have been looking the people up in order to induce them to come. While doing so found a poor boy had to appear on bail at 2 sessions for obtaining goods under false pretences – some trumpery brooches which he had given to two maids who, I believe, had instigated him. Knowing he had not been right in his head for some years, owing to a bad fever, wrote to the Chairman of the Quarter Sessions, and am told by a lawyer in court (the boy was undefended) that my letter had the effect of getting the punishment narrowed to 14 days in prison.

October 24th

I drove the Duncombes to Mr Mills of Claremont[2] (late the shooting seat of the Duke of Wellington) to see his valuable collection of paintings & remain to luncheon. There are about 50 originals of Old Masters, some of which by Murillo & Velasquez are of the size of life. The Dutch school is well represented & there are six beautiful Canalettos. But the gem, to my mind, is a Madonna by Sassoferrato, even more beautiful, and if possible, realising the ideal better than the famous one by C. Dolci.

October 27th [Great Yarmouth]

Saw the new Fish Wharf, where lay some hundreds of herring smacks from Holland, Scotland, France etc. It is 780 feet in length, under cover, with offices etc. This year the catch is so prodigious that there is not enough salt for the fish, or casks in which to pack them, & dealers complain as much as if the supply was scanty!

December 1st

The Prince of Wales is lying between life & death of gastric fever at Sandringham. It is supposed to have been caught at Lord Londesborough's, near Scarborough. Lord Chesterfield, one of the party, is dead – also a groom – supposed to be from bad sewerage.

December 11th

A 'prayer' only written at Privy Council in London at 2 this morning arrived by telegraph at 9.30! It was for the P. of Wales whose decease is hourly expected. I had, of course, to transcribe it, in order to use it in Church, but either through hurry of composition, or mistakes by telegraph clerks it was, here & there, no sense at all, so I had to put it into shape as well as I could.

December 31st

The Prince is now on a fair way to recovery.

1872

Revd Armstrong's children in 1872
L.to R. Helen, Bertie, Lilly. In front, John with Grip, the dog.

February 11th

The small pox has unfortunately been introduced here from Norwich, & we have 14 cases & 2 deaths. One of these deaths occurred this

214

morning and at 9 this evening I committed the poor fellow to the grave. Although I have passed through every phase of duty at various epochs, this is the first time I took a funeral by torchlight.

February 16th

Brought a boy before Magistrates for breaking fences. Explained that it was with great reluctance that I did so, & that it was simply a warning to prevent a great nuisance. Fined, or a fortnight's imprisonment in default.

February 27th

Buried another by torchlight who had died of smallpox the same morning. This makes 6 deaths out of 20 cases we have had.

March 23rd

To Norwich, to a conference at the Palace. The Bishop gave an excellent luncheon to the whole party. I heard two clerical anecdotes. Dean Pellew went to shoot, at Sir E. Kerrison's. The keeper said 'we've had Dukes & Lords & suchlike & I know how to address them but we've never had a Dean'. Presently up got a cock pheasant – when the keeper cries 'Cock! Shoot, your Holiness'. Also someone complaining to Bishop Wilberforce that Archbishops were the Most Rev., Bishops the Right Rev., Deans the Very Rev. but that there was no distinctive title to Rural Deans. 'Oh' said the Bishop, 'they might properly be called "the Rather Rev." '

March 31st

Going to Norwich on Saturday heard that handloom weaving is still carried on to a considerable extent at Wymondham, who do it by piecework for masters in Norwich. A hamlet near the station called 'The Lyzards'[1] is full of weavers. It is said of this hamlet that there is not a house from which someone has not been transported, from which it may be inferred the weavers are an impoverished & improvident lot.

June 17th

Off to London to see my father and to attend to his affairs. Finding his assurance not paid and knowing his life to be so precarious went by cab to his Bankers and obtained the necessary sum – another cab to Fleet Street and saved the closing of the office by one minute only!

June 24th
Went to the opening of the Bethnal Green Museum by the Prince & Princess of Wales. The Prince looked pale after his illness, the Princess looked charming. It is the receptacle of a most superb collection of art treasures which has come to Sir Richard Wallace.[2]

June 25th
Dr Peregrine told me that Sir Richard Wallace is the natural son of the Marquis of Hertford.

June 28th
To my father, and accompanied him in his Bath chair into Regent's Park, which is greatly improved. A beautiful drinking fountain provided by 'Bomejee Readymoney Esq., a Parsee gentleman of Bombay'. The name 'Readymoney' would seem to be a soubriquet for one who had made a rapid fortune in trade, but William Challice says it is an English translation of his other Indian name.[3]

July 22nd
Went to a pleasant garden party at Necton Rectory and met poor Walker's widow, who was staying with her uncle in what would have been her home if her husband had lived. A pretty, stylish young thing, but not suited for a parson's wife.

October 27th
Preached in the afternoon at St James's Pockthorpe – a vile neighbourhood full of factories and low dwellings. Tried to persuade some idle fellows to enter church, without effect. They gave me a good-natured laugh and a wink, as much as to say 'We're not as green as that!'

December 30th
It is most reluctantly that one would go to London at this time, but circumstances transpired connected with my sister which demanded my presence there. It seems that an adventurer, calling himself the Duc de Roussillon, under cover of affording information in the compilation of her work on French Palaces, has succeeded in obtaining considerable sums of money from her while she, unfortunately, insists on the validity both of the obligation and the title. Found the servants had been in the habit of conveying money and letters during my sister's long illness. In short a crisis had clearly been reached which rendered prompt action indispensable, or my sister be

compromised. My father being quite hors de combat, the responsibility rests upon myself.

December 31st
Called on the 'Duke' & left a message (he being in Paris – so they said) that he was denied the house. Put a detective on his trail, gave the butler a month's warning, with loss of character to any future master if he carried more messages to the 'Duke'.

1873

January 1st
The cloud which hung over the old year has not yet dispersed. A sad scene with my sister, who declares she will leave the house if she is not allowed unrestricted intercourse with her friend. I remain firm & my precautionary measures are approved by her son-in-law, her friend Mr Barford & her lawyer, Mr Paed of Storey's Gate.

January 3rd
Plunged again into this unhappy affair & had an interview with a General Blunt who is marking down the same individual & has several similar cases against him. Mr Paed, the lawyer, has obtained suspension of hostilities on the part of my sister till next Monday at 4.00p.m. which will enable me to return to Dereham.

January 6th
In London, again. My firmness & resolution never so tried, but thank God I had strength to utterly forbid the entrance of the 'Duke' or to let the servants take any message to him, even at the risk of my sister leaving the house. Mr Paed the lawyer & Mr Barford, a friend, endeavoured to make me modify this. The result was that she did not leave the house, & the victory was won. Interview with General Blunt, Montagu Square, chairman of the society for detection of such miscreants, undertaking to pay the expense of a detective. Men however firm seem to fail when they are brought in connection with my sister.

January 19th
The post brought the news that Herbert would be appointed to a regiment as a Sub-Lieutenant in a few days!

January 27th

Letter from Horseguards today to say the Commander in Chief offered Bertie a Sub-Lieutenancy in the 97th Foot, stationed in Dublin. Offer of course accepted, on learning from Capt. Bathurst that it was a very respectable, though not crack, Regiment, & that he knows the Colonel, who was a gentleman.

March 5th

Again telegraphed to go to see my father, who it was thought was dying, but by the time I arrived he was so much better as to enable me to return on Saturday. Occupied the three days in his affairs and, on one of them, walked into St Alban's Holborn. There was a very large crucifix, coloured, on a quasi Altar by the Chancel step. A priest (in surplice and violet stole) was confessing a female in the aisle, the confessional consisting of curtains instead of boxes & both priest and penitent were fully exposed to view.

April 14th

In consequence of the Prince and Princess of Wales coming to Elmham to lay the foundation of a County school, the Vestry was heard at the early hour of 9.00 a.m. There being two candidates for the people's churchwarden, viz. Everington and Gidney, and the latter being the favourite by 1 hand, a Poll was demanded for the former, and the most excited Vestry I have ever presided over was the result. Afterwards, all Dereham went to Elmham and had a good view of the Royal party, the Princess looking terribly pale and the Prince just as much too fat.

April 21st

Poll for the Parish Warden took place this day. This affair, which began rather gloomily on April 14th ended in the greatest triumph of Church principles over Dissent and Low Church that I have known since living in Dereham. This being the point of the contest, every effort was made by the clever resident Baptist Minister to return the candidate who would 'thwart the Vicar' – he wrote letters on the 'rampant Ritualism' at Dereham in the county papers, and issued a Bill announcing his intention of preaching on the subject of the Election. I was at my post at 8.00 a.m. and Gidney seemed likely to win in a canter during the first two hours, but after that Everington crept up and soon passed him, and won by a large majority – Everington 592, Gidney 280, majority 312!!! It was curious to see how the countenances of the Dissenters fell, and how the most respectable went away and did not return, how the Baptist Minister came hectoring into the room and above all, how a dissenting draper paid up the rates of a voter at the booth, feeling sure he would vote for Gidney, when, on my asking him for whom he wished to vote, he exclaimed 'Everington for ever'. Squibs[1] were being sent about, a band played, and our little town showed more excitement than it did at the county election. I forbad the bells being rung beforehand.

The ci-devant Warden (Hyde), the lawyer (Cooper) and the Doctor (Vincent) who have always worked against me, more or less openly, have now received a defeat which they richly merit.

May 13th

During my brief absence Mr Hyde died. As people's warden he differed widely from myself in religion and politics – I am thankful that I visited him the day before leaving home. He has been rapidly failing but it is thought that his recent parochial defeat contributed towards hastening his end. His great energy and capacity for business ensured for him a certain respect even where he was far from being loved.

May 25th

On the Queen's Birthday, Bertie carried the Colours of the 97th at a grand Field Day in the Phoenix Park, Dublin.

15th June

My second curate, Rev. George Dean Dundas Watt, who was ordained last Sunday, officiated for the first time and seems likely to turn out to be a valuable curate, but no sooner does he come than Mr Norwood, the senior, gives notice to leave, objecting to work with another curate.

1st July

Took my wife, John & Lilly to Yarmouth for a week. Had excellent lodgings on the South Beach. The place not as full as usual, accounted for by people being kept in London on account of grand doings consequent on the visit of the Shah of Persia. Part of the Channel Squadron passed Yarmouth on the Sunday afternoon after seeing him off to France. They were going to Leith – a grand and solemn sight.

July 19th

Bishop Wilberforce, the 'greatest monument of the English Church'[2] (as the Times calls him) was killed by being thrown from his horse, while riding in Surrey.

August 1st [London]

A pleasing feature of this visit was that my old curate Dove (now an honorary Canon of Adelaide) dined at Wimpole Street. On our return we broke the journey to see Ely Cathedral again after many years, and were present at service, at which Bishop McDougal read the service. We were not much impressed with his bearded face and lounging habit.

August 12th

Another old curate who has a living in Hampshire, Atkinson, called. He has exchanged with a neighbour for a couple of Sundays, and will dine with us – singularly enough a third old curate, who is staying with his family at Hunstanton (Skeat), invites himself from Saturday till Monday. It shows, at all events, that I have never quarrelled with my curates!

August 23rd

This has been a trying week, on several counts. There has been a sad fracas among the Challices even to their summoning me by telegram to check it, which I did, however, by letter. Then I find my father's annual expenditure exceeds his income, chiefly on account of his having let his properties get out of repair. Then I find my eldest boy has formed an attachment to a clergyman's daughter who has not a sixpence, and that Lilly has done the same with a clergyman's son, who is no better off. Then I found the sympathy of my wife enlisted on her children's behalf, giving Lilly permission to correspond with Arthur Nelson, and consenting to chaperone Miss Bell, whom I have not seen, to a dance to be given in Dereham next week, and both without my knowledge.

August 26th

My wife and Lilly accompanied me to the meeting of the Dereham & Fakenham Archery Club, of which we are non-shooting members. Our chief object was to see Raynham Hall, in the park of which the meeting was held. It is a mansion, by Inigo Jones, of far greater importance than I had supposed, second only to Houghton among the palatial residences of Norfolk. It belongs to Marquis Townshend, whose father is represented as a bluff old seaman in Admiral's uniform. The present Marquis is a trifle cracked, his hobby being to haul all mendicants before the Magistrates & get them punished. His wife ran away about three months ago with a man old enough to be her father, but has returned, and went to Church arm in arm to show that the reconciliation was complete.

September 16th

Miss Neame's wedding is interesting because her father 'was once a gentleman', kept a pack of hounds in Kent and ran through his fortune – also because her suitor 15 years ago transferred his affections to her sister, whom he married, and both of whom were present on this occasion. Miss Neame after this affair went to China as a Governess, and has now married a wine merchant of Sheffield who has been attached to her for some years. Thus the ruined family is recuperating itself. Mr N. gave a capital breakfast and presided thereat with the ease and courtesy which marked his origin.

September 28th

Took the service at St James' Pockthorpe[3], a terribly low and squalid place, shops open (such as they are) groups dirty, idle, smoking and very few except aged at Church. Conversed with one of these groups and invited them in. One man, who had a huge basket of fresh water-cresses said if I would give him the price of them he would come, otherwise he should sell all of them in the time he would have to lose by being in Church.

October 7th

My wife, Helen and myself dined at Rev. Collison's one of his great parties. He is admirable in all matters not connected with his profession.

October 17th

Met W. Challice at his room in the new section of the Post Office – a very splendid building and marvellously fitted up with every possible scientific improvement, e.g. telegraphs, and letters sent through tubes by blasts of air. We went to see Gerald Challice who, greatly to his credit earned for himself a commission in the Army Service Corps by competitive examination – 200 candidates and 20 commissions to be contended for! He has got good quarters and 170£ a year pay, being 80£ above that of a Sub-Lt. in the line. The uniform, (dark blue and white), not very attractive, the nature of the service cavalry rather than infantry, and the horses (in stables holding 50 each) more useful than ornamental.

October 30th

My wife and I dined at the Langton's – rather a dull affair, though the dinner was excellent. I begin to doubt whether the game is worth the candle of this sort of party at this time of year.

November 1st

Drove Mr Watt, the junior curate, to lunch at Necton and take part in the Annual commemoration. Was sorry to find that Miss Mason, sister of the departed High Church Squire, has got under Low Church influence through a brother-in-law, and also her companion – the latter not even attending the service, though she was at the luncheon, and indeed persuading Miss Mason to drive to a neighbouring Church on Sundays, because the service at Necton is Gregorian!

November 6th

Went to Parochial Work Association in Norwich, subject the church in relation to the labour question, chosen in consequence of the serious strikes going on among the labourers. The debate, in which I took no part, was feeble, the general impression being that the clergy had better let it alone and that the question would, in time, rectify itself after the law of demand and supply.

Herbert's Regiment embarks today for Jamaica, but he, with the depot, sails for Portsmouth, whither, it is thought, they will proceed to Colchester or Maidstone for a year and then join their comrades in the West Indies.

November 19th

Du Port said he had reason to believe that the Dean and Chapter would be glad if I would take the Vicarage of Great Yarmouth! It would not be so good a living, without my beautiful park of Glebe, the people would not tolerate my 'line of things' and I am getting too old to begin afresh in so large a post, so told him I should decline the honour at once!

November 27th

News came that the Rev. Carson, Vicar of Scarning, is dead. Last week he fell down in the road on his way to an act of charity, and was carried home by some parishioners who were called to the spot by his dog. Poor Carson's forte was good nature and, though without earnestness, or with any decided views, he will be much regretted by a large circle of friends.

Old Mrs Hipperson, my parishioner at Hoe, has obtained 30£ per annum as a result of my writing among influential people on her behalf. She insisted on my accepting a Queen Anne's Guinea as a token of her appreciation.

December 16th

Mr Angerstein's Staghounds met at Dereham today. Turned out at Hoe, the deer turned back and made across our Glebe where Lilly saw it quietly sniffing the air by our kitchen garden, till scared by the baying of the dogs and the sound of the horn.

December 20th

About 4 o'clock news came that my dear boy had passed his examination and immediately and with thankful heart telegraphed the information to Thatcham, where he is to be curate.

Dec 23rd [London]

All day about my father's business, and my son's fitting him up with cassock, surplice, set of coloured stoles & Biretta.

December 29th

The long dreaded telegram has come. On returning form my pastoral visits at 6, my dear wife told me that my excellent father was no more!

1874

January 3rd

The mournful day has come. At 11.00 a Hearse and two mourning coaches started from No. 7 for Highgate Cemetery. The morning was terribly wet, but just as the coffin was being lowered a bright gleam of sun broke out, and a robin perched himself upon a tomb close by to sing his little requiem.

January 4th

The remainder of the week was occupied in valuation for Probate of my dear Father's will – separating plate divided between my sister and self, sorting and destroying old papers and letters. On account of the great exposure to the Challice family, he had nothing at his Banker's, and yet, as his sole executor and residuary legatee, all expenses of his funeral, repairs of his houses etc. must be paid by me. I found a deposit receipt for 400£ at the Banker's (which turned out to be true, and with 28£ interest due on it) and also some 3 per cents worth 1,000£ which I will share with my sister.

January 31st
Our dear Herbert, who was on leave from the camp at Colchester for two months, was unexpectedly ordered to Sandhurst. Accompanied him as far as Norwich and had him photographed in his tunic with sword and accessories.

March 18th
Last night attended the most rowdy and uproarious meeting ever assembled in Dereham. The case was this – a tract of land, called Rush Meadow, is open to the poor as a 'fuel allotment' on which they may cut sedge-grass as turf, but, as it is almost always under water & the sedge valueless the poor do not think it worthwhile to go for it. A London man has offered the Vicar & Churchwardens, who are the Trustees, no less than 40£ a year for this swamp, to grow water cress to be sent to London – the only purpose for which it is worth anything, except for snipe and occasional wild duck. There is also a considerable and larger portion which is not to be parted with and which has fair pasture. The 40£ we proposed to spend on coals for the poor.

It seems, however, that a number of horse dealers, dicky buyers, fish cart people and hucksters are not only in the habit of turning their own horses on to this tract, but of receiving payment for turning on the cattle of other people who do not belong to this parish. A meeting was called by these gentry to protest against the action of the Trustees. We found the room full of 'roughs' and the chair taken by an active dissenter who was perfectly incapable of keeping order. I attempted to explain the case, but they gave me only a partial hearing, interrupting by groans, cheers & counter groans and cheers. I said my say, but to no avail as they had made up their minds to 'no enclosure', and the meeting ended in disorder.

Fortunately half a dozen young fellows came with a view to protect me from the mob who, as we left, hooted and yelled. I took refuge in the Reading Room, and afterwards got safely home. Everington, the other Trustee, (who had not been at the meeting and was most unpopular because they thought he wanted the land) happened to drive through the marketplace just as the mob had let me go, in a tandem, his wife being with him. The mob got round him and so alarmed the horses that they took fright, though happily without accident.

April 20th

So much dissatisfaction at my continuing to sing the Nicene Creed that I am forced to compromise the matter by agreeing to sing it only at Festivals – it is sometimes the part of a good general to retire as well as to advance.

April 24th

The return luncheon to the Watts and the Baileys – the party included Mr & Mrs Hyde & Miss Hill, who is staying with them. What with these early dinners and late suppers one misses dinner at the wholesome hour of six, the only one when I care for food.

May 15th

Went over Skipper's Leather Factory near the station – a vast place employing 100 men who dress leather in every from, colour and stage. The work is chiefly done by steam. This is quite a new feature in Dereham, and alien to all former proclivities as a purely agricultural town. It has called into existence a population, part dissenting and part antagonistic to any form of Christianity and it is a most serious and difficult problem to solve, how such people can be got at or any influence be brought to bear on them. There is also a shoe factory which I have not yet seen.

May 20th

Archdeacon Hopper's visitation at Litcham. There was an agreeable debate after luncheon on keeping the Lord's Day, on which speakers took both the Puritan and the Catholic side. It was insisted that the Holy Communion ought to be celebrated every Sunday in every Church in the land, and that cricket was a good thing after the service. But the puritan side would not listen to this. The Archdeacon, who is staying at the King's Arms dined with us in the evening and our dear Herbert came home again, preparatory, we fear, for foreign service.

May 26th

While on the way to the Club Dinner, a telegram was put into my hands to say that Herbert was to sail from Liverpool next Tuesday, to join his regiment in Halifax.

June 1st

Herbert & I left the Vicarage at 6.30 and went to Liverpool via Ely, Peterborough and Sheffield. The only feature noticeable on the way was the awful pandemonium of misery, dust and smoke of Sheffield.

The trees, the sheep and everything was black with the prevailing smoke. In Liverpool, the beauty and importance of the public buildings, the magnitude of the docks astonished me. Everyone one meets seems to be Irish, German or American, the number of Roman Catholic priests again makes the place un-English, and the liquor shops, which are very numerous, display the singular device of a huge glass puncheon, lighted from within and suspended by a crane.

June 2nd

The good ship 'Circassian', one of the Allan Line, lay in the middle of the Mersey to take ordinary passengers and 7 young officers of the 20th and 3 of the 97th to Halifax.

At 2 we had got things on to the pier and at 3 we got aboard the tender. A long time ensued before the immense lot of luggage was transferred, and then came the sad bell for parting. Even poor 'Grip' [Herbert's dog] felt it and refused food all evening. It was intended that he should go but, in order to discourage dogs, they said he would be charged 3 guineas. So he will return with me to Dereham.

June 3rd

Left Liverpool by the 8.30 train and arrived at Dereham at 6.30. Passed through a very long tunnel[1] which goes by the name of 'the backbone of England'. Had for a fellow traveller a wealthy mill owner who told me that a boy of 14 years old can earn 10/- a week, women 20/- and men from 40/- to 100/-. Then he said, on the other hand, that the surplusage was all spent on whisky, and that the men seldom lived over forty years in consequence of drink, work and the dust and filings of the iron producing chest complaints, and from the absence of fresh vegetables, those they had being blackened with smoke and crushed. He said he knew a man (it might be himself) who from earning 1£ a week as a hammerer was now worth 4,000£ a year. This man ate a pound of steak daily for dinner with a bottle of champagne which enabled him to do prodigies of labour. Our poor fellows who are leaving East Anglia for these regions must find out that an increase in wages is not everything.

June 26th

Received a letter from Herbert announcing his safe arrival at Halifax. He had so fine a passage that he was not once sick, and is to proceed to Bermuda in a few days.

July 10th

My dear Lilly is wanting her engagement sanctioned which she has formed with Arthur Nelson, and my dear John is in the same case with regard to a Miss Bell, daughter of a Norfolk clergyman. This is a great trial in a parent's life. Gladly would he promote the happiness of his children, but then there is the future, as well as the present happiness to look to.

July 14th

A letter from Herbert at Bermuda, he says very little of the coral reefs for which I understand it is celebrated. He complains of the heat, and for want of occupation.

The Archery meeting at Quebec – the usual people etc., the next is to be at our Vicarage, and a good place, too.

July 15th

Athletic sports by Pilling's boys on the cricket ground drew a large concourse of spectators and were really interesting. The contest of leaping the bar with a pole was very spirited between a boy, Rodwell, & Clouting, a smaller boy, who beat the other by clearing 6ft 11 inches without touching the bar.

July 21st [at Sandringham]

The Church is the tiniest thing possible, but in good order, with cross, flowers and candlesticks on the altar. The Royal people occupy the Chancel, but the Church is so tiny, I know not where else they could sit. The Princess has given a brass eagle, on which is written 'When I was in trouble, He heard me'. Dear little thing – this trouble was when she fled to the Church to pray for her supposedly dying husband. There is also a cross to the groom who did die when the Prince was so ill of the same complaint.

The new 'Hall' is of red brick, plentifully relieved with stone, and commensurate with an income of about 3,000 a year.

August 2nd [Hunstanton]

In the afternoon preached at the old Church. Some gypsies were present in their gorgeous dresses of yellow and scarlet. Their name is Mace and they camp out on the beach all the summer. They behaved devoutly and made an offering although I saw them yesterday telling fortunes and selling trifling articles.

August 6th
Called on Sir Thomas Watson Bt., Queen's Physician[2] and who occupies the pinnacle of his profession. He is staying with some poor relations in Dereham. He is 80 years old, and is in full possession of his faculties, knows everybody and is very lively and communicative.

August 9th
Sunday. A very satisfactory service, contrasting favourably with Hunstanton last week. My two curates and self, all in long cassocks, short surplices of the same make, all M.A.s and they both six feet high and not Irish gave a look of respectability not often seen in a county church, or in a London one either.

August 20th
The School Feast, for which we had a most lovely day. 250 children marched with flags and banners, headed by an excellent band, to the Church gates, where they were met by the choristers and clergy. After service the procession re-formed to the Vicarage. The children sat around the flowerbeds for their tea. The teachers had tea within the Vicarage, and then came the usual games, dancing, swings and what not till long after the moon had risen. Several hundred people were on the ground during the day.

August 24th
Received two satisfactory letters one from dear Herbert from Bermuda, saying he was well and happy, the other from John Challice [his nephew] dated Brisbane, where, after going the round of the world, he has settled down as a colonist and seems to be doing well. Lilly returned from Derbyshire where she has been staying with the Nelsons, and has brought Mr A. Nelson, her lover, back with her.

September 1st
Went to London to see my lawyer about Lilly's marriage settlements and my sister's lawyer about her affairs. As usual in Norfolk saw no signs of shooting, though it was 'the first'.[3]

September 11th
A railway accident of most fearful character took place at Thorpe by Norwich last night[4], which has thrown the whole neighbourhood into consternation. The London express and the Yarmouth train dashed into each other at speed.

'Extracting the Dead and the wounded'
Illustrated London News 19th Sept 1874

September 15th

Miss Edith Pilling's wedding – a very smart affair, followed by a breakfast and Ball in the evening...My dear Lilly's affair is in strange contrast to this. It seems that the money which it was always understood his father would give him to set him up in his farm is now only to be lent and interest paid for it. To start on borrowed capital would be ruinous, and consent must be withheld.

September 18th

A stationmaster at Wymondham told me the late railway accident would cost the company a quarter of a million sterling! [5]

October 5th [Swaffham]

Rev. Houchen took me over the gaol. Visited several of the cells where the prisoners are kept in solitary confinement, and also the dark cell, the very idea of a man being kept in which filled one with horror. It seems to have been used but once, and that for a flagrant offence, viz. the attempt of a prisoner to kill the Governor by breaking his back on the staircase rail, and which he would have succeeded in doing but for the friendly succour of another prisoner. There are several names of French prisoners with the date 1798 cut into the bricks.

To me it seems very incongruous that such eccentric and ill-informed men, as some of the county magistrates really are, should have the power of sentencing prisoners to such an awful penalty as solitary confinement. Here, e.g. was a man who was going through a year for the crime of stealing a watch!!! It is but justice, however to add that he had been in gaol before.

November 11th
Sent my dear wife and Lilly off to Brighton as the latter needed a change after her recent disappointment.

November 26th
Walked home after lunch at Gressenhall to find dear Helen sobbing, and with a telegram in her hands. Telegrams almost always forbode evil rather than good. It was to the effect that Arthur Nelson had discovered the whereabouts of Lilly – that he had followed her, procured a license, called at 8.30 this morning, induced Lilly to go out with him, and that they returned at 9.30 just as my wife was coming in to breakfast and announced that they had just been married by the Vicar at the Parish Church.

My grief and indignation knew no bounds, coupled with much sympathy for my wife. How many sins were concentrated in this unhappy act! Deceit and lying on Nelson's part – a direct infringement of the 5th Commandment on Lilly's part and cruelty to her mother on both their parts. We were both of us confounded and broken-hearted. A second telegram informed us my wife had left Brighton and taken refuge with John at Thatcham. We telegraphed in return to meet us at St Pancras Station tomorrow.

November 27th
When Helen & I met my wife and John at the Station it is needless to say she was in great distress, which was only alleviated by my exonerating her from all blame in the matter. Took an advert of the wedding to the Times office the same evening.

November 28th
The usual letters requesting forgiveness arrived but shall not reply for a day or so, and make it conditional on future conduct. Called on my sister, Mrs Challice, who was pleased to regard the matter in a romantic and cheerful way.

November 29th

Went, as usual, to All Saints Margaret St where I have before poured out my sorrows for the loss of my father and mother, and now for the disobedience of my child. In the Lesson came the passage 'I have nourished and brought up children, and lo, they have rebelled against me'. I felt the application to existing circumstances.

November 30th

Endless correspondence with friends as to my dear Lilly, whose marriage has appeared in the Times and the Norfolk Chronicle. May God forgive and bless her.

December 8th

Letters for reconciliation have come from A. Nelson and Lilly, who are now at their home in Sulhamstead, near Reading. Lilly describes it as pretty, but the question is how are they to keep the farm on? It is not wise, however, to anticipate evil.[6] A letter from Bermuda today. Our dear boy, thank God, is well. He has lost one of his comrades, young Elwes, a Norfolk man, and was one of the pall-bearers. On enquiry at his agents in London I was thankful to find he had not outrun his income.

Today's Times records the condemnation of Mr Machonochie for processions, lighted candles, wafer bread, vestments and East position, grounded on the late decisions of the Privy Council. But the judge allowed that the law was in an uncertain state, and an appeal was made.

December 12th

Called on Sir T. Watson, Queen's Physician Extraordinary. He told me some anecdotes of the death of the Prince Consort, with whom he sat up the night before he died. The Prince always said that he was so delicate that while he could get on tolerably well yet, in the event of a serious illness he felt that he would succumb. There is no truth in the report that he refused to take the prescribed remedies.

December 15th

Dined at Sir Thomas Watson's, who lives only a few doors from us. Met Mr Richmond of the Royal Academy – a delightful person, full of anecdote and a good churchman withal. Also a Rev. Dr Coghlan, Minister of Vere St Chapel, a very conceited shallow fellow of the Broad School and got up in ultra costume viz. breeches and silk stockings, buckles and an Episcopal sort of coat. He said his mother and wife (with whom he does not live) are Romanists, and with such an example before them I should think likely to remain so.

December 19th

To Oxford, to see my dear boy ordained priest tomorrow.

December 26th

Somehow Christmas always seems to be accompanied with calamity. This week 30 persons were killed in a railway accident near Oxford, and as many more by a colliery explosion and 475 lives lost by a ship on fire.[7]

1875

January 6th

At 7.00 a.m. a telegram to say that my sister was in a most critical state. Knowing how often I had been the victim of exaggerated telegrams in my father's case, I contented myself with sending off Ethel Challice to London and said service. But on my return a second telegram had come announcing that she was 'sinking fast' so I went to London via Peterborough, arrived at Wimpole Street at 10.30 and found Annie reduced to the last stage.

January 11th

William Challice came to my room at about 3 o'clock to say all was over. Father, mother, sister all gone, and only I remain. She was a woman of sweet temper and most generous disposition, but, alas, vanity amounting to monomania which induced her to seclude herself, forbad interest in her children, or in any matter of business. Regardless of expense she indulged herself in food and drink, taking no exercise and not even to Church for many years, in fact, killed herself. I believe that had she been spared she might have been the ruin of her family.[1]

January 20th

The Church Association[2] (on the invitation of one or two disaffected members of the congregation) held a public meeting in the Corn Hall, to hear a lecture from a Rev. Mr Concannon, an Irishman and now incumbent of a church in Brixton. Great efforts had been made to induce a Churchwarden to take the Chair and appeals had been made to Mr Hyde, our J.P., without effect, so the post was filled by a Mr Berney, a neighbouring low church squire. The Rev. Dawson accompanied me to the meeting to reply to the Lecturer if necessary, and which was found to be so much so that the meeting was prolonged from 7.30 to 11 o'clock. Six or seven of the extreme low church clergy of the neighbourhood occupied the platform, Dawson, my curate, Watt, and myself sitting beneath. The lecturer started with a sound exposition of the Divinity, then diverged onto the excesses of the ritualists and was going on to the secrets of the Confessional when, observing symptoms of distaste on the part of the audience, he went off into the claptrap of the glories of Protestant Institutions and the fact that 'Britons never would be slaves', followed by the usual applause.

Immediately at his conclusion I rose to reply, but should not have gained a hearing from the Chairman had I not reminded him that the Lecturer had promised one! On this there were loud cries of 'fair play' and I ascended the platform to the hearty cheers, although half the audience were dissenters.

The meeting agreed, nevertheless, that there should be a branch of the Church Association in Dereham.

February 15th
The meeting on 20th January has resulted in a spirited controversy between others and myself, week by week, in the Norfolk Chronicle.

Called on the Rev. John Nelson, Lilly's father-in-law, who is staying with a parishioner. He assures me he was equally in the dark concerning the marriage, and seemed to view the matter in an easy-going, hopeful light. There is no doubt they are supremely happy at present, but I very much fear for the future.

March 13th
The house in Wimpole Street, and all its contents was sold this week.

March 20th
Saw an immense shark which was caught off the Norfolk coast a few days ago – a hideous beast 15 feet in length. A whale was washed ashore near Cromer about the same time 75 feet in length, and thousands went to see it. We have been obliged to kill Herbert's dog, Grip, on account of his fighting and cat-killing propensities.

April 6th
After Evensong dropped into the Corn Hall to hear the famous Mr Arch[3] who was haranguing a vast concourse of labouring men to join

the Union. Arch was a farmer's labourer and is now a paid delegate for the union all over England. He is a thickset coarse sort of man of about 40. His address was decidedly revolutionary. He let off the Church better than I expected. A few of our small democratical people were on the platform, dissenting shopkeepers, and frequently cried 'That's it!' when any telling remark was made by the speaker. The heat was intolerable and I felt green all evening from the steam arising from so many with whom cleanliness is not always accounted next to godliness.

June 1st

Archdeacon Hopper cane to dine and stay. Invited the Rev. Pilling to meet him. Left them in the evening to attend a public meeting of the parishioners to take into consideration the present condition of the organ in the Parish Church, which Messrs Hill of London want to spend £500 upon and which will make it worth £1,000. To my great surprise £400 was promised in the room. The zeal exhibited was the more gratifying because Church matters have been a trifle depressed here of late on account of the aggression of the Church Association. Capt. Bulwer promised £50 and myself £25. The Archdeacon was astonished at the result.

July 7th

A letter from Bertie's agent which has filled us with anxiety to the effect that Bertie has drawn on his agent for £40 over and above his balance! I have paid it, but what causes misgiving is the suddenness of the call and the largeness of the sum. I sadly fear he has been gambling.[4]

July 21st

In France many millions of property and many hundreds of lives have been lost by the floods. In England the rivers in some parts have overflowed the whole country, and the hay crop has been almost everywhere destroyed – including ours.

July 29th

As we intend taking a month on the Continent, we wished to have the school feast over first, but the weather has been so fearfully wet that we hadn't the courage to fix a day. Realising that the evenings would be drawing in by the time of our return we resolved to fix it, and were rewarded with a splendid day, bright sun and no rain. The Fête, which included a rifle-shooting gallery which was extensively patronised, went off to perfection. Had a first rate band and came through the market place with banners flying, one or two determined dissenters looking anything but gratified!

August 2nd

Started on a trip to Antwerp, the Rhine and Brussels, taking monthly returns at 40/- each. Went on board the 'Harwich' at 9.00 p.m., a very slow, inferior boat so we did not arrive in Antwerp until midday on Aug 3rd, when the ladies having been very ill in the night took a long siesta.

August 5th

Left Antwerp for Aix La Chapelle. Our fellow passengers consisted of three old ladies, a cavalry officer in uniform and a monk. The officer did not quite come up to the description of a gentleman, as his nails were dirty, he answered brusquely, and he spat about the carriage. Nothing can be more uninteresting than the whole country from Antwerp to Mastrict [sic].

August 6th

Aix is not as interesting as Antwerp. Some portion is very modern, and others being dirty and smelling disgustingly. It is as well to walk in the middle of the street, or you may be damaged from the windows above!

The Hotel de Ville very fine. At Table d'Hôte one does not exactly understand fish coming round in the middle of the meal, or why venison and chicken should be served in one dish. The Germans are stout fellows, eat enormously, never passing a dish over, talk incessantly, and light cigars immediately after dinner notwithstanding the presence of ladies.

August 7th

Among other objectionable German habits (such as dining at 1, spitting, etc. etc.) they have that of getting up at 5 or 6 and setting the house in a Babel to the great discomfort of the more quietly disposed.

August 8th [Cologne]

To the Jesuit Church. The sense of depression great and no service going on. Where is the Order? Bismarck[5] has expelled them from the country on account of their sympathy with France, and they are probably in London. In four years the ruthless 'reformer' intends to banish the innocent nuns and it would seem he means to stamp out the old religion, in which case Germany will become wholly Rationalist.

All the shops are open on Sunday and all people who have Orders or medals wear them, though in private dress. German beds are uncomfortable, sloping down from the head. Doubled the wretched square pillow and made it into a bolster.

August 9th
Got on the Rhine boat at 8.30 – a large vessel with raised deck, having an awning and tables for the convenience of the various parties. For 8 of the 12 hour voyage there was an uninterrupted panorama of lovely scenery. My wife and Helen confessed that it greatly exceeded their expectations. The only passengers with whom we conversed were a young officer who knew a good deal about Herbert's regiment, a Scotch clergyman whom Helen mistook for an R.C. priest and a prosy old party who had been staying at the hotel. We disembarked and went on to Weisbaden in an omnibus belonging to the hotel.

August 10th
Called on General von Gerstein Hohenstein, with a letter of introduction. The General had been at Gressenhall this spring, and knew Dereham some years ago. He had been in the Franco German war and was Commandant of Hamburg. He speaks English fluently and was very kind and hospitable. He likes England and the English and tries to make his lawn 'smooth, like ours' but says this drier climate is an obstacle. In the afternoon he paid the return visit in the garden of our hotel and was very agreeable and amusing.

In the evening to the Kursaal Gardens which are very pretty and well-lighted, a good band and tables everywhere for anything you like to, order. There were crowds of people and lots of officers, between one of whom and a belle we were much amused at a wonderful flirtation! There was a rival as a chaperone, but the officer was clearly the favourite, though we all agreed that probably the man in plain clothes loved her better! It is clear that there are flirts in Germany, as elsewhere!

August 12th
The ladies went shopping so I took a walk to Sonnenberg under trees all the way, plums and walnuts growing everywhere, and apparently 'pro bono publico'. The village is chiefly inhabited by 'blanchisseuses', the girls standing in the river with naked legs, which must be pleasant in this weather, and the others laying out the things on a huge drying ground.

Went to a village restaurant and got a bottle of a red wine called 'Assmanshauser', which, like most German wines, was very poor stuff, though being hot and tired I was very glad to drink it. The hostess spoke French and told me she had 9 children, one of whom (Little Helène) sat on my knee and helped me finish the wine – a little cropped thing with a sweet mouth and German blue eyes.

At 5.30 took a carriage to the Grand Duke's hunting lodge, uphill all the way through interminable forest in which I did not see as much as a rabbit, though the guide said it contained stags, roe deer and wild boar. The Lodge is tenantless as the Duke prefers to live in Vienna. In fact the Grand Duke's territory has been absorbed into the new Northern Empire[6], and he has taken £50,000 from the Government by way of compensation.

August 14th
Dined at the General's at 6 and met an agreeable party, chiefly English, one being a Mr Huntley who had taken the Duke's forests for wild boar. The General received us with his star on his coat, and there was also a young Lieutenant of Infantry, a nephew of the General, in full uniform and decorated, having been at the battle of Sedan.[7] The dinner was in German fashion. Six different sized wine glasses were set before each person, and were replenished rapidly by waiters before they were half finished. There were endless courses, and the table was far too crowded with plate and flowers. There was a profusion of lights in the chandelier over the table, and as the doors and windows were closed, as their custom is, the heat was very great. Nothing however could exceed the kindness and hospitality of the host.

The gentlemen and ladies sat together a long time after dinner, and rose together, but the men went into a room to smoke, while the ladies had coffee by themselves in the drawing room.

August 16th
So hot we could do nothing but sit in the garden. This is a very first-rate hotel and, in addition to the Russian Prince, who plays at cards night and day, Lord Derby and the Countess of Winchelsea are coming. General von Gerstein dined with us.

Why, in Germany, do they eat olives with duck, and stewed prunes with poulet? But it might be asked why we eat gooseberry sauce with mackerel and apple sauce with goose? We live and learn!

237

August 20th [Cologne]

At Table d'Hôte a Priest joined us, and made a famous dinner out of very questionable food. Indeed not only the German food, but the wines, the language, the hours, the uniforms, the beds etc. are all inferior to those in France or Belgium.

August 24th [Brussels]

There is an extraordinary family in our Hotel, who sup each evening at 10. They are 'Walloons', and said to be noble. They quarrel, gesticulate, beat the table and conduct themselves in a way that one would think must lead to fisticuffs. An intelligent person here tells me that they are not quarrelling at all, but that Walloons always conduct themselves this way!

August 27th [Antwerp]

Here are a few stray jottings – the natives have got in the way of saying to everything you ask 'All right' though they cannot speak another word of English. You ask them, in French, 'Is this the way to the Cathedral' and they say 'all right', when you soon discover it is 'all wrong'. Always eat at the Table d'Hôte as it is the best and cheapest dinner in the end. Four francs a head is the usual charge. Always have the barber shave you in your bedroom – it is impossible to shave yourself as the looking glasses are always against a wall instead of the window, and so of no use.

Belgium is known as a stronghold of the Church.....we saw one of the little cropped headed fellows who play in the Place Vert make a 'long nose' at a Priest who had passed by. Another boy, told of this, followed the first and without saying a word to him, administered to him a tremendous kick behind. The curious part was that the first walked on without expostulating, taking it, I suppose, as a just punishment for his crime. The good boy then returned to the ladies, and took off his hat, by way of indicating that he had vindicated the honour of the Church.

August 31st

At 4 in the afternoon got on board 'The Pacific' and after 17 hours in a gale of wind, the ship pitching and heaving all the night, with waves occasionally breaking over the deck, arrived at Harwich.

September 13th

Had the happiness of reading in the Times that Bertie was gazetted Lieutenant. I believe the boy has been working hard to pass a good Exam. The fact of their being a dozen Sub-Lieutenants and only two promoted, leads me to believe that they were at the top of the exam list.

November 18th

My dear child Lilly, whom I have not seen since her marriage just a year ago, came on a visit accompanied by her husband. I am thankful to say they seem happy and prosperous and there is no prospect of a family.

December 27th

I encountered, in the dark and in the churchyard, a man and a woman having a high dispute. Before I could prevent him, such a move being unsuspected by me, he struck the woman with a thick stick at the back of her neck, which made her reel and stagger. The brute was about to repeat it, when I parried further blows with my stick, and diverted the attack on to myself. Fortunately he was drunk, and presently lowered his weapon. During the conflict the woman escaped.

1876

January 3rd

My wife accompanied me to Norwich to buy glass and china for dear John who comes this week to his new curacy in Brome, near Scole, Norfolk. He has a nice furnished house and £120 a year. All I fear is that the foolish boy will urge having a house as a reason for marrying.

January 10th

To Norwich to purchase a second-hand Brougham, this being the only extra in which I mean to indulge in consequence of succeeding to my little patrimony, especially as I must be very careful for my children's sake, there being no sign of their improving their worldly status by marriage.

January 11th

The carriage soon came into use as we have engagements for almost every day.

January 12th

Pilling, my neighbour's son, preached in the evening and, in conversation at the Vicarage afterwards gave an interesting account of the extraordinary increase in Church principles in Manchester where he is located. He says that the clergy of all schools meet on friendly terms and that all sections (even the Roman Catholics who are very numerous) give those 'Tea-Drinkings' which elsewhere are monopolised by the dissenters. They have recognised the teapot as a very powerful engine, and so it is.

January 24th

A young man, Brunton, got me to sign a paper to get him the benefit of Tancred's Charity.[1] He is the son of a painter and glazier in Dereham, who sent him to Holt Grammar School.[2] There he won all the prizes, got to the top and obtained an Exhibition to Cambridge. He is now a Sizar[3] at St John's, and wishes the charity (100 a year) to eke out his finances.

January 28th

Rev. Mr Bell from Snoring called with a view to facilitate dear Jack's marriage with his daughter. The only impediment is the matter of ways and means. Mr B. is ready to risk that, by doing which he has nothing to lose, and everything to gain, and the dear boy indulges in the 'love in a cottage' dream, and expresses his determination, with much filial tenderness to marry no one else, especially as he has been engaged more than 2 years. It is hard, however, for a father to be asked thus to consent to his son being rendered poor all his life, while had he been more prudent, he might have done so well. Must consult my lawyer.

February 15th

My long contemplated supper to the Officers and men of our Volunteers was given at the Kings Arms Hotel, at which 75 sat down, the Officers at a high table, and the privates down the room. I fear it will be an expensive affair, but having been Chaplain for more than 10 years without having given an entertainment, I thought it high time to give one and moreover it may not be without a good influence in a Church direction among the men.

February 16th

Mrs Collison and her daughters took a family dinner with us and accompanied us to a 'Spelling Bee' – a new American importation. A 'Bee' means a gathering of people for any industrial or literary pursuit. Mr Pilling was the interrogator and Hyde & myself were the referees, sitting at a separate table with folios of Johnson, Walker, and the imperial Dictionaries. There were 25 competitors for the prizes, of whom my wife was one. She was, however, 'sent down' through not understanding the asker, he not being over articulate. He asked her to spell 'rueful' and she understood him to say 'woeful'. The novelty of the occasion attracted a large body of people.

February 21st

My dearest John, getting very urgent as to my sanction for his engagement, writes to say that neither his wishes nor his honour would ever permit him to forego it. I write to say that though the pecuniary difficulty is in no degree closed, yet it was the only objection, and that if he deliberately chose to make a poor man of himself, for life, the responsibility was with him, and that I would do the best I could for them and wished them every happiness.

March 6th

Mr Watt, my curate, has become a teetotaller for the sake of securing another, in the shape of a confirmed drunkard, an act of great self-denial, but I cannot see why moderate men should be called upon to forego God's gifts, simply because there are those who abuse them.

March 14th

An eventful day in the family as John came with Miss Bell from Snoring, on a visit. She is a very agreeable and ladylike person and I hope will make my dear boy's life a happy one. I should have wished the dear fellow to remain unmarried a few more years, and, in the meantime to have seen something more of the world, and then to have made a prudent match. Anyway, Miss Bell is a lady, and her connections highly respectable.

A chemist has been selling bottles of scent, each one of which is warranted to contain a sum of money from a farthing upwards, and one bottle contains £5. Most of the coins are farthings of course, but several have found sovereigns or half-sovereigns, and a poor woman yesterday actually bought the bottle which contained £5. She is half-mad with joy!

March 23rd

A dark day, having received a letter from Herbert's agent to say he had overdrawn his account £40 again. This fills me with sad misgivings.

April 2nd (Sunday)

At Hoe, in the afternoon, found that the countryside had gone to Swanton to hear Mr Arch, the Labourer's Union man. Even my schoolmistress had fled, and only one man in Church, to whom I gave 1/- for his steadfastness.

Mr Lombe, the Rector of Swanton, voluble and bad-tempered generally, very conservative and Low Church, is said to be almost beside himself at this aggression on the part of Mr Arch, but as he does not scruple to aggress into the Parish of his brother clergyman in the interests of the Church Association, I don't much pity him.

April 6th
Met my dear boy in Norwich and accompanied him to his new curacy in Brome, Nr Diss. He has a comfortable and well-furnished house and garden, well suited for young people beginning life – all they want is more income.

April 7th
Inspected everything in Brome, and my impression is that everyone is too well off. The Rector is a very moderate Churchman, inclining to High and his wife talented, agreeable and of high connections. Their Rectory is an emporium of art, almost overdone, and their stables and garden perfect. They went round the village to distribute among the poor some rabbits (which the Squire had sent) in an open carriage and pair with a servant, just fit to drive in Hyde Park. They have no children.

Next drove to Oakley Park, the seat of Sir Edward Kerrison, quite a palatial structure. Sir Edward was very agreeable, he is a very philanthropic man, and has a Reformatory at some distance containing about 60 whom he hopes to benefit.

Next we visited Brome Hall, likewise the property of Sir Edward, but they do not reside here, leaving it for pleasure purposes. The horses are kept here and communication with Oakley is kept up by private telegraphic apparatus.

April 10th
The marriage of my elder son to Miss Mary Penrice Bell of Great Snoring. The villagers had erected some triumphal arches, and there was a great concourse in the Church. Although Jack might have 'done better' (as the saying is) yet there is a certain energy and self-possession about his bride which indicates that she may be an efficient and real helpmate.

April 19th

Some idea of the increase of Dereham may be gleaned from the fact that, whereas in 1873, there were 7,000 letters per week sent to our Post Office, in 1876 they amount to 25,000!

April 30th

A letter came informing me that Herbert had drawn bills to the amount of £45 beyond his allowance (£100 a year) and his pay. I have no doubt he finds it difficult to make two ends meet, and the 97th is an expensive regiment, but this matter fills me with anxiety as to the boy's future.

May 9th

A letter from my daughter-in-law informs us that, on their return home they found a carriage and pair of greys provided for them at Diss Station, and that when the carriage neared the Curacy House some peasants, who had been previously supplied with ropes, took out the horses and pulled the carriage. From a triumphal arch a basket of choice flowers was lowered into the lap of the bride.

May 11th [London]

To the House of Commons where was great excitement on account of Dr Kenealy M.P.,[4] a notorious charlatan, presenting a petition for the release of 'Sir Roger Tichborne'[5] the notorious prisoner now in prison.

May 12th

Visited a Miss Kate Thomson residing with her aunt at Highgate. She was formerly of Little Stanmore and it seems that I had prepared her for confirmation, though I had lost all remembrance of the fact, and, to tell the truth, of the lady herself. She is living in comfort, not to say style, and had accidentally heard of me through a friend in Dereham. Hence some correspondence and a promise that I would call when in Highgate. The aunt is a ladylike little old maid who has completely lost an eye by the explosion of a bottle of beer at a picnic party!

May 19th

In the evening to Maskelyne & Cooke's[6] celebrated séance in which there is an automaton figure, on a glass tube (to prevent suspicion of collusion) who played whist with three of the visitors and performed the most difficult arithmetical problems. It ended in Mr Maskelyne floating over the heads of the audience while several tambourines rattled around the room – too marvellous to be amusing!

May 21st

In the evening to hear Cardinal Manning at Spanish Place. The Cardinal in scarlet cope and biretta of the same colour and white stole, is emaciated in appearance (he eats and drinks nothing) and his voice is feeble, indeed I thought his sermon feeble also.

May 25th

My wife and self went to Sulhampsted by the Great Western Railway to pay our first visit to dear Lilly since her marriage a year and a half ago. They met us at the station and drove us to their home, a very pretty farm, but not the sort of home we could have hoped for our child. Nelson seems to have plenty of stock, 8 cows, pigs, 250 sheep, and the stables etc. are in good repair.

June 28th

A grand day for our parish – the grandest since my Vicariate. Occasion – the opening of the new organ by Hill of London – a splendid instrument commensurate with the requirements of our splendid old Church.

July 1st

Quite a setting up day for our dear boy and his bonnie little wife. Yesterday I bought him a nice strong cob-pony, and a new harness, he having bought a cart.

I took my dear daughter-in-law, whose good qualities become more and more apparent, to Norwich, to effect some business in the plate line and to furnish them with a hamper of port.

July 14th

The Carbineers rode into Dereham a few days ago, en route from Norwich to York – plain uniform & brass helmets. Called on the Commanding Officer as to making arrangements for the men to come to church on Sunday, but he said they would be 'too busy'. Found afterwards the regiment was raised in Ireland and almost all the privates are Roman Catholics.

Dined at Quebec today to meet Mr Price, Recorder of York, and Judge of our County Court. Rather a bumptious little gentleman, who prides himself on 'knowing everybody'.

July 16th

Rev. Key '10 years missionary in Kaffaria' preached an S.P.G. sermon, and a very short, poor sermon it was. A few more such 'Keys' and the Society would be brought to a dead-lock!

July 31st

Received a satisfactory letter from Herbert in Bermuda, thanking me for increasing his allowance to 120£ a year. His letter speaks of the red and blue seabirds there, the marvellous and varied tints of the sea – in short, is more intellectual than usual.

August 7th

My wife accompanied me to the dinner to the Haggards at Bradenham. A grand party of all the elite in the neighbourhood to meet their son's American wife, who he picked up at Washington when he was with the embassy, to which he is an attaché. 24 sat down to dinner, and though we didn't begin till 8.30, the heat was intolerable. The American was a very 'fast' specimen, and although young, was much rouged and frizzed, and wore very little above the waist. When it is considered that she is a divorcée, I think young Haggard was a bold man to take her, notwithstanding the very large property she is said to possess. She is a fine woman and pleasant to converse with.[7]

August 30th

Annual treat to the Choir, Yarmouth as usual was the attraction for them. We were not aware that this was 'Race Week' and I had some difficulty in providing so large a party with dinner, on account of the hotels being so full. And full indeed the place was, chiefly of the genus 'snob'[8] with a large mixture of billiard playing and Racing gentlemen. The only plan was to pay the men 2/6d each and let them provide for themselves while my curate and I took the boys to a Cook's shop on Church Plain where they had plenty of hot roast beef, cheese and potatoes for exactly half what I have been accustomed to pay at the hotels.

September 14th [at Lagley]

Mr Harris, a Banker, and his wife came to dinner. She is niece to Earl Russell and nearly related to the Duchess of Bedford. He is a Quaker, but retains no vestige in dress or manners of his sect. They have not been married many months and the lady is 'not very handsome, nor very young' – the fact, palpably, being that the aristocrat married the

Banker (who is not aristocratic in his personal appearance) for the sake of his money and he married her for the sake of her grand connections.

September 28th

An attempted reconciliation, and in part successful. A well to do parishioner, lying on his death-bed was very bitter against an only son whom he had not seen for many years. The son (now over 50) had been articled to a lawyer, ran away to sea, was got back, enlisted into the cavalry and was bought out, had forged upon, robbed and even tried to poison his father. Still I urged upon the father that he ought to forgive him, but he had not seen or heard of him for many years and could give me no address. This person, however, presented himself yesterday at the Vicarage, and wished me to obtain an interview with his father.

Today that interview took place, but nothing availed with the parent. Would he see his son in my presence? No. If a policeman was in the house? No. However, he extended his full forgiveness to his son, and said that despite his conduct he would have 'his portion'. I told the son, who seemed so well satisfied that I fear lest the 'portion of goods' was not the main inducement in seeking the interview.

October 8th

Received a letter from Herbert in which he announces the removal of his regiment from Bermuda to Halifax in December, also that he is first on the rota for leave.

October 16th

Went to Downham Market to preach at the Harvest Festival and was entertained by Capt. & Mrs Read at Crow Hall, the property of Mrs Bulwer. I was told by Sir William Bagge M.P. and Sir J. Hare Bt. whom I met in Downham that Crow Hall derives its name from having been an Inn with the Crow for its sign. Called on little W. Everington, who is at school here, took him for a walk, and treated him. Sir William, on finding that his father was a voter, tipped him. Willie, I imagine, wondered why a perfect stranger should be so generous.

The place is full of Meeting Houses, one reason for which may be the utter indifference of the Rector, who never goes into the Church or subscribes to any of the charities. He is, of course, deranged.

Capt. Read told me that close by there is a village called Southery, where there are but 3 names in the parish, one of which is Porter. This is so inconvenient that, in Union returns etc. they are obliged (the Christian names often being the same) to describe the individuals by some soubriquet, e.g. 'Moley' Porter because he has a mole on his cheek. This betokens a bad state of affairs, isolation, intermarriage and many very serious evils.

October 30th

Roger Challice, my nephew, has, for many years, been the trouble of his family. He has had three fresh starts in life, and all to no purpose. Lately he has been drawing bills on me for small amounts, say £5 on various people, mostly strangers, representing that I had money in hand for his Grandfather's Will – an utterly false statement as he sold his interest to Mr Sedgwick. His dupes were a Mr Forsyth, a Dr Pollock of Harley Street and Mr Tookey, the undertaker at my father's funeral. I refused to pay these (except Tookey) knowing that if I paid, it would surely lead to further, more extortionate demands. Now I get a letter from Mr Martin, my solicitor, to say that he was in custody at the instigation of Dr Pollock for obtaining money under false pretences. Mr Martin will appear at the court to obviate the need of my going to London, and worse, appearing in the papers.

November 3rd

A letter from Mr Martin to say that Roger Challice was committed yesterday, but bail accepted. He seems to think R.C. may bolt and leave his bail in the lurch.

November 7th

Roger Challice was brought before at the Middlesex Sessions, but was discharged, in consequence of the absence of his uncle to substantiate the charge! I really think that what my solicitor calls 'this happy blunder' has procured a miscarriage of justice. It is now proposed to send him to America, towards which project I am already being asked to contribute, and of course must do so.

November 28th

Sorry to say that letters received from our dear Lilly arrived to say their farm was a losing affair, and that they thought of giving it up. History repeats itself but I hope and trust that this may not be a new edition of my sister's case in consequence of an indiscreet marriage.

King James II told Chief Justice Coke, the ancestor of the present Lord Leicester, that he had quite enough land at Holkham and elsewhere. Coke begged His Majesty to allow the addition of another acre, which moderate demand was granted by the King. But the 'acre' turned out to be Castle Acre, a very extensive and valuable estate.

December 9th

Amy and Mary Frazer [step-daughters of his brother in law, William Duncombe] have been paying us a long visit, during which my curate, Watt, has been more frequently seen than ever at the Vicarage. We had not observed the slightest passion on the part of any of the young people, but it seems to have been smouldering. Anyhow Watt proposed to Mary this evening, and was accepted. Then of course followed mysterious disappearances on the part of the females, slamming of bedroom doors, brandies & water, and all the usual concomitants of 'declarations'.

1877

January 9th

Married my organist at 66 to a Miss Smith at 28! This disparity is in every respect most unsatisfactory. The curious part of it is that the bride, now a fashionable, accomplished and good-looking person, was once quite a poor girl living with her widowed mother on Toftwood Common. Some say she was educated by a distant female connection in better circumstances, but others that she is the illegitimate child of some gentleman who supported her. Her brother, a private in the 5th Dragoon Guards, and in, uniform, was present at the wedding and at the subsequent breakfast, which was given by the bridegroom. I proposed the health of the newly married ones in very excellent champagne!

January 18th

The Nelsons, having visited some relations of his in Norfolk, are again with us, and attended the Dereham Subscription Ball with Helen, by invitation, but my wife and I thought it better not to go. Today Nelson was allowed to walk the Gressenhall courses though they are exhausted of game for this season. He managed to kill a cock pheasant, a woodcock, a hare and a rabbit.

January 24th

Although I dislike going to Balls (late hours not agreeing with me) and do not dance (having a great repugnance to the clergy doing so) I yet accompanied our party to Mrs Hyde's 'drum' at her special request.

January 27th

Somehow I do not think our Vicarage is a very successful field for courtship, remembering two instances of breaking off of engagements. This has now taken place with my curate Mr Watt, and Mary Frazer, the eyes of both being opened to the fact that they are entirely unsuited to one another. She is said to be cold, apathetic, capricious and exacting – all of which came out at Mrs Hyde's Ball on the 24th. The curate seems like a man who is relieved of a burden!

February 9th

Heard that A. Nelson was a bankrupt, though he told me during their recent visit (to be renewed tomorrow) that he had merely sold off on advantageous terms and had been re-leased by his landlord. Their runaway marriage began in deceit, which it now seems is being carried on to the bitter end.

To complete a dark day, letters from the Challices that Roger was a beggar and had pawned his last coat. Proposed to send him to South America, as he was a pest to his sisters. The old question, could I help? Agreed to send £25 to pay his passage.

February 10th

The Nelsons returned. He confesses that his affairs are in liquidation, but that he hopes there will be 20/- in the £ for all his creditors. He attributes his failure to the poorness of the land, the scantity of crop, the high price of labour, and his having spent too much in improvements. What is to be done with them now?

February 14th

We had a long letter from Herbert to say he was well and happy and enjoying the numerous gaieties of Halifax. Next came a letter from my niece Jane Challice, thanking me for my offer of paying Roger's passage to South America, but adding that I should not be called upon to do so, as someone had given him the post of overseer in some slate mines in Perthshire.

My parishioner, Mr Halcott Cooper, who is solicitor to Arthur Nelson's father, has just come from Reading where he has been searching into the true state of Arthur's affairs, which are found to be infinitely worse than he had represented. The fact is he had not included in his debts a sum of £2,500 which had been advanced him by his father, and the consequence is that instead of paying 20/- in the £ he will not be in a position to pay 5/-. Meanwhile the affair has got wind in Dereham and, though people are sympathising and kind it is a very bitter pill.

February 19th

When my niece wrote the other day to inform me that Roger Challice had obtained a situation I said in reply that the news was almost too good to be true. Alas, so it has turned out! The Manager of the mine naturally wanted a 'character' from the last employer, which is just what Roger has not got. So the South American project is resumed and I sent off the £25 today.

February 23rd

To my great astonishment, William Challice sent back £20 of the 25 sent him to deport Roger to South America. They had met at my lawyer's office and Roger had signed a paper expressing his wish to go, but he cried off at the last minute, while he and his brother were on the railway platform all ready to start for Liverpool! He is now absolutely destitute and joined with some low gamblers, it is said.

April 4th

The day appointed for the Vestry. Unusual excitement has prevailed on the subject of vestries on account of the labourer's movement and the attempt on the part of the Union to get one of their men into office. All passed off happily in the end, though the atmosphere looked very threatening at the beginning. A radical dissenter, one Brett, had got about 20 roughs – one of whom was not sober – to back up his resolution that the Vestry be adjourned until 7 p.m. for the convenience of the labouring men. I said at once that the consent of the Chairman was necessary for this, which I would not give. I was glad to see the labourers taking an interest in these matters (I suspect they were all paid their day's wages by the union) and they would be treated with the same courtesy and consideration as their betters, but I could not inconvenience another section of the ratepayers to suit theirs. Besides the great number of labourers present showed that others could have been present if they liked. This was met with loud cheers by the Church party. Business being at length commenced, I named Mr Carthew for the 19th time, and by previous arrangement Mr Elvin was proposed for the people's warden. No other candidate being brought forward I declared him elected.

April 6th

The two surgeons in neighbouring parishes, Mr Sprigge and Mr Clouting have both died within a week, quite suddenly. The latter, a few days before, was in attendance on the former, but died from a totally different complaint.

April 11th

Col. Duff gave his annual dinner to the Officers of our Battalion at the King's Arms, about 35 sat down. Sat next to Col. Harenc – a curious name, Jersey I believe, who said he was 18 years in the 97th and was with them at Halifax, and also at the taking of Redan.[1] Spoke highly, as everybody does, of Halifax, but says that the custom of young ladies being 'muffin' to the young men (i.e. their companions on public occasions without chaperone) is a dangerous thing, as the obtaining for a husband a British Officer is the grand object of a Nova Scotia girl's ambition.

April 17th

Saw the Nelsons off by train, they are going on a visit to Bradenstoke in Wiltshire, where his father has a living. They have now been with us three months and, as Arthur Nelson's affairs are not only unsettled but rendered more complicated by the lawyers, our poor child is without a home of her own.

April 26th

Russia has today declared war on Turkey – the war is ostensibly a religious one. Although the Conservatives (with a very few exceptions) are on the Turkish side, as upholding the ancient policy of England, I confess to being a Christian first and heartily wish success to the Cross against the Crescent.

May 3rd [London]

Took Helen and my dear boy's wife to the Lyceum to see Irving in Richard III. I never was an admirer of Irving and imagine his popularity arises more from the extraordinary absence of good actors, than from merit. Anyhow, to one who remembers C. Kean, and who did actually once see the elder Kean, the whole thing seemed very inferior.

May 4th

In the afternoon my wife and I accompanied our dear boy to Liverpool St station to see him off to Brome. This station, which I had not seen before is very inferior to the magnificent structure at St Pancras.

May 5th

Took my daughter-in-law Mary and my niece Ethel, to Moore & Burgess's Minstrels – singing excellent and the jokes not bad. Am much pleased with my dear boy and also with his little wife. It is delightful how she enjoys everything.

May 7th

Started from Charing Cross for Paris, rushed through the hop-gardens of Kent. Thought there was a lack of fine timber and few if any gentlemen's seats. At Folkestone the tidal steamer was waiting, steam up, for the train and we were on the sea in no time.

May 14th

Took my nieces to the porcelain factory at Sèvres, going by boat. The factory is a new building and the ateliers have only been opened very recently. There we saw every process from the rough lump of clay in its natural state, and which comes from Limoges, up to the finishing touch. One of the workmen, quite a youth, was moulding and re-moulding this paste into the most artistic and classical shapes with his hands until he made an elegant tazza[2] with it, which was then set to dry. The shops for mosaic work were very curious and interesting, but the finished objects were astonishingly beautiful. Most of the huge vases were made to revolve so that the painting could be seen all round.

May 16th

Left Paris at 9.00 and arrived in London at 7.30! Country around Chantilly pretty, but the rest uninteresting to a degree, the cattle few and lean, the peasantry looking poor. What a contrast to France was the country between Folkestone and near to London! Sheep fat and fleeced, trim hedges, well-to-do farmers, peasants well clothed etc. but the contrast turned in favour of Paris as we got into London! Clouds and fog, interminable dumpy black houses, smoking factories, bad management at the station with our baggage contrasted unfavourably with the gay city we had just left.

May 29th

My wife and I lunched at Gressenhall to meet Reginald Hill and his wife, who had come from Thetford to shoot rooks. I surprised the tenant and the gamekeeper by knocking over 6 birds in as many shots.

July 2nd

Had a garden party and luncheon, fortunately a very fine day for it. Lawn tennis, which has entirely superseded croquet, was the order of the day.

July 3rd

We have all been suffering great anxiety in consequence of the very unusual interim since hearing from Herbert. I had already determined to telegraph, or even go to Canada if matters had been in a bad way when, to our great delight a letter came on this, his birthday. The Regiment had given a grand Ball – he had obtained an extra, but temporary garrison appointment and hoped to be with us at Christmas. A letter had miscarried, which accounts for his silence. Wrote to Herbert paying his tailor's bill, as a birthday present.

July 10th

R. Challice resumed his game of going to clergymen and getting money through his connection with me. The only chance for him would be his committal to prison!

July 21st

A note from Mrs Bulwer to say that she had just received a telegram from London to say that Capt. Bulwer's father, of Heydon Hall, died in London this morning. This will be sad news for Dereham if it involves our Bulwers going to Heydon, for the tendency for some time past with this, as with other towns, has been the elimination of gentry and their places being filled with the tradesmen who abandon their shop residences for more pretentious mansions.

July 22nd

My dear wife accompanied me to Hoe to open the new harmonium. So much does a little novelty please that the whole church was filled, and many of the labouring men re-appeared, who have been allured by Mr Arch.

July 25th

Started to join the camp at Yarmouth. Col. Gurdon's 4th regiment formed part of the camp but they were neither our equal in numbers or appearance. Met Lord Suffield, Col. Duff, Major Boileau and many old friends. Dined in the Mess which was badly served, and was glad it was only for once as the tent was draughty and the dinner indifferent. During the afternoon I visited the new Aquarium and thought it inferior, there being a great scarcity of fishes in the tanks – in fact natural history seems to take quite a secondary place to the concert room and the restaurant.

Mrs Stoughton of Bawdeswell Hall travelled in the same carriage and told me that one Stoughton ancestor made it his custom to go into Church at 10.00p.m. for private prayer. Leaving his lighted candle at the West end, he went to the altar for that purpose, but was terribly alarmed by seeing a light advance gradually up the Church to where he was. It turned out to be a rat, who had made prize of the tallow, carrying it still alight, but dropped it on seeing the stranger and left him in the dark.

July 30th
Mr & Mrs Scott Chad of Thursford Hall having invited us to stay there for 3 days, we were compelled to limit the time to one night on account of the visit of H.M.Inspector to the Schools at Dereham. We all three went by rail and had an open carriage from Fakenham to the Hall. Lady Leicester and her step-daughters (one of whom is older than herself) were visiting when we arrived. After dinner the Squire said prayers in his pretty Oratory, which was quite filled with the family, visitors and domestics.

July 31st
The Dereham & Fakenham Archery Club had their meeting in the park and we lunched with them in the tent. Being of the 'Hall party' we came off better than would otherwise have been the case, the set out being of a very ordinary kind – so much so that I shall avoid the luncheons if we continue in the club.

August 5th
Ernest Duncombe is spending a few days here, to meet John. He says that being a Lieut. R.N. on half pay he is cut down to £75 p.a. It would seem that the Army, though not by any means a lucrative calling, is better than the Navy.

August 11th
Went to Norwich to buy my dear John a gold watch that should last his life and Lilly some port wine. Saw a specimen, dead, of the

Colorado or Potato Beetle whose ravages in Canada are almost as destructive as those of the locusts of Scripture. They have appeared in Germany, and great consternation is felt about their getting to this country.

August 17th
Received information from Jane Challice that her brother John, Lieut. R.N. has arrived in England from New South Wales hopelessly insane, and that his brother Willie has had him conveyed to the Naval Hospital for officers so circumstanced, at Yarmouth. I have known of his insanity for two years past but have been forbidden to disclose it to his sisters. He could not be in a better place for one in his condition. He was always very eccentric and went by the name of 'Mad Jack' while he was at sea. So it is with this family that either their faults, like Roger, or their misfortunes, like John, are a constant claim on our anxieties.

August 24th
Saw poor John, who was looking very thin and pale, with restless eyes. He asked after all at Dereham, and, for some time, I began to doubt whether his mind was really affected, as he did not evince more than his usual eccentric manner. After a while, however, he rambled away as to whether 'sobriety was consistent with honesty' (and vice versa) perhaps so, perhaps not, well, he didn't know etc. I asked him why he interrupted the performance at Sydney, by making love to the heroine on the stage? He said 'he wanted to marry her there and then'.

As regards the stage heroine it has transpired that, during an intimacy with her, she had extracted large sums of money from him, and had then transferred her affections to someone else. Thinking this someone must be the professional 'amoreuse' in the play, poor John went mad with jealousy.

September 14th
The Norfolk women have a slovenly habit of throwing refuse water into the streets regardless of who is coming, so that one sometimes narrowly escapes being covered with it. In this instance the splash coming under the nose of a horse which Mr Fulcher was driving into Dereham for the market, accompanied by his son, the animal took fright and, dashing against a post, upset the gig and flung them so violently into the road that the old gentleman fractured his skull, and

died next morning. He was 80, and presented a most ghostly appearance when I visited him at the 'public' where he had been taken.

October 9th
Went from London Bridge to Croydon for the Church Congress, and was surprised at the little army of city clerks and men of business who got out of all the stations.

October 18th
During the cyclone on Sunday night Cleopatra's Needle which was being towed from Egypt to England to be set up in London parted company with the towing steamship in the Bay of Biscay and is probably now immersed at the bottom of the sea, but hopes are entertained of her drifting to shore. Six lives were lost in the attempt to save it.

October 19th
Learnt that Cleopatra's Needle had been recovered, drifting about by itself, about 90 miles from where it had been abandoned.

The Russians have gained a great victory over the Turks in Asia, but the Russian army in Europe has been repulsed from Plevna[3] three times, and it is now being approached by siege and not by assault, as it ought to have been.

November 19th
Took the Chair at the first meeting of a Debating Society. About 50 young men present. Subject – 'Abolition of Capital Punishment', suggested by a twofold murder recently at Wymondham[4], in which a journeyman blacksmith killed his master and a fellow workman, and for which he will be hung at Norwich tomorrow. A conceited young fellow called Gamley spoke well in favour of abolition – the other side very poorly represented, but the votes were in favour of the existing law. Gamley being a stranger, I asked him whether he was a Churchman. Said he was, but his master, a dissenting draper, expected him to go to Chapel, so he did.

December 7th
A telegram from Herbert to say he had arrived in Liverpool and hoped to be with us this evening. Went to meet him at 7.00 p.m. but he did not arrive by that train. Went again at 9 and sure enough, there he was! The joy of all of us could not easily be expressed after 3½ years absence!

December 11th

Herbert and I met dear John by appointment in Norwich. Herbert looked every inch the soldier and John looked every inch the priest. I felt proud and happy and very grateful for them both. Had a bottle of champagne to celebrate the occasion.

1878

January 2nd

About 10 years ago our Bishop prohibited our chief Chemist from coming to Holy Communion because he had married the sister of a deceased wife, which caused much talk in the parish. Now the mother of the young woman, who lives with them, is in a critical state of health and wishes to receive the sacrament and the daughter wishes to receive it with her. All I could do is to make another application to the Bishop, urging the peculiar circumstances at present, but he is, rightly no doubt, inexorable, to the great grief of the Chemist and his so-called wife.

Herbert & Helen went to the Grand Ball given by the 5th (Royal Irish) Lancers – my wife and I dined with the Bulwers on a splendid swan from their estate at Heydon, which had been fatted at Norwich.

January 26th

Our complete family party began to break up today – John and his good little wife going home. The Nelsons stay another week. Arthur has been out with his gun, making a pretty little bag in the vicinity of the Vicarage including snipe and woodcock, but then he misses nothing.

January 28th

The political world in a great ferment on account of the Russians having obtained Adrianople & progressing towards Constantinople itself. Lord Beaconsfield very bellicose and sent the British fleet into the Dardanelles, but Lords Derby and Carnarvon resigning their places in the Cabinet in consequence, they telegraphed its recall.

February 6th

The Dissenters here are moving towards the church in consequence of their internal dissentions. The Baptist Minister having married a rich woman and built a grand house, snaps his fingers at his Deacons and retires into private life. The Independent Minister has an idea of taking

Orders, which being B.A. (London) he would have no difficulty about.

On Sunday there was a regular row in the chapel as a consequence of his introducing Church Collects – a protest was read, defiance given, the epithet 'humbug' and 'liar' used, blows nearly come to, and a lady member fainted away. Poor Mr Tyas was charged with plotting to go over to the Church of England, but another declared it was the Church of Rome!

February 15th
Mr Tyas, the Congregational Minister sought an interview with me relative to his leaving dissent and asking to be put in the way of becoming a clergyman of the Church of England. Promised him all the aid in my power. The dissenters are dreadfully angry about it & he has resigned his charge.

The British ironclads, six in number, have passed through the Dardanelles and anchored before Constantinople, against the protests of Turkey.

March 8th
To Westminster to see the site where Cleopatra's Needle is to be set up on the edge of the Thames, which, though it may be effective when viewed from the water, is not so when viewed from the land. Afterwards to Westminster Abbey, and thence to the Aquarium, which seemed very incongruous with the venerable precincts. Like others it has been diverted into exhibitions of all kinds, which go on for 3 hours without intermission, e.g. jugglers, acrobats. Swiss singers, dogs and monkeys, Sword-swallowers etc. the whole terminating with the truly astonishing feats of Miss Zazel,[1] a splendidly made girl who does anything on the thin wire and the trapeze. She pitches, as if taking a

Theatre poster, March 8th 1878
© The British Library Board - Evan 263 (1877)

258

header, from the roof into a net beneath, contriving to land on her back. She is shot from a cannon with a velocity which is astonishing.

March 9th

Heard the terrible news that young Empson, till recently in our choir, had accidentally killed his father on the evening we left home. Empson Snr was walking, gun in hand with his boy and, wishing to pick up a large piece of coal which had fallen from a cart, handed the gun to the boy which somehow exploded and killed him. Excitement is great and a sum being raised for the widow etc, whom I must see on Monday.

March 19th

First meeting of our Branch of the Church of England Temperance Society. Waived the proposal of my being Chairman in favour of Mr Watt, my curate, he being a total abstainer, which I have no intention of becoming. The 'shipwrecks' I have known in Dereham from drink are numerous and appalling and it would be a great mercy if by any means it could be arrested.

March 22nd

I am thankful to be able to record that Arthur Nelson has obtained an appointment at the forthcoming Paris Exposition[2], at a guinea per diem & his travelling expenses. Quite a new era for Lilly.

March 29th

Weather so bad that on Sunday last the ship Eurydice[3] was capsized in a snow storm off the Isle of Wight through having full sail. Nearly 300 men were drowned, all sailors returning from training at Bermuda. Young Nicholson, a parishioner – a promising young fellow and engaged to be married to a very nice girl, among them & I fear another young parishioner from Hoe, likewise.

In my correspondence with the Bishop of Manchester about Mr Tyas, I sent him a copy of my Church Report. The Bishop, in acknowledging it is very enthusiastic and complimentary – my own Bishop has never commended it, though Archdeacon Hopper told me that his Lordship always reads it with much care – probably to spy out 'Ritualism'!

May 4th

Calling at the Collisons of Bilney saw a young elephant, stuffed, in their Hall. The mother was shot by Harry Collison in Africa, lately, and the calf taken alive, but it died for lack of milk on which to rear it.

May 10th

Herbert has arrived at Edinburgh and will embark from Liverpool for Halifax with about 170 men. I'm thankful that another officer from his own regiment will share the responsibility and also be a companion.

May 28th

The Bishop of Norwich held a confirmation in Dereham Church. Met him at the station in the Brougham & had the Churchwardens and other guests to lunch with him. I was glad to escape the dispraise of the Bishop, who must have disapproved of our elevated altar with gold and white frontal, to say nothing of the bouquets of white flowers, candlesticks and credence. It is, I imagine, as perfect as any altar in his diocese, but I doubt very much if he appreciated it, which, considering his views, could not be expected.

June 12th

The public mind had scarcely got over the Eurydice capsizing off the Isle of Wight when last week, off Folkestone, two of the monster ironclads belonging to the German Navy 'rammed'[4] and the monster thus assailed went down in 10 minutes with 250 lives lost. An explosion from fire damp has taken place in the North whereby nearly 300 men have been destroyed. The aged Emperor of Germany (82) has been twice shot at in Berlin, being wounded in the face and the arm.

June 17th

My dear wife and Helen accompanied me to London for our month's holiday. No beds to be had at Charing Cross & slept at Ashley's Hotel, Henrietta Street. Americans everywhere for the Paris Exhibition.

June 18th

Started for Paris at 11a.m. & arrived at 9.00 p.m. having lunched with the Bathursts in Boulogne. We are located on the Avenue de la Grande Armée, where we met Lilly and her husband. Our 'flat' is a thoroughly French affair – laid out more for show than comfort, but it will answer our purpose.

June 19th

Dined at a restaurant in the Rue de Rivoli and were astonished at the Avenue de l'Opéra being illuminated with electric light, which made everything look as white as day – the gas, by comparison was yellow and dingy.

June 22nd

We visited the Exposition, by far the most vast kind that the world has produced. Through Nelson's influence we went all over the Pavilion erected for the use of the Prince of Wales – a quaint Elizabethan structure exquisitely furnished. The outdoor central avenue, called 'The Street of all Nations' is perhaps the most interesting thing. I observed that Germany is the only country not represented. The crowd is enormous, 20 or 30 thousand visiting every day, but so vast is the area that there is room for all. Not so, however, in the Restaurant which is, literally, besieged, as are all the means of public conveyance.

Went to see the French, Swedish, Italian & English pictures, amongst the first of which there was a great superfluity of nudes.

June 27th

Took Helen to the Exposition to see the pictures and was interested in a portrait of M. Gambetta[5] who played so important a part in the late revolution.

June 28th

My treat to the Nelsons to Versailles. Sought some refreshment at a stall. A stout, bumptious, pushing Frenchman came up for 'Pale Ale' and rather rudely got himself served first. I thought him remarkably like the picture of Gambetta I saw yesterday. On returning to our coach, the coachman said 'Voilà! There is one of our foremost revolutionaries, M. Gambetta'! But, he added 'he is only using the revolution to suit his own ends. His rudeness at the stall shows that he does not practice 'Liberté, Equalité, Fraternité' though he adopts it as a cry.

July 12th

Herbert's Regiment is probably at Montreal, with five others and artillery to quell an anticipated riot between Orangemen and Catholics on the anniversary of the former. The number of troops indicates the seriousness of the affair.

The Berlin Congress is over. England is to hold Cyprus, thus obtaining prestige of the whole Mediterranean, and in return to defend Turkey in Asia, and to manage it! A great enterprise, but also a most serious responsibility. Lord Beaconsfield is a bold and remarkable statesman.

July 17th [London]
Business with the Banker and with the lawyer. Temple Bar gone, and the new Law Courts prodigiously risen – a magnificent pile which ought to my mind to have been erected on the Thames embankment.

September 20th
Went over Mr Brown's boot and shoe factory in Church St – quite a new feature in our town, as we have no other factories except one for leather and two for agricultural machinery. He employs 50 people, and pays away £50 in wages, and, by machinery, by which everything is done, can make a pair of boots from the uncut skin, fit to put on in two hours! All the different parts of the boot, the cutting out the soles, making uppers and heels and toecaps are done in separate rooms.

September 23rd
Dined at Quebec & met General & Mrs Bulwer, General & Mrs Lennox. Conversation about Afghan War which seems to be inevitable as the Amir has refused to let our military mission enter his state. What added interest to this was that Lord Lytton, Governor of India, is uncle to the Bulwers, and is said to have occasioned the situation by mismanagement. Who knows?

October 28th
At Norwich met Herbert who had arrived from Halifax. The Colonel had suggested his coming to England to qualify for an Adjutancy by going through the course of musketry at Hythe.

December 21st
This week I have supplied with coal and called upon every parishioner in Hoe, and given Christmas dinners to those who are communicants as well.

1879

January 17th
North Norfolk is in great electioneering excitement in filling the place of Col. Duff. Candidates are Sir Fowell Buxton, the brewer, Liberal and Mr E. Birkbeck, Conservative. Capt. Bulwer proposed the former, but said on the hustings that, though a Liberal, he disapproved the foreign policy of his party. Now, as the election turns simply on this very pivot, it is a curious illustration of how men, for party ends, will

go against their own convictions. The contest is likely to be a severe one – the Afghan War is another count against Lord Beaconsfield's government by the Liberals, and here again our Captain stands awkwardly with his party as his brother, Lord Lytton, Governor General of India, is said to have brought it about.

January 19th

Two sermons by Dr Hills, Bishop of British Colombia, of the ordinary Missionary type the chief point of interest being that a small church on the Frazer River, built by our congregation in response to a previous appeal, had long been completed and when not served by a regular clergyman, the service is done by converted Indian chiefs.

January 25th

In the Northern Division of the County Mr E. Birkbeck, Conservative, beat Sir Fowell Buxton by 490 votes. The contest assumed great importance as it turned on approval or disapproval of Lord Beaconsfield's foreign policy.

January 29th

Dined at du Port's where was a fine haunch of venison given by Lady Bayning. Though I have known him a long time this is the first occasion when I have met C.S.Reade M.P. at dinner. As all the party were Conservatives there was much congratulation at the result of the late election. Mr Reade showed me a letter he had received from Lord Beaconsfield in which he attributed the result in no small measure to the speeches and exertions of Mr Reade.

February 6th

Gave a lecture to the Churchman's Club in Norwich which was well attended, the audience being warm and enthusiastic. Not having been invited anywhere, slept at the Royal Hotel and, being Assize time, had difficulty in getting a bed – had to pay double for it, as seems to be always the rule during the Assizes.

February 10th

My curate, who is rather riding his hobby-horse Temperance to death, or rather, total abstinence, got up a meeting in the Corn Hall on the subject, which was well attended. As I do not concur with the fanatical views of total abstainers, viz. that all should be such, I always feel that in speaking on the subject, I may be doing great harm instead of good.

With a view to not allowing people to suppose that I object to the Society, I have taken 10 shares in a Dereham Coffee Tavern, though feeling it will not succeed.

February 12th
Mr Rivett, who has long resided in Zululand, brought disastrous news which was confirmed in today's paper, viz. a great defeat of British troops![1] We know so little of defeats, and that from uncivilised tribes, that the news has produced a complete shock. 500 of our men and 30 officers were killed in the engagement. All our supplies and the regimental colours are in the hand of the enemy. Six or seven regiments are being sent out as reinforcements. I hope our dear boy's regiment may not be one of them.

February 18th
The Nelsons left us to visit his father. Arthur says he has been promised an appointment in South Kensington in two year's time and the interval may be spent in going to an impending Exhibition in Australia. A poor look-out, I fear, likely to prove the nemesis of disobedience.

February 21st
Payson,[2] the American who is walking all round England, passed through Dereham at 8.00 a.m. after completing 40 miles. He gave a lecture at the Corn Hall and walked on to Lynn, 27 miles on. He is to walk 2,000 miles in 1,000 consecutive hours. He got to Lowestoft the same night, via Norwich and Yarmouth – and lecturing at both places. It seems incredible.

Visited the Coffee Tavern – the last novelty in conjunction with the Church of England Temperance Society. It has been opened as a Joint Stock company, in which I have taken 10 shares. I don't think it will answer, but it would not do to hold back. The bar is very comfortable, there are good meat dinners and the sleeping rooms are exquisitely clean, but I thought the coffee execrable.

A very hot letter in the local paper against me for a sermon I had preached. These local papers are great nuisances, as there is not enough news in the place they make up for it by writing letters etc.

February 22nd
Buried Ed. Barwell, who killed himself by drink, to which his trade as a wine merchant naturally conduced. He was a clever artist, linguist

and musician, and a man of taste, coming of a large family in Norwich with similar abilities. Everyone liked – and everyone pitied – 'poor Ed. Barwell' who was 'nobody's enemy but his own.'

February 28th
Herbert left to go the School of Musketry at Hythe. Prince Louis Napoleon has gone as a volunteer to join our army for the Zulu war. Who would have thought the time would ever come when a Bonaparte would be fighting on the side of the English.

March 6th
The notorious convict, housebreaker and murderer, Peace[3], was executed a few days ago. The papers making capital out of his confessions, adventures etc. a fellow about here has taken it into his head to imitate Peace, and has committed burglaries night after night. Tracked through Dereham, he visited the Coffee Tavern; a mounted policeman took him, but not before he had fired 6 shots and wounded the policeman's horse.

March 18th
Took two parishioners in later life to be confirmed at Fakenham, where I soon saw that everything from the Vicar's surplice was far behind Dereham, e.g. a choir of women.

April 5th
Was much scandalised that a Madame Card intended to give an entertainment at the Corn Hall on the evening on Good Friday. Wrote a protest to the proprietors, pointing out the scandal.

April 6th
Preached on the solemnity of Good Friday and warned the people against entertainments, without alluding, of course, to Madame Card.

April 7th
Mr Gidney, the whilom discomfited Churchwarden called, accompanied by Madame Card, he being Corn Hall Manager. He agreed with my strictures and says that the Hall was let in ignorance that the 11th would be Good Friday. Madame is a very fine and masterful woman, evidently regarding my suggestion of transferring her entertainment to Easter Monday as a pecuniary question. She feared that being a Bank Holiday, and the Prince of Wales being about to open a new hospital in Hunstanton on that day, all the holidaymakers would go there. However the 'Mesmeric Enchantress', as she is described in

the Bills, in the end yielded to my remonstrance and transferred the day. This she did on my promising not to publish a remonstrance, as she knew I intended, in the local paper, and my promising to attend the performance on Easter Monday.

April 14th

In consequence of my forbidding the bells to be rung in Lent, even on the occasion of the Royal marriage, there was a threatened strike of ringers. It seemed for a long time that there would be no joyful peal this Easter. The uneasy and jerky motion of a single bell or so indicated that there was a commotion among the ringers. However, at 9.30 – out they went.

May 15th [London]

Dined with William Duncombe at his club. A friend of his invited us to visit the Junior Garrick Club, as Thursdays happen to be their best evenings. At the time we arrived the amusement was at its height and carried on with unflagging energy. The room was clouded with tobacco smoke, and the members consist of actors, authors, painters and the like. Not a word or jest was spoken which might not have been uttered in the most refined society, yet no ladies were present.

May 19th

I went to a meeting of the Additional Curates Society, at which Mr Hubbard (founder of St Alban's, Holborn), Mr Gladstone and the Bishop of Peterborough were to speak. Though I arrived 20 minutes before the time the programme had attracted such crowds in Willis's Rooms[4] that I had to stand. The Archbishop of Canterbury presided. Mr Gladstone delivered himself in that slow, emphatic, thoughtful style, common to all great speakers.

May 20th

Called on Mr & Mrs Wilson in Harley Street. Mr Wilson told me that Mr Haweis, who was to have preached to the Volunteers a fortnight ago, has sent his resignation to the Colonel on the ground that he would not be Chaplain to troops who seemed to 'require umbrellas'! The order for Church Parade had been rescinded because it was a wet afternoon.

May 24th

In the evening took Lilly to Christy's minstrels. Moore[5], who is the head of the thing, and is 'Bones', had splendid brilliants in his shirt-front and wrist bands, which flashed and gleamed like glow-worms all over the place. Probably a whim, like that of an omnibus conductor who wore a diamond ring worth £40, or that of a fish-hawker from Yarmouth, whose pride is a chronometer to the value of £50.

May 26th

Saw W. Challice, who told me that his brother Roger had 'broken out again' and has betaken himself to his evil ways. He is certainly now past hope! Saw Herbert off to Liverpool as the ship sails tomorrow for Halifax. He has had a long holiday and it is high time he was at work.

June 20th

Very afflicting news in the paper about the death of Prince Louis Napoleon who had joined our army as a Volunteer in this lamentable Zulu War. He was one of a small reconnoitring party who were suddenly surrounded by the enemy and the Prince and two troopers were killed. It seems most imprudent and unnecessary to have thus risked a life on which the Napoleonic dynasty depended, but I suppose it was done to please the French. He is described as 'brave to rashness'.

June 25th

William Duncombe and his wife, on leaving us, went to Yarmouth for a week, where the Prince of Wales was inspecting the Militia Artillery of which he is Colonel. The Gaiety Company were there, and two of the ladies occupied a house next to the Hotel where the Duncombes were – the Prince supped with them each evening, leaving at 3.00 a.m. 'Not quite the thing', as William says.

July 8th

The drains being out of order it became necessary for the family to vacate the house for three days, Helen to stay with the du Ports and my wife and myself to Yarmouth, chiefly that I might visit my poor nephew at the R.N. Asylum. Found him rather better in body, but more feeble in mind. He wanted some 'Cavendish' tobacco and some paper and pencils, as he writes all day long. Provided him with these and wrote a careful estimate of his condition to his brother William.

July 31st

Attended the Church of England Temperance Society meeting. A certain Herr Cohen, a small converted Jew intruded on the platform, but with permission. This gentleman combines Phrenology with Tee-totalism and is evidently a charlatan, and made a ridiculous exhibition of himself.

August 1st

Having heard yesterday of the death of the Rev. Cubitt, called on Mrs Cubitt and at her request remained an hour. She was in a sad state – he was only 40 and leaves four children. I fear he has not done much good, as he never seemed to have a sense of the office of a priest. Whisky at the hotel at 11.00 a.m. and pipe smoking are not practices calculated to raise the Church in people's minds.

August 7th

Found Hoe in a state of excitement in consequence of Mrs Hipperson's wretched daughter-in-law (in rags and either half-drunk or mad) threatening the old lady who was pale and nervous with fear. Getting the woman by herself she said she had walked from London to discover where her two little girls were, and to get money from the old lady, whose son had married her while he had a wife yet living, and who is living now. As I had been the means of getting one of these girls into the Royal Albert Asylum and the other into Sister Mary's orphanage, I was able to tell her that one of them is dead (I gave her the memorial card) and the other well provided for in a wealthy family – that, as for money, Mrs H. had not enough to support herself. The poor creature was satisfied with this explanation and at my request walked back to Dereham with me, where I got her a lodging for the night. On our road, hearing a great shout, on turning I discovered that we were being followed by an infuriated ox, and only just managed to escape him. As luck would have it, going through the town, met 'everybody' who looked not a little surprised at the companion I had with me.

August 8th

Met the poor creature by appointment at the station, took a ticket for her, gave her 10/- and was glad to see the train move off to London. She was profuse in her gratitude and promised never to disturb the old lady more, which promise I sincerely hope she will keep.

September 9th

Letters from our two distant children, Lilly & Herbert. I am sorry to say that the former bids fair to become a mother. How they are to support a family on such small means I do not know. It is the natural nemesis of imprudent marriages. Poor Herbert is suffering from a repulse in love – not from Miss Drayson, daughter of the Colonel of the Artillery at Halifax, but from the Colonel who, very wisely I consider, will not hear of it on account of insufficiency of means.

September 11th

Dined at the du Ports' to meet his brother who has just returned from Egypt. He describes the Harem of the recently deposed Khedive as consisting of 1,200 persons, including the servants, and says the value of the jewellery owned by the ladies is upwards of two millions sterling. The expenses have ruined the country, as well they might.

September 25th

John accompanied me to Little Blakenham, where we have a considerable interest in a farm, in consequence of a request from the tenant for a reduction of rent on account of the late disastrous harvest. Conceded the point and went over the land. Mr Ransom, the tenant, works with his sons and his wife attends to the butter and poultry, quite in the old-fashioned style.

October 1st

Dined at the Bulwers and met a South African settlers' party. They seemed to think that the capture of Cetawayo – recently effected – and the war itself, was an absolute necessity as the colony of Natal was at his mercy, and if he had followed up his victory over us at Isandlwana, he might have taken possession, in which case every white would have been murdered. There was an African tinge over the party, the Bulwers having a son with Sir H. Bulwer, Governor of Natal, and the Collisons having a son in the wine trade there, and who diversifies business with elephant shooting and other big game.

Curiously enough we are asked to meet Sir Theophilus Shepstone[6] in a day or so, to whose policy the war is attributable.

October 8th

Dined at Nathaniel Girling's and met, among others, Rider Haggard and his sister. Haggard has 1,000 acres in South Africa and says that John Dunn[7], who has been made a ruler of one of the new dependencies under Sir G. Wolseley, is a thorough scamp. Speaking English & Zulu with equal fluency he was of immense use to us in the late war, but he has cast off Cetawayo the moment he saw which way the wind was blowing and what is worse, has cast off the Christian religion, taking to polygamy and ordering every missionary out of his jurisdiction. He made a fortune by supplying the Zulus with guns.

October 26th

Heard from Herbert at Halifax, who has not written for an unusually long time. The poor boy is in love with the daughter of a Colonel, who will not hear of the match and Herbert thinks it would be better for both to avail himself of the opportunity of going to the depot at Maidstone. He hopes to sail from Halifax on the 28th.

In the afternoon took duty at E. Bradenham for E.Winter who has just become Vicar on the presentation of Capt. Adlington, an old Eton chum. Etonian friendships seem to be much more strong than any which are formed at the Universities.

November 7th
A letter from the ship conveying Herbert from Halifax, satisfactory as announcing his safety, but, alas, he again informs us that he has spent a considerable sum beyond his pay and allowance.

November 10th
Mr Watt having it in contemplation to take a secretaryship of the Temperance Society, I have offered John the curacy in that contingency, and also to furnish a house for him, but the matter is, as yet, in abeyance.

December 23rd
Mrs Field applied to me some time ago to get Col. Bulwer to use his influence with his brother, Sir H. Bulwer, Governor of Natal, to aid the promotion of Mr James Field Walker, her husband's nephew, in the Cape Town Mounted Force. The Colonel gave me despatches to show that the young man is insane and, among other things, fired his carbine into tents which were full of soldiers. Is it drink or exposure and hardship which sends so many of our young fellows in the Army and Navy insane?

1880

January 6th
My dear wife accompanied me to some private theatricals at Bradenham Hall, and a dance afterwards. 'Everybody' was there and the performance was really excellent. Came away immediately after supper, the number of carriages rendering departure difficult, and the night being very foggy.

February 19th

To Norwich to select a testimonial for Watt. On my return heard that dear Lilly had a little girl. I'm thankful the mother is doing well, but in the low state of their finances they would be better off without children.

Read that the life of the Czar had been attempted for the fourth time by another Nihilist conspiracy, by blowing up part of the Winter Palace when the occupants were supposed to be at dinner. Providentially the Imperial family were half an hour behind time, waiting for a guest, so escaped.

February 25th

Watt preached his farewell sermon. Thus I part with a curate who has been longer with me than any other (seven years) and who was a very valuable help until he took up with teetotalism to which he has since devoted all his interests.

March 10th

Letter from Lilly – she and baby well, but containing misgivings as to how they are to live in the future. Poor child, she was warned of this by me, before she took her fate into her own hands.

April 9th

Hoe gives me a vote for W. Norfolk, as Dereham does for S. I therefore drove to Mileham to vote for the Conservative candidates & to take luncheon with Rev. Cartwright. A liberal candidate has been put up – a fox-hunting squire whose only qualification seems to be that he affords excellent sport with the hounds, of which he is Master.

The Hon. Mr Cole, son of Lord Enniskillen, a splendid specimen of an Irishman, was at luncheon, having come for the same purpose as myself. After luncheon my old parishioner W. Mayes wanted to see me. He had come as an escort as a row was going on at the Polling place, at the notice of which Mr Cole seemed delighted, tucking up his cuffs and flourishing his stick in the theatrical Paddy's way. The roughs, however, to his regret, had departed.

April 29th [London]

To my lawyers, Messrs Norris, Allen & Carter in Bedford Row about my freehold house 39, Hatton Wall, the tenant of which has become insolvent, and the place left. Accompanied one of the clerks to look over the premises, which I have not done for 40 years! It is an excellent house with a stone staircase and large rooms which the late tenant had sub-let to various artificers, mainly Italian.

Called on my solicitor, who by virtue of illness has transferred this business to Messrs Norris. As the nominal prosecutor in Martin v. Machonochie we always avoid religion.

May 1st
In September last year I visited H.M.S. Atalanta[1]. The public are at this time in a feverish state of anxiety as to what has happened to her, as she is overdue, nearly a month and no tiding of her whatever. It is feared she has gone down in the Atlantic with 300 on board.

May 12th
At Gressenhall shot 25 rooks by invitation as none of the young Hills were at home and could not hit them if they had been! Alas! The Atalanta is now given up for lost, though no vestige of wreckage has come to light.

May 18th
At the Oddfellows Annual Dinner, 250 sat down with Col. Bulwer in the Chair, supported by myself, Capt. Haggard and Dr Jessop. Everything harmonious and complimentary, but the speeches were too long and somewhat egotistical. Sat down at 4 and rose at 8.30 – the town was very gay, but little or no drunkenness.

May 29th
Mrs Gurdon of Letton Hall died this week. Poor Mr Gurdon has so lost his mind that he is under the impression that it is he, not his son, who is returned as M.P.

June 27th
The Machonochie and Martin case which has been protracted over 12 years has utterly collapsed, Mr Martin declining to prosecute any further now he finds that a verdict in his favour would mean imprisonment for Machonochie.

July 25th [Volunteer Camp at Yarmouth]
Dined at Mess after which we all went into the garden. Moon bright, and the sea a sheet of rippling silver. All prognosticated fine and settled weather except a young officer who said he possessed a delicate French 'aneroid' which announced rain. This was received by all with incredulity.

July 26th

On waking, the rain was descending in torrents, and, as it subsequently turned out, kept up during the whole week.

August 3rd

As last year I had to record the defeat of the British Army at Isandlwana, so this I must mention in Afghanistan, General Burrow's Brigade of 3,000 has been defeated by Ayub Khan[2], only a third escaping. The excitement is intense, the more so because Mr Gladstone, the Premier, is dangerously ill.

August 6th

The world's talk just now is about the Baroness Burdett Coutts[3], at 66, marrying Mr Bartlett, a rising young man of 30, who manages her affairs. By this act she foregoes the enormous sum of £100,000 per annum, he being of American extraction, which is forbidden by the will.

A friend of Mary Girling's told me that Rylands[4], the famous engraver, who did my 'Meeting of Edward IV with Lady Grey' (of which I have also the original) was hung for forgery. Alas he employed his eminent talent in engraving Bank Notes, and suffered the penalty of the law.

August 16th

Dear Lilly, who has been staying with us for 6 weeks with child and nurse, left this morning for Ripley, Derbyshire, where her husband has obtained a situation in some factory which it is supposed will lead to something – it seems so sad for the poor dear to have no fixed home of her own, but to live in lodgings, especially now there is a baby.

August 18th

The Collisons, under the name of Luncheon, gave an early dinner and garden party. This kind of entertainment is very much in vogue of late.

August 23rd

Luncheon party at Miss Girling's and garden party subsequently at the Haggards. This going so often to these entertainments I should not allow myself, but it is now full harvest, the school is dismissed & there are hardly any sick in the parish.

The Old Vicarage, Dereham, little changed in 2012
(Photograph by kind permission of Mr & Mrs Nigel Matthews)

August 30th

My dear wife wishing to give a garden party, like all the rest of the neighbourhood, it came off today. About 60 persons accepted and the amusements were Archery, Lawn Tennis and Pool Croquet, the latter being very popular.

September 6th

The Burials Bill is passed, whereby any dissenter may be buried in the Churchyard by whatever Minister and with whatever service the relatives may desire. I am not sure that penalties may not attract if we refuse to do so. This is disparaging and humiliating to the Church and the worst of it is that the two Archbishops and several Bishops have advocated the Bill.

September 8th

Our troops in Afghanistan have now obtained a great victory, destroying Ayub's army and re-capturing all the guns (27) that had been taken from them. This victory was gained under Sir Frederick Roberts at Kandahar.[5]

Several disagreeable matters have taken place at Dereham. Goods conveyed away in large quantities from one Ironmonger and received by another, an attempt to burn down a seed shop in the market place, and in which gunpowder was employed, extensive smashing of windows.

September 17th

A Norwich weekly paper of a scandalous nature, and having correspondents in each town, has of late been attacking me, and my dear son & curate, for 'Romish' proceedings. Today, having to go to Norwich, I determined to call on the Editor of the 'Daylight' and demand the name of the contributor, on whom I told him that an action would be brought if the thing were repeated. He said his justification was his belief was true, but on my describing the nature of our services, the fact that the bishop joined in them, my being on good terms with the Parishioners and even with many dissenters, he confessed to be labouring under a mistake and that more caution would be exercised in future. It is clear that I have an enemy, also judging from his writing – one who is a regular attendant at Church.

September 30th

A case of belief in sorcery. An old lady had said the Lord's Prayer backwards to cure herself of an infliction which had been 'put' on her. She promised me to say it forwards, thrice daily – but added 'Unless the trouble comes back & then I say it backwards again'.

October 5th

We decided, before winter began, to obtain lodgings in Ripley, where Lilly and her husband live, and to make that place a centre for seeing Matlock, Dovedale, Haddon & Chatsworth, so we travelled there today. But on arriving our hearts sank! Not only is it a horrible place, with a coarse population, but the apartments which Lilly had provided at the Inn, the only accommodation that could be had, were wholly and altogether below par. It was an error in judgement & the worst of it was, we feared she had taken them for 10 days! Went to bed in a terrible state of anxiety as to what was to be done.

October 6th

We summoned the landlady, and she acquitted us, we paying 13/- beyond our bill, which we were only too thankful to do, in order to get away. After lunching with the Nelsons, we left for Matlock. I never felt a greater sensation of relief than when, in a fly, we drove out of Ripley with its hideous coal-furnaces and its town wholly given over not to idolatry, but to dissent. We arrived at the Royal Bath Hotel in time for tea. It is a splendid hotel set in the gorge of Matlock.

November 2nd

A telegram told us that William Duncombe died this morning at 3.30. Thus I have lost my earliest friend whom I have known since we were 12, and with whom for nearly half a century, I never had a quarrel, though our ideas of life and duties differed widely.

November 16th

Herbert, who only left us six weeks ago, came home on long leave before his Regiment goes to Gibraltar. We are delighted to see him, but verily the gentlemen of the Army are not hard-worked, and as pay goes on all the same, they ought to be well off too.

November 20th

Called a meeting of the English Church Union to consider the case of Rev. T. Pelham Dale, now in Holloway Gaol for contempt of Lord Penzance's court,[6] to which he will not pay obedience. It is certainly the result of a compact between the Queen and the Archbishop to stamp out Ritualism.

November 26th

Baptized a child by these names – John Capel Marjoribanks Courtenay Locke – his father is a Lieutenant in the United States Army and his mother is about to join him. The surname is Hurstlynn.

Norwich Cathedral under a quasi re-consecration in consequence of the principal singer (Minns)[7] committing suicide in a remote part where the archives are kept and which is seldom visited. A Chapter being held and some documents needed the discovery was made otherwise poor Minns might have hung there three months without anyone knowing.

November 30th

Dined at Bylaugh Hall – a very recherché dinner – real turtle and swan & French cookery. The Lombes very cordial and kind. On our way a hawk who had captured a pigeon was scared at our carriage lamps and let it fall on the roof of the Brougham, from whence it fell into the road. On our return our man said that the hawk had no doubt returned and eaten the pigeon as the road was covered with feathers.

December 15th

Mr Dale and Mr Enright have both been sent back to prison, all the technicalities of counsel on their behalf having broken down and Lord Penzance pronounced a lawfully constituted judge. We are helplessly under the rule of the civil power, represented by a Parliament consisting largely of dissenters and Roman Catholics.

December 27th
What a year has this been! Frightful Colliery explosions, Railway accidents, shipwrecks, war broken out again at the Cape, Ireland on the verge of rebellion, and two English clergymen in gaol, reminding one of the Elizabethan, rather than the Victorian age.

1881

January 14th
Helen, Herbert and myself joined a friendly party at Quebec 'to eat swan'. At dinner Mr Jex Blake, a Norfolk Squire with a wooden leg, whom we met at Bealugh in the autumn, told how his leg had been smashed by a cannon-shot at Waterloo and had been humanely treated by a staff officer, in the field. He never knew who his benefactor was, till he accidentally met him at a dinner party a year ago, when the story of the 'poor boy with the mashed leg' was told by the benefactor himself – 'and I' said Mr Jex Blake, 'was the boy'. They are both very old men, but neither had forgotten.

January 18th
Mr Waters, my principal tythe payer at Hoe, has been shamefully defrauded by a Steward in whom everyone felt the utmost confidence. He was a most regular attendant at Church, and a Communicant, and has added to his sins by seducing quite a young girl who was living at the Waters'. Such cases are very discouraging, the more so as this man acknowledged former extravagance to me, but had now 'seen his error'.

This extreme cold does some good, as Mr Waters' flock of sheep (300) all suffering from foot and mouth disease are cured by it.

January 28th
Herbert left us for the depot at Maidstone. I should have preferred him sticking to the Regiment, which is about to arrive in Natal, and certainly should have done so myself.

January 31st

Another reverse for our troops in the Transvaal[1], through haste and bad generalship. A Colonel, 2 Majors, a Captain & 3 subalterns killed, and 100 men. Two of the officers are Norfolk youths. In proof of the wonderful power of Telegraph in these days, news of this battle was printed and circulated in London, before the contest was over. The General was Sir G. Colley.

February 7th

The King of Ashanti has declared war against us. Verily, the army has enough to do – Kandahar, the Transvaal, Ireland! Strange times!

February 10th

We are unable to drive out of our gates on account of excavations being made for the drainage scheme. Today I assisted in exhuming a poor fellow who had become buried by the earth caving in on him.

February 15th

Herbert called and announced that he had received orders to sail for South Africa with troops on Saturday.

February 17th [London]

Yesterday was spent purchasing mackintosh sheets for camping out and a revolver from Colt's in Pall Mall. Herbert came to dinner and to say good-bye, but none of us had any appetite for a meal. He stayed until 10.30 and then left for Colchester where his draft of men is. He is bringing them to London tomorrow and is to sail from East India docks in the 'Lapland' on Saturday.

February 23rd

Very unpleasant announcement from Herbert's agents that he had overdrawn his account by upwards of £100. It was agreed he was to pay up everything before sailing, but I had no idea it would reach this!

Took Helen to the Lyceum to see Tennyson's 'The Cup', which was very beautifully put on the stage, followed by 'The Corsican Brothers' a tale of vendetta by Dumas, with ghosts, duels and what not, but I never admired Mr Irving.

February 25th

Went to the Haymarket to see 'Masks and Faces'. Excellent acting and sumptuous dresses. The Duke & Duchess of Connaught and the Prince & Princess Mary of Teck were present and seemed to enjoy the play immensely. The Duchess, who was always stout, has become enormous.

February 28th

News of a great battle[2] and defeat in the Transvaal. Thankful Herbert is not yet there. The General killed, and only 100 of one of the Regiments got away alive. Great consternation in London – meeting of authorities and determination to send out 10 more regiments. Paul Kruger declares for possession of the whole of S. Africa for the Afrikaaners on the model of the U.S. The fear is that the Orange Free State may join the Boers and, if so, a long and bloody war.

March 7th

Received a letter from Herbert written from the Lapland, 'off Madeira' on 24th Feb. He says that they have had a splendid passage, but will not reach Durban until March 26th and the front by the middle of April. It is good to hear, in the face of his extensive overdraw, that 'on his Colonial allowance, he can live on his pay, especially as one has to live on Government rations, which one gets free'.

March 10th

Dined 'en famille' with Rev. & Lady Mary Currie on the last pheasant of the season, saved from January, and afterwards preached one of a course of Lent lectures in the splendid parish church [Hingham] to a very numerous and attentive congregation. A blustering drive home, over swollen fords, of which 4 crossed the roads, the latter being in a wretched state. Found that Lilly and her child had arrived on a visit, her husband, who has lost his position, having gone to his father, where I hope he will remain – but fear not.

March 14th

The daily papers announce the assassination of the Czar at last, after several attempts. A bomb was thrown under his carriage and destroyed it, the Czar being uninjured, but a second bomb was thrown at his feet which blew off both his legs and soon ended in his death. These Nihilists are an awful and fiendish power.

March 16th

Preached in the parish church at Yarmouth, dining previously with Rev. G. Venables who had gout so badly that he was carried into the room by two men, and could not go to Church. There was a very large congregation and I found the huge pulpit, or rather, scaffold, very pleasant to preach from – being able to walk around imparting a freedom of action and of utterance.

March 17th
After breakfast to see my poor nephew John Challice, whose unhappy case shows no symptom of improvement. After getting him some tobacco, went to Southtown to a ship's chandlers to buy a St George's Ensign of the largest size, for our clock tower. The dealer recognised me at once as the preacher yesterday evening.

March 19th
A Mr Spark, B.A. Oxford & Ely Theological College came about the curacy. This is the third candidate we have had.

March 20th
Mr Spark read the Lessons very nicely. He will do, but really candidates in these times seem to think that Vicars should alter arrangements to suit their ideas, so it is true that it is not so difficult to govern, as to prevent being governed!

March 22nd
Answer from Ely to say that Mr Spark's Principal could not recommend his young friend to accept a curacy where there is not a double daily service. Mr Spark had evidently not read the printed programme of services which I had previously given him. Telegraphed at once to Mr Peskett, B.A. Cambridge who is now studying at Lincoln and is recommended by Mr Gaye whom the Bishop rejected.

March 23rd
I trust I am getting out of the curate difficulty at last. Mr Peskett returned to Lincoln perfectly satisfied and having accepted the curacy.
Our General in Transvaal has arrived at terms of peace with the Boers, for which one cannot but feel grateful, for Herbert's sake. The public satisfaction however is by no means universal. Our troops having suffered three distinct repulses at the hands of the Boers, and the General being killed, they call it 'Peace with Dishonour'. Others say that as England was wrong in annexing the Transvaal in the first place, there is no dishonour in making an amende and averting bloodshed.

March 26th
Letter from the Bishop accepting Mr Peskett as a candidate but couched in colder language than usual. This may be partly because I declined to accept Mr Daubeny, who is on the Bishop's special and

private list. I fear I can never get on with the Bishop. Although I based my objection on Mr Daubeny being a married man with family, and no house for such, my principal objection was his being of the Low Church, or he would not have been on the Bishop's list.

April 7th

Voting papers were counted up for the election to the Local Board today, and I was elected.

I'm sorry to say a fire broke out at Toftwood last evening and some wheat stacks are destroyed, belonging to Mr Ray who is a kind master. From the stacks having been fired in three places, there is no doubt that it is the work of an incendiary.

April 20th

Took my seat, as a re-elected member, at the new Local Board, and was sorry to learn from our Medical Officer that we had a case of smallpox. Unfortunately it is at the Post Office where, of course, everybody resorts.

Today was the Easter Vestry which was unusually well attended on account of the Churchwardens putting a notice in the paper respecting the negligence of the organist, and the expediency of electing another. Now, though the whole Parish had been complaining about the organist, yet no sooner was another known to be endeavouring to supplant him than they all rushed to the rescue. I was glad of this as I distrust the new man altogether. It will do good, as Martin will be more careful in future, and the complaints of the parishioners will be silenced by their permitting him to remain in office.

April 28th

The result of the census came out and showed an increase of 456 from 5,107 in 1871, and in 1881, 5,563. From this, however, must be deducted a large number of navvies now employed in the sewage works but who will leave Dereham at the completion of the work.

April 30th

Received a letter from Herbert at Maritzberg. He reports himself safe and well, and in camp. He has had to march from 10 to 20 miles in a day, and speaks of the tremendous thunder showers. He has only two between him and his captaincy.

May 5th

Unpleasant letter from the Bishop and another from the new Curate that is, or rather was, to be, to say the latter had failed his theological exam at Cambridge. This puts me in sad difficulties.

May 24th (Rogation)

It is curious that round London there are vestiges of the old Catholic customs which are extinct in Norfolk – one would have thought it would have been just the reverse, e.g. the Sweeps at May-day and the mummers at Christmas. All these, I imagine, were suppressed by the rampant Puritanism of the Eastern Counties.

May 28th

Dear Lilly, baby and the little maid left us after a three months' visit. We were all very low at her departure as her husband has no employment, they have no settled home, and he is living on her money – no more than might have been predicted of such a marriage.

June 1st

Wrote to Herbert in reply to one received from him yesterday. He is in camp under Majuba Hill, near where General Colley was killed in action with the Boers. He has been made a musketry instructor and consequently will be mounted. He describes a friendly visit from Pretorius, Joubert and Kruger – the three leading Boers – who came up with the officers when the latter were playing at 'rounders' for want of something better to do & who accepted their invitation to luncheon.

June 30th

Many of our neighbours were kept away from the meeting of the E.C.U. to enable them to attend the funeral of the Rev. Thomas Fellowes, Rector of Honingham with whom I had a tilting match at the Rural Decanal Chapter on the 'vestment question', though he was far more in the agricultural and poultry line.

July 5th

We live in an age of horrors. Of late years attempts have been made on the lives of the Kings of Spain and Italy and on the Emperors of Germany and Russia, but the news today is that the President of the United States, Garfield,[3] has been wounded by two pistol shots by one Guiteau, a disappointed place-seeker, and his death is almost certain.

July 16th

The Archery Club came to the Vicarage – a pleasant garden party of 40. The thermometer read 90 in the shade. The papers report that the heat exceeded the maximum of Bombay or Calcutta last year.

August 8th

A satisfactory letter from Herbert, sent from Newcastle, Natal. He has taken up his duties as Musketry Instructor and has a Captain's pay. He says there is only one intervening between him and that rank. Had bought his predecessor's horse for £20, but sold it for £25 when a brother officer lent him one.

August 18th

Attended the funeral of the Revd Collison of Bilney, at 90! A large number of his tenants, parishioners and the neighbouring clergy attended. Mr C. was possessed of valuable vineyards in South Africa and was more a merchant than a priest, going up to business every Monday morning till Saturday. He did not marry until he was 60 but has lived to see all four of his children grow up. He was greatly given to hospitality.

September 3rd

Two sudden deaths – one a most respectable parishioner who died unexpectedly of paralysis and the other, alas, through frequent fits brought on by drinking as much as two bottles of spirits per diem! The son of a clergyman, he kept a school just opposite the Vicarage gate. His poor little wife is the daughter of a barrister and they were both under 30.

October 16th

This day 31 years ago I began active ministrations in Dereham. May God forgive all my shortcomings.

October 19th

A meeting of the Burial Board to meet a deputation of Odd fellows and other societies begging that burials might take place on Sundays.Represented to the Committee that as we generally had 6 regularservices on that day, saying nothing of occasional ones, it would be a hardship to the clergy to walk up to the Cemetery and to the mourners if they are kept waiting, which would then be the case. The deputation retired in a rather sulky humour – they were chiefly dissenters.

November 9th

Amongst our guests for dinner today were the Rev. and Mrs Barry with a Miss Brodrick. She is a very clever person (aged 23) who has taken up with the higher class of women's work. Her father is architect of Salisbury Cathedral and she is one of the secretaries of Professor Fawcett, the Postmaster General. He is wholly blind from being shot accidentally by his father while rabbit shooting many years ago. She gave some amazing proofs of his memory in quoting statistics in speeches etc. She has to read the papers to him and often takes him out to dinner.

November 13th

At a wedding both the bridegroom and his best man were so drunk that I would not do the service, and turned them out of church. I never met such a case before.

Baptized a child privately yesterday whose screams while in its cradle caused the mother to undress it – a rat had been feeding on its little arm!!

1882

January 12th

My dear wife, Helen, and Arthur Nelson accompanied me to dine at Miss Girling's to meet our old friends the Haggards. They have had much trouble – their eldest child married an American divorcée & she has now got divorced from <u>him</u>, gone back to America and married a third time. The eldest daughter is insane and in safe keeping, a son in the army got married without the knowledge of his family, another has thrown up the navy, a daughter-in-law is ill, and Mrs Haggard herself in poor health. Also a son who had settled in South Africa lost his investment.

February 2nd

Dined at the du Ports and met the Rev. & Mrs Fielden. Although an old man, Mr Fielden has recently been appointed to Honingham, and is much given to growing orchids, just as his predecessor was addicted to poultry – a highly respectable, easy-going man – and enjoys a good dinner.

February 15th

Busy getting up the annual Church Report (44 pages) and in administering the endowed charities for which we had 700 applicants whose claims had to be looked into.

February 16th

A movement is being got up to present our Bishop with his own portrait on attaining the 25th year of his Episcopate. Mr Burton, Barry and I thought it uncalled for, and a specimen of that 'toadyism' which largely affects the Norfolk parsons. At first I determined to have nothing to do with it, but next day sent in a small sum because Dereham is too important a town to be omitted from the list, and also because, having been pointedly passed over – in the estimation of my brethren – in the distribution of Honorary Canons and Rural Deans, I preferred rendering good for evil.

February 18th

My annual Church Report came out. During the year we had 18 visiting preachers, there were 80 celebrations of Holy Communion, 148 Baptisms, 34 marriages and 56 funerals. Sent a copy to the Bishop but the fact, I suppose, of my being Chairman to a branch of the English Church Union is enough to prejudice him against my work.

March 2nd

Letter from Herbert saying he was about to sail from Durban on Feb. 14th in a mail steamer instead of a troopship, which is far more comfortable. The Regiment is to go to Dublin, but as half the officers are to have leave, he will soon be home again. He says he has worn nothing but his uniform for a year, and has been using kitchen forks and knives, and tin cups!

March 8th

Buried Edward Coker, an old favourite at the Vicarage who – and his mother before him – used to receive money from the endowed charities, and his mother from outdoor Parish Relief. He has left £450 – the savings from a gravel pit he hired! This is by no means the first case of the kind, but not so large an amount!

March 12th

Two or three days ago an elephant broke out of a travelling menagerie in Dereham in the early morning, and, proceeding to a neighbouring house, demolished the windows and, inserting his trunk, demolished the contents of the larder.

March 14th
Telegram from Ernest Duncombe to say that the 'Balmoral Castle' mail packet is due in Plymouth today, with the 97th on board, and asking for letters to Herbert to be sent to him, he being the Lieutenant of the 'Assistance' which is to convey the regiment to Dublin. A coincidence that the cousins should so meet.

April 18th
Meeting of the Dereham Branch of the English Church Union at Soham, where the Rector, Mr Coker Adams, entertained us. The meeting was occupied in passing resolutions concerning the continued imprisonment of the Rev. S.F.Green who has now been in gaol more than a year. Matters are in such a fix that neither Queen, Prime Minister nor the Bishops seems able to get him out. Only the prosecutors, the Church Association, can do it, and such is the narrow-mindedness and bigotry of that party that this is the thing they won't do. The anomaly is so great and the unconstitutional character of the Public Worship Regulation Act that there is no doubt this continued imprisonment will hasten disestablishment.

April 19th
The Times today carries the Gazette with Herbert as Captain.

April 23rd
Herbert has gone to his new Battalion at Aldershot.

A troupe of undoubted Japanese who have been performing in Dereham attended Church both morning and evening, and behaved in a most exemplary manner, having Bible, Prayer & Hymn Books with them, and turning East at the Creed.

May 7th (Sunday)
Received from Count the Bookseller a copy of a telegraph saying that 'Lord F. Cavendish, Chief Secretary for Ireland and a Mr Burke, Under-Secretary, were both assassinated in Phoenix Park Dublin in broad daylight. They were stabbed in several places and died after a severe struggle. Bodies shocking to contemplate'. Excitement in London said to be intense. Singularly, the subject of my sermon was 'Cities of Refuge' and I could not avoid alluding to this matter, at which the congregation were visibly excited.

May 10th
Attended a public dinner of the Dereham Fire Brigade – the toast of its prosperity being confided to me. Upwards of 90 sat down. It is said that this unusually large number was attributable to the speeches being allotted beforehand, many often keeping away on these occasions from fear of being called upon to speak. But I think 'the Whip' was much used.

May 16th [London]
Being at Lincoln & Bennett's the hatters, the shopman knew me well, he said. He often travelled to Norwich but always spent the Sunday in Dereham for the sake of the Church and its services, which I did not think were appreciated in Piccadilly!

May 19th
Called on Mr Martin, my solicitor, about the Challices' affairs, and particulars as to my Will, giving direction for a codicil in favour of my eldest son, as he is the head of the family, and has a son himself, and has not had preferment purchased for him, as my dear father did for me.

May 20th
Took my dear wife and Helen to see 'Patience' at the pretty little new theatre called the Savoy - a clever skit on the aesthetic tendencies of the age.

May 31st
Went with my wife to visit the Tower of London. The arrangements are greatly improved since I was last there, the public being permitted to range where they will & to stay as long as they please, and not even to give up umbrellas etc. at the entrance.

June 22nd
Interview with a young woman boarding at a proprietary school who is a regular communicant. The poor girl is quite blind – her mind is a curious jumble of belief and disbelief. She expressed her devotedness to Ritual, which I could not understand, she being blind, but she said that she conceived the whole thing when a companion explained what was going on, and that it was a great help to her devotions.

June 29th

Meeting of Sunday School teachers at Hingham. Sixteen went from Dereham and the Rev. Currie kindly sent his carriage and also a huge van to Hardingham to convey them to the Rectory. I doubted whether I should get there, for, on arriving at the station I was too late for the train. Another was going in half an hour, but does not stop at Hardingham. There is nothing like being well known in a place & on good terms with its people, to which I attribute an order from the Station Master to the driver to stop at Hardingham and let me out. On arrival I found that our party had gone ahead and there was nothing like a conveyance to be had, Hingham was three miles off, and the day was hot and sultry. Just then a butcher's cart drove up, and the driver having deposited a hamper of meat for London on the platform, announced his intention of returning to Hingham. Availing myself of this opportunity I arrived in the middle of the service, to the surprise of my friends.

July 8th

Herbert's Battalion has received warning to be in readiness to start for Egypt on the shortest notice. Arabi Pasha, with the army at his back, is seeking to dismember the Turkish Empire and to threaten our vast and most important influence, especially in regard to the Suez Canal. A political riot broke out in Alexandria the other day in which hundreds were killed and the British Consul dragged from his carriage and beaten![1] The Fleet is there, ready to bombard, and almost every European has fled in consternation.

July 14th

The day before yesterday Admiral Sir B. Seymour opened fire on the forts of Alexandria and reduced them to a heap of ruins. The usurper Arabi withdrew his troops to the interior, first releasing the convicts and leaving the town to be burnt and ravaged by them, and ordering them to kill the Khedive, who somehow escaped and got on board a British man of war.

August 3rd

Letter from Herbert who is at Aldershot to say his Battalion is ordered for Portsmouth tomorrow morning, to embark for Egypt in the 'Catalonia'. The order is so sudden that he cannot run home to say 'goodbye'. I had written to him in the morning to make his mind easy about money matters, about which he is not careful, but, fearing the

Regiment might start before the letter arrived, I telegraphed to him. God knows when the poor fellow will be home again, if ever.

August 5th

A brief note from Herbert to say the Queen had been on board to say goodbye to them.

The Rev. Mr Stracey told me he had three sons and a son-in-law in Egypt, and a neighbouring squire also has a son there.

The ex-King Cetawayo, whose troops beat the British at Isandlwana has been brought by the Government on a visit to London with a view, some say, to his restoration.

August 16th

Read in the newspaper that Herbert's Regiment had arrived at Alexandria. The Norfolk newspapers have lists of all the local Officers who have gone out to the war, in which Herbert's is conspicuous as 'with Sir Evelyn Wood' from which many suppose that he is on the staff, which is not, however, the case.

August 28th

Another letter from Herbert in which he says an action is imminent, but of course the 'news' in private letters ceases to be news as the Telegrams in the papers outrun it. It is very difficult to understand the movements, even when one reads them, but there must be hard fighting very soon. The letter is dated 'Cunard Royal Mail Steamship, Catalonia' which we saw by the paper had grounded in the Suez Canal but was got off again. As usual when he is on service anywhere abroad, Herbert came across his cousin Ernest, whose ship is in Aboukir Bay. He describes the demolition of Alexandria as complete.

August 30th

There have been two engagements since my last entry, but both were chiefly affairs of cavalry and did not involve our dear boy. The Haggards said their son was to go to Egypt directly. Cetawayo starts for his kingdom tomorrow, to be restored to it under conditions.

September 7th

Letter from Egypt. Herbert had still received none of our letters. Filthy water, myriads of flies, the sand for a bed. By this time he must be in quarters.

September 13th

Returning from a Local Board saw a telegram announcing a great victory at Tel-el-Kebir[2], Arabi's forces completely routed and his position stormed, 40 guns and immense stores taken, also 3000 prisoners. As a portion of Herbert's Regiment was left to guard the camp, we trust he was not in the actual fight which, wonderful to say, took place in Egypt this very morning and we knew of it in Norfolk before luncheon, whereas the news of the Battle of the Nile took six weeks before it arrived in England!

September 16th

Our bookseller in Dereham kindly sent us copies of two telegrams from Egypt – troops all surrendered unconditionally, Cavalry occupied Cairo, Arabi arrested and handed over to the English.

October 14th

In the Prince's garden at Sandringham there is a huge bronze idol which was shipped to Lynn and placed where it is as a curiosity. The Prince, thinking it would improve the appearance, ordered a kind of canopy to be erected over it, but in making the foundation for it, the workmen found that the rabbits had completely undermined the image, which had to be laid flat for a time. During this operation a great 'jingling' was heard inside the image, which turned out to be a quantity of native coins which had been offerings to the idol. They are now arranged in glass cases and are hung up in the Hall as desired by H.R.H.

October 16th

A letter from Herbert, dated 'Cairo, Oct 1st'. Nearly 200 men and 8 Officers of his Regiment have fever or dysentery, but he was never better. The Regiment, whatever be its future mission is not to go to India as supposed. Herbert will get two medals for this war, one from the Khedive and one from our own government.

October 21st

My old friend Carthew died. He had been my Churchwarden for nearly a quarter of a century. When I first came he was the only intelligent churchman in the place, and though my position was a very difficult one in those days, he always supported me. He was a great archaeologist and a man of considerable taste.

November 11th

Herbert is quartered in the Harem at the Khedive's Palace in Alexandria! He describes the magnificence of it as being great, and the fleas numerous. He is greatly troubled with boils, which seem to be one of Egypt's scourges.

November 20th

Mr Watt preached for the Temperance Society. In the first Lesson (Amos. III. 5) the following occurred 'Can a bird fall into a snare upon the earth where there is no gin?' Rowland Hill would have made fine capital out of this!

December 3rd

Dr Tait, Archbishop of Canterbury died, after an illness of some weeks. Broad Church and Erastian and with Presbyterian proclivities, he was tolerant and remarkable for his common sense. It is satisfactory to know that on his death bed he induced Mr Machonochie to resign St Alban's Holborn and to accept St Peter's, London Docks, putting Mr Suckling into St Alban's. Thus the contention with the Church Association has collapsed and 12 years' litigation, and an expenditure of many thousands of pounds goes for nothing.

1883

1st January

Received a letter that a pupil at a Ladies School in Dereham who had been transferred by her Guardian to a school in Kent had absconded, and it was thought not improbable, might have returned to her old quarters. Immediately assumed 'the detective' and, after some trouble, found the girl. On returning to her school in Church St and finding the proprietors not returned from Christmas holidays and the house shut up she was filled with despair, but a respectable little tailor and his wife living nearby had compassion on her, and took her in, turning out of their own bed in their tiny cottage. Here I found the imperious young damsel, aged 16, partly of Creole and partly of Irish extraction – an odd mixture. She had run away on account of her extreme love for her old mistress & her love for the services at Dereham Church – both thrown into violent contrast by her detestation of the people – extreme Calvinists – into whose hands she had fallen. Her poor heart was full, and she wept passionately.

Meanwhile the lady of the new establishment had followed the scent, accompanied by her brother, who, after a powerful appeal to the Almighty after the manner of Dickens 'Chadband' insisted on the girl's return. I was inclined to resist this, and to take her to the Vicarage, but the elder lady produced written orders from the Guardian for her return. After obstinately refusing to comply, I at length persuaded her to accompany me to the station, and saw her off with her friends. It is fearful to think what might have happened to the girl, who is very attractive, on her going from Kent to Liverpool St station. She cried so on her way to Dereham station that the people I met must have thought me an inhuman monster – but they knew me, fortunately.

Herbert arrived, looking thin after his privations, & brought me a well bound copy of the Koran[1], which he had 'looted' out of a Musselman tent during the war!

January 11th
Col. Bulwer who is to be Sheriff of Norfolk this year asked me to be his Chaplain, to which I assented. I have preached in various churches on every possible occasion, but never an assize sermon before the judges, as I suppose I shall now have to.

January 14th
Mr Trundle, Precentor of York Minster sang evensong with that peculiar and indescribable vibration which always seems to be a speciality among those who form the staff of a Cathedral.

January 20th
Meeting in Norwich on the proposed alteration of the Marriage Law to enable a man to marry the sister of his deceased wife. Mr Reade, who is spiteful towards the clergy for abstaining from voting for him at the last election, because he voted for the P.W.R.A. wound up a speech with allusions to Ritualists being law breakers as much as the farmers. I always took an interest in him as a rising man, but after these performances I cannot vote for him again.

January 22nd
An excellent Magic Lantern exhibited on the events of the Egyptian War. Herbert, who is in London for a few days, we all think postponed his return to avoid this. H. is so shy that he shrinks from saying a few words at any public meeting & this he would probably have been expected to do, having been one of the army of occupation.

March 15th

We certainly live in lawless times. A terrific explosion of dynamite took place at the local Government Office, not far from the Houses of Parliament, the floors of which were ploughed up.[2] All is shrouded in mystery, but it is believed to be the work of Fenians.

March 27th

At 7.00 a.m. poor Lilly gave birth to a second little girl. Our old friend Hastings, the doctor, stayed at the Vicarage. I am thankful to be able to afford Lilly a home, so that she may have every comfort, but this addition to her family fills me with sad apprehensions about her future.

1st April

Last week Dr Benson, the new Archbishop, was enthroned at Canterbury. He and Mr Gladstone are on a visit to the Prince & Princess of Wales, and the Queen is coming there this week. Norfolk can no longer be considered remote and obscure.

Undated, April

I must record the sad conclusion of poor Lilly's affair. She went on well after her confinement for some days, indeed until April 6th when, on paying her my accustomed visit, I found she had undergone a change for the worse. Hastings acknowledged the fact of non-improvement but could assign no cause for it. The following day I was convinced that the hand of death was upon the dear child and telegraphed Dr Beverley of Norwich, who came in a wonderfully short time and I could see that he considered the case hopeless. He at once pronounced the evil to be 'Embolus' a rare complaint arising from clots of blood originating in different parts of the body, but gradually congregating at the heart.

Growing rapidly worse the poor darling breathed her last about 8.00 p.m. Her husband had been telegraphed, but had not arrived in time.

April 8th

It is a cause for gratitude that I freely forgave poor Lilly for her disastrous marriage, that I made her an annual allowance and increased it, that she was with us three months before her death and consequently had every comfort and advantage, that her death took place in Norfolk & not in Wiltshire, that she was surrounded by her parents and all her brothers and sisters to the last.

April 16th

Arthur Nelson left, for which I was not sorry as he has been the cause of much unhappiness. He left the two children – so the nursing is started again with a new generation.

April 23rd

Being in Norwich I saw the 'triumphal' entry of General Booth, who had just come from London by the train. He drove in a carriage with a pair of greys and stood on the seat waving his handkerchief whenever there was a lull in the cheering. Two 'Halleluia Lasses' followed in a wagonette, dressed in scarlet, looking and behaving like anything but respectable females. There was a brass band, of course, the whole accompanied by a body of 'roughs' extending from the houses to the opposite side of the street. There is something absolutely painful in such a travesty of religion. None of the respectable tradesmen to whom I talked had anything but misgivings about the whole movement.

May 7th [London]

There was family business which needed to be attended to, e.g. Mr Martin about the effects of Lilly's marriage settlement – about the lease on the Southall house & dilapidations, and also about the Challices' affairs. Then to Mr Furben to go over some of the Challices' houses and Mr Allen about my own house in Hatton Garden, for which I cannot get the rent. Went to the clerical tailor to be measured for Robes to preach the Assize sermon.

May 19th

Received dear Lilly's baby into the Church. It was a melancholy performance opening up much of our late grief. Dear John had two of the choristers at the Font to sing hymns, but my heart was too heavy to enjoy them.

June 10th

Troubles never come singly. Two days ago, while I was preaching at Hoe, my dear wife became very ill and the Doctor said it was 'Erysipelas'. She is progressing favourably, but this, added to poor Lilly's death, failure in house rent and dilapidations in Southall – the surprise that Nelson seems to have a life interest in Lilly's marriage settlement, make the year so far unfortunate.

June 20th

A most appalling and afflicting accident has taken place at Sunderland[3] whereby 200 children, aged from 5 to 10, lost their lives. About 1,000 children had been witnessing the performance of a conjuror in the theatre, who, at the close of the performance, announced that a present would be made to every child, in a room below. The natural consequence was a great rush of the little ones to get to the room. Alas the door at the bottom of the staircase was only open sufficiently wide to admit two at a time. The children came pouring down the stairs urged by those behind and 200 were trampled (or smothered) to death.

July 11th

At Mr Bailey's funeral there were 13 clergy in surplices exhibiting, as usual, that wonderful want of conformity in headgear which is always observable in Anglican processions – 'pot-hats', college caps, 'wideawakes',[4] birettas, zucchettos, ritualistic cords and tassels, black velvet nightcaps and some with no covering whatever.

July 25th

The Salvation Army have sent a detachment into Dereham who are carrying on an 'Assault and bombardment against the Citadels of Sin'. Whether the Citadel is the Parish, or only the theatre which they have hired I don't know – but the bombardment seems to be of the most quiet character, and there is no diminution of the congregation in Church. I doubt the immense number of instantaneous conversions recorded in the 'War Cry' a copy of which I purchased from an 'Hallelujah Lass', price a halfpenny, in which, by the way, much profanity was interspersed.

August 6th

To Norwich with Colonel Bulwer, High Sheriff, for the Assizes. The Col. having assumed his uniform and I my Canonicals we proceeded from the Royal Hotel, our quarters, in the State carriages to the Judges' Lodgings. Here the trumpeters set up their fanfare and all the usual form and ceremony were gone through with.

August 7th

Conducted both the Judges from their Lodgings to the Court, the carriage being driven at walking pace and the rabble accompanying it. A trial for Breach of Promise of marriage – the plaintiff, a Miss Blenkinsop, who used to live in Dereham, only got £30 damages. The

High Sheriff gave an excellent luncheon in the courthouse, and a grand dinner at 8 – soup, venison etc. to some of the Grand Jury. In fact eating & drinking and driving the Judges about were the chief features of the week.

September 11th
Temperance Society Choral Service in the nave at 8.00 p.m. The sermon, a very long but eloquent one was preached by Mr Horsley, Chaplain of Clerkenwell Prison. Having so much to do with criminals his evidence is valuable as to drunkenness being the cause of so much crime. He is a singular looking man with long hair behind, and a red beard down to his waist.

November 16th
The new Landlord of the King's Arms being a Churchman – and an acquisition – I accepted his invitation to be present at a Market-Tea, with Mr Reade, ex M.P., in the chair. These Market-Teas are, in fact, excellent cold dinners, in which tea performs a very subordinate feature. They are generally protracted to a late hour, and the speeches are slightly political and of an agricultural character, and the Farmers will sit and listen to them with delight. They are interspersed with songs & music.

November 26th
Herbert left to join his regiment in Alexandria after eleven months leave. His orders are to go to Dublin, and thence to Queenstown to take up a draft of men. He will embark them on the 'Poonah', taking in more troops in Gibraltar and dropping them at Malta, Cyprus and Alexandria. This active sort of employment must be more congenial than having nothing to do.

December 20th
It generally seems that when Herbert is ordered abroad there is fresh cause for anxiety respecting events. The Mahdi – or false prophet, claiming to be the Messiah – has raised the Southern Egyptians to a stated of fanatical revolt. They have utterly annihilated the newly formed Egyptian army, only one man escaping. In Upper Egypt, as it is supposed, the situation will be awful indeed, as his followers are well nigh numberless. In anticipation, we are sending out more troops.

February 16th

Arthur Nelson came to stay. Glad that his 'little Helen' took to him, though she is a shy child, and it is nearly a year since she has seen him, As usual, he is in no sort of employment and seems in excellent health and spirits. As he is naturally loath to work I do not pretend to feel the anxiety which I did for his prospects when dear Lilly was alive. He is very good-natured.

March 1st

News arrived of our victory at El Teb[1] in the Sudan, in which we killed 3,000, with the death of 5 officers and 124 men wounded on our side. It is hoped that this will check the Mahdi, who has raised the whole country into rebellion by persuading them he is the true Messiah. It appears that the Arabs fought desperately, being urged on by religious fanaticism.

March 11th

Having observed a slight diminution in the congregation consequent on the winter months and the attractions of the Salvation Army, was pleased to see the Church quite full in the evening. With respect to the Salvation Army, the wife of our stationmaster, a Churchwoman and Communicant, assured me of 4 undeniable conversions among the Railway servants by that means and men, hitherto drunkards and blasphemers, turned into really religious characters.

March 14th

News came from the Sudan of the battle of Tamai[2] in which we were victorious over the Mahdi's troops. It is described as complete, but hard won, on account of the desperate valour of the Arabs, inspired as it is by Moslem fanaticism. The British guns were captured, and re-captured. It seems that 2,400 rebels were killed, while we had 100 killed including several officers.

March 31st

Heard from Herbert that the du Ports called on him on their way home from Egypt. He showed them all over the forts at Alexandria, & dined with them at their hotel, as Miss du Port was not admissible at the Mess.

April 23rd

The Bible Class for young men has developed itself into 'The Church-man's Society' and contains upwards of 40 members and yesterday was the wind-up of the winter session – in the summer they are to play cricket. There was an exhibition of Brasses, Photos etc. and songs and little addresses. All seemed much pleased. I confess I never personally enjoy this sort of thing, though I find it necessary and expedient to bring all classes together on the common basis of Churchmanship. There is so much shyness to be overcome – and so little really in common that it is no small difficulty to bring about an amalgamation of all classes. They must be constantly amused either with eating and drinking or by a succession of songs and speeches that I have a doubt in my mind whether such entertainments are any more real pleasure to the entertained than they are to myself.

April 25th

Mary Skeat, daughter of the Professor, my old curate, left after a week's visit. A regular Cambridge girl, doing algebra for amusement!

May 1st

Dined at the Barry's. Du Port told me that Herbert's quarters at Ras-el-Tin palace[3] are sumptuous, that the Palace is close to the sea and that the Officers have a boat on which they disport themselves – a good, clear sea.

May 10th

Suddenly met with Ethel Challice who, to my great astonishment, was walking with young Bidwell of Dereham, in Oxford St. What can be the meaning of this?

May 11th

In the afternoon called on my nieces, when it turned out that Ethel is actually engaged to young Bidwell, who is staying at the Challices'. There could be no objection to the match, so far as I am concerned, but nowadays not one in ten of these engagements comes to anything.

May 19th

Baptized the infant child of our Organist, the father being 77 years of age!! His previous son (by another wife) is upwards of 50! The present Mrs Martin is young.

June 22nd

Was summoned to the bedside of a dying woman just before Morning Service and the poor thing actually passed away just as I finished the Commendation Prayer. This was not calming and then I found that the adult members of the choir had actually mutinied just before the service because they had to vest in a side chapel in order to allow more space for the Bishop! They came back, however, in the evening – they shall hear of this again.

June 26th

In the evening an accident befell me. While un-dressing, standing, my foot became entangled in my trousers, and, losing my balance, I fell against furniture with my whole weight. I felt sure I had dislocated my shoulder and spent the night in misery.

June 27th

By the united efforts of Dr Vincent and Mr Hastings, the 'ball' was pulled into the 'socket'. They seemed to be a long time about it, but when the result took place we all distinctly heard it.

July 4th

Young Mr Bidwell, who is in connection with the brewery here, having become engaged to Ethel Challice during her visit to the Hydes, we thought it right to ask him to join our family party at dinner. I don't think anything will come of it, as he is some years younger than Ethel, and though there is money in the family, yet the family is numerous. He is very agreeable and conversational.

July 20th

I desire to record my thanks to Almighty God for a highly satisfactory letter from Herbert. I had sent him £5 for a birthday present and in reply he said he 'didn't owe a cent' and that his Captain's pay together with his allowance were amply sufficient.

August 4th

A Bank Holiday, making our town as triste as a Good Friday. There were the usual Athletic and other sports, but they were not so well attended as usual, owing to the early harvest. The prizes were considerable, and athletes competed for them from Northampton, Liverpool, Hull, London, and Sheffield.

August 6th

Sunday School Treat. The proceedings were the same as usual, except that the parishioners sent such a number of presents for the children that I had difficulty in disposing of them. Several balloons were sent up in the form of animals, a fine elephant soaring away towards Scarning. We had an excellent band and fireworks and, the moon being full, the amusements were protracted until an unusually late hour.

August 11th

A letter from Herbert tells that he and brother officers were invited to the Khedive's palace for luncheon. The Khedive, who is an insignificant looking person, was very cordial, speaks English fluently and has sent his sons to Germany to finish their education. There is hope that the expedition to the Sudan may not be undertaken.

August 19th

After notice of only a few hours, Herbert's battalion has been ordered from Alexandria to Cairo, where it is 10 degrees hotter! The policy of the authorities is so shifting and uncertain that now there seems to be no doubt that the expedition to relieve General Gordon will take place.

August 20th

People about here seem to be quite wild about garden parties. Yesterday there was a large one at Quebec, and today came our turn. My dear wife, who never does things by halves, invited the whole neighbourhood, including the 'great houses' of Bylaugh and Elmham Hall, who both came. About 60 were in the grounds. Ices and fruits were supplied from Norwich, for which I suspect there will be something to pay.

September 30th

In the afternoon was the Church Parade, and a larger muster of men than I ever saw before. Colonel, Captain, Lieutenant, Adjutant, Doctor were all there. I preached in my capacity as Chaplain and marched back with the men accompanied by the excellent band of the Corps. The Salvation Army, who generally monopolise Sunday afternoons with their marching and music did not put in an appearance.

October 6th

The Bishop made an official visit to Hoe Church at 10.00 a.m. He expressed himself as very much pleased with it – the new seats, the roof, the new Vestry and the choir stalls all coming in for approbation. Concerning the flowers and candles on the altar he made no remark, though I'm sure the approbation would not have extended to them.

We had a letter from Herbert a few days ago, fearing his regiment would not accompany the Nile expedition for the release of General Gordon, but another came today, saying they had orders to start. Meantime the papers say that General G. has obtained a great victory and released himself! Getting up the Nile seems a most hazardous experiment, and more than one steamer has already been wrecked at different rapids. In trying to rectify one of these disasters the passengers had to land, and were at once slaughtered by the Arabs. Among them was Colonel Stewart, who was second in command of the expedition. Our wars, of late years, have been most unsatisfactory.

November 17th
In consequence of the Agricultural Depression there are now very few dinner parties compared with 20 years ago, but I have got to that age as to regard this as no loss in winter months.

December 3rd
Letter from Herbert, written near Luxor. He is well, and speaks in raptures about Karnac & Thebes, and of the vast size of the Obelisks and Temples. It is very few lives that are privileged to see sights such as these. They are pushing the expedition forward which he describes as the greatest undertaking of the age.

December 4th
In consequence of our Annual E.C.U. meeting taking place at Soham, the tradesmen and daughters thereof who are members seldom have an opportunity of coming together, on account of the distance, and because Mr Coker Adams, the Rector, an old bachelor, objects to entertaining females. My dear wife and I therefore invited them to tea and refreshments after the services of the day were over. All seemed delighted, but it is difficult work to entertain a party of this kind who, having very few resources, and being very shy, seem to think that the host and hostess ought to keep up a succession of amusements for them – for they are incapable of entertaining themselves or one another!

December 25th

In the afternoon went to Hoe for the service, but found that the stove pipe had slipped and the smoke, instead of going up the chimney all came into the church, so with my dear wife, who acts as organist, could only return to Dereham.

December 31st

The last act of the year was a provision that, at my death, the money I left by will to dear Lilly should be tied up to her children by Trustees.

1885

January 1st

Dined at Quebec – a nice friendly dinner consisting of swan, woodcocks and other rarities. Considering how often the Squires and the Parsons are at feud the sentiment suggested itself 'Ecce quam bonum et jucundum'[1] etc.

January 7th

Called on Mr Freeman, the Baptist preacher, who I heard was not likely to live, having been seized with paralysis. He could not be interviewed, but I had a satisfactory conversation with his wife, a very rich and somewhat aged spinster whom he married a few years ago, and with whose money he has built a commodious and luxurious abode, with a handsome fountain in the front court, and a smoking divan at the top of a campanile! He is said to have been an actor, a bookseller, a newspaper editor etc. but is a really clever man.

This week Prince Edward came of age, and there were grand doings at Sandringham in consequence. Among other things Sanger's Circus was engaged from Norwich with its performing elephants, passing through Dereham by train at 6.00 a.m., the poor creatures returning to Norwich the same evening for their usual performance.

January 12th

Received a postcard from Herbert, dated from Ambigol 21st Dec, written while the boats he is in command of were being towed through the rapids 'All well, have come thus far without the slightest mishap and in good time. Arduous work'.

January 22nd

This morning's paper contains an account of the success of General Stewart's force in an engagement with 10,000 rebels which resulted in 'a great slaughter of the enemy'. It took place at Abu Klea Wells.[2] This is taken from Lord Wolseley's telegram to the Secretary of State for War. We had 8 officers killed and 6 severely wounded, but the enemy lost 1,200 killed or wounded. Thankful Herbert had not arrived, he being with his boats and men, probably at Korti. God grant him a safe return.

January 24th

Today was rendered famous for three audacious dynamite explosions in London[3], but this being a Saturday, we did not obtain full particulars until Monday, though rumours were in the air. The attempt was to blow up the Tower of London and the Houses of Parliament, the Tower at 2.00 p.m. and the Houses 10 minutes later. Saturday being the day for visitors it is wonderful that no one was seriously hurt beyond the Policemen. Much damage befell the interior of the House, the windows and doors being shattered. A lady found a bag on the Crypt staircase and pointed it out to a policeman who took it upstairs into the Hall, almost immediately after which the tremendous explosion took place.

January 26th

Took the Chair at the Annual Farmer's Tea, at the King's Arms, where 95 sat down to a substantial repast – a very joyous and amicable party. When I had responded to the toast of 'The Chairman', someone cried up for 'Three Cheers for the Captain in Egypt' [Herbert] which were given enthusiastically.

January 27th

Annual Choir Supper at the King's Arms, at which 30 sat down. Poor old Philo, Parish Clerk, though quite blind, was there and sang the comic song 'Johnnie Sands' as he has done for many years.

Heard from Herbert – the main difficulties are over and he is sailing in peaceful waters, under a deep blue sky, beyond the palm trees which line the bank. His, the Captain's boat, goes in front & hoists a flag. On their way they encountered a hippopotamus which seemed terribly incensed at the intrusion of boats into his sacred Nile.

January 31st

The papers record the Battle of Metemmeh[4] in which the British gained another victory over the Arabs, the preponderance of casualties amongst officers being remarkable. General Stewart was dangerously wounded and the well-known and adventurous Colonel Burnaby was killed. Lord Arthur Somerset has died of his wounds and Lord S. Vincent has subsequently died of his. Two correspondents of London newspapers were also killed. This victory has the effect of opening up the communication with General Gordon at Khartoum.

February 5th

Terribly disquieting news as to the Sudan, which has thrown London into a state of the greatest excitement, indeed the paper says that 'the statement was so terrible in its significance that the public were unable to accept it.' Khartoum has fallen, the city is occupied by the Mahdi and the fate of General Gordon is unknown!!! A concentration had been made by the Mahdi around Khartoum in order to strike a blow for the capture of the town before the British forces could be got up. There seems no doubt that this result has been obtained through treachery, the officer in charge of the ramparts opening the gates to the enemy! Why on earth could this country ever have been induced to send Gordon there, or have anything to do with such brutes?

February 8th

A letter from Herbert at Debbeh, dated 10th January, en route to Korti. He said that he couldn't resist 'the temptation of camping in the prettiest spot he'd ever seen – thick jungle abounding in every kind of tree and shrub – cactus in full bloom, bread fruit, pears, oleanders etc.' He'd never seen 'so many different sorts of birds before, singing in trees over his head – the Nile blue, with two crocodiles basking in the sandbank'. The inhabitants came to see what 'extraordinary creatures' had turned up, had probably 'never seen a white man before' and were amused at his washing, and astonished at his washing his teeth!

Finished reading the life of George Eliot – a great genius whose books will be standard literature for all time. But what a scandalous thing it is, not only that this woman was an unbeliever, but also that she lived in adultery for many years with a literary man named Lewes, he having a wife living all the time. She is great in impressing moral axioms and high ideas of duty, but, alas, the practice! She married a Mr Cross at Lewes's death, who seems like all the rest of her associates to have been an unbeliever.

February 15th

The fate of the chivalrous General Gordon is no longer uncertain. The hero, for such he was, is dead. General Stewart has succumbed to his wounds, thus adding another to the long list of officers who have been killed in this campaign

February 20th

Buried Azariah Waters at 82, at Hoe. He was a wealthy man, a respected parishioner & my largest tythe payer. His children were constantly receiving accessions of fortune from their bachelor uncle, but the young people derived rather more harm than good thereby. The eldest son drank himself to death, the eldest daughter made an unsatisfactory marriage with a man who was evidently attracted by her money, the husband of another daughter killed himself through the accidental discharge of his own gun while pheasant shooting. Mr Waters was counted one of the best farmers in Norfolk.

February 24th

Herbert wrote from Korti. As the letter was written three weeks ago, he is by this time probably at the front. The campaign seems to me inexplicable, and no one seems to know what is being done, or, now Gordon is dead, what is the particular object in view – nevertheless there seems to be a determination to go ahead with hostilities, seeing that the Grenadiers and Scots Guards left this week for the seat of war.

March 4th

The Bishop having put out a service for 'Humiliation of our sins', it was proceeded with this evening. There were a great many present and would have been more, had not a man previously announced that he was going to ascend a tight-rope in the marketplace at the time of the service.

Herbert is at Korti, the forces are assembling there. Those of General Brackenbury's column, who have been in the desert, have been limited, officers and men, to a pint of water per diem for drinking and washing!

March 25th

Arthur Nelson returned to Wiltshire. He is doing nothing but stay at his father's, and to my belief, he never will do anything but go around with a gun or fishing rod.

There was terrible fighting in the Sudan on the 22nd, near Suakin.[5] Our troops seem to have been taken by surprise while constructing a zariba. Everything, say the papers, was against our force. The situation was desperate, and a hand to hand mêlée of the fiercest nature ensued. To make matters worse, the camels and mules became so alarmed at the firing that, in one confused mass, they broke out of enclosure and 600 of them were killed. The British casualties were 165 and the dead bodies of 1,000 Arabs were counted on the plain. A victory, but at what a price? Is the game worth the candle?

April 2nd
A letter from Herbert to thank me for regularity in paying his allowance, & requesting me not to pay in any more after June as he expects he has £80 or £90 to his credit!

Called on Lady Congleton, widow of the late Baron, who is staying with Mrs Actelik. Lady C. is very wild about religion – she went to the Salvation Army at Dereham on Sunday morning and to the Parish Church in the evening, but she did not make any remark to me about either. I'm told the Congletons are Plymouth Brethren.

April 8th
We are on the brink of war with Russia, about the Afghan boundary. There has been an actual conflict in which 500 were slain. Surely the country cannot bear the strain of this in addition to the Sudan war! That the Government is alive to this is shown by the embodiment of the Militia and the reserve forces!

April 24th
Ethel Challice's brother Gerald – in the Army Service Corps – has been ordered to Suakin. If the papers speak truth, however, he will not be there long as it is likely that the troops will be recalled and the Sudan expedition abandoned.

Sorry to hear that the wretched ritualist prosecutions, of which all thought there was an end, have broken out at Liverpool, in the harassing of Mr Bell Cox.[6]

April 30th
There seems to be little doubt that our troops are to be recalled from the Sudan, where the poor fellows are smouldering, with the thermometer at 112 degrees. The Mahdi and his best man Osman Digna have vanished and there is no enemy to be found.

June 2nd

Attended the District Union of the E.C.U. at Norwich. The Rev. S.F.Green, who was imprisoned 15 months in Lancaster Castle for disobedience to the Privy Council, was the preacher. A very fair preacher, but the chief interest lay in the man, who still looks jaded and haggard from his treatment.

June 12th

Mr Gladstone's government, having been defeated on the Budget by several votes, have resigned. An augmented wine and spirit duty was the cause.

July 1st

The Mahdi is dead! But it doesn't seem to influence the withdrawal of the troops.

August 6th

It sometimes happens that very clever and learned people are devoid of common sense. My friend Coker Adams, Rector of Saham has been indiscreet enough to excommunicate a parishioner in his church, just before the Communion Service. The papers are, of course, taking the matter up and someone has reported it to the Bishop. It does not appear that this old man has done anything except that he persistently refuses to attend church!

The Bishop of Norwich has given £30 towards the restoration of our Church which is going on.

August 10th

A note from Herbert to say he has got his company to Wadi Halfa, but, finding he has got a touch of fever he had gone into hospital. This may end in his being sent home on sick leave.

August 11th

Large Garden Party at Quebec at which the elite of the whole vicinity were present. A lovely and agreeable afternoon as, from long residence in the county, there were very few we did not know.

August 12th

The sister of the excommunicated farmer at Saham told me that the Bishop had induced the Rector to call upon the culprit and apologise. Thus Mr Adams has made himself ludicrous in the eyes of the County and disliked by the body of parishioners. This will do the Church, and especially the High Church section no good.

August 26th
A long list of promotions in the army in Egypt, among which appears Herbert's name as Major (Brevet Rank). He is also honourably mentioned by name in despatches. He will be entitled to a gratuity of £60 for the part he has taken in the Sudan. There are only two other officers in Herbert's Regiment mentioned, the Colonel and another Captain.

August 27th
Congratulations from all quarters on Herbert's success.

August 31st
A sad thing in the papers about my former curate, Vaughan. A harvest-man passed as he was holding his pony at a cottage door, who fell from the wagon in which he was riding with his pitchfork in his hand, which entered Vaughan's heart and killed him instantaneously.

September 23rd
Herbert is in London, but delays his coming home for a day or so in order to replenish his wardrobe, having left his heavy baggage at Wadi Halfa and finding, on his way back, that the white ants had eaten his things up, even his boots!

October 1st
It is sometimes difficult to recognize that all is for the best, Ernest Duncombe's wife has produced twins – and, what is worse, twin girls!

November 2nd
Letter from a Mr Cock of Shipdham, finding fault with my sermon on disestablishment, in that I stated that among the disadvantages would be the loss of pastoral work on the part of the clergy, which the dissenting ministers somewhat neglect.

November 5th
Mr Cock continues his correspondence and I suspect that he is a 'fighting cock'. This sort of writing is a great trouble and never satisfactory.

Yesterday visited 'Old Susan' a servant of the Hydes, who has become half-crazed by the Salvationists who had got her in their power in

Norwich, from which Mr Hyde rescued her. The Salvation people were related to the poor old woman and probably had an eye to her money.

December 9th
Re-opening of the nave of our Parish Church, the galleries having been removed and the substitution of a wagon roof for the old ceiling makes it look a different building. The Church was warmed for the first time, which was a great comfort.

I am truly grateful for today's proceedings which I did not contemplate would take place in my Vicariate, but they form a splendid episode towards the close, which cannot now be very far off.

The election is now over[7], and most important it was as including the new electorate for the first time. To judge from the specimens exhibited at Dereham, however, it seems a perilous thing to entrust the franchise into the hands of 'roughs', many who can neither read nor write (my own gardener among them) and who have not the capacity to comprehend the bearings of political questions. I voted for Mr Fellowes as being opposed to Disestablishment. Mr Arch, the dema-gogue and agitator, and deceiver of the labourers has gone, the papers style it, from the plough to the Senate!!

December 25th
Today was a little clouded. Found my dear wife crying at breakfast because our grandchild had been ill in the night. Then John had such a frightful cold that he could do very little in the way of duty, then our unamiable organist played atrociously at the service, and would have sung the _Easter_ anthem had he not been corrected by one of the senior members of the choir. Then the attenuated choir had very little voice from singing carols in the cold night air. On the other hand, there were excellent congregations.

1886

January 6th
Took the chair at the annual meeting of the Athenaeum and made a short speech recommending the members to read works of history, biography and travel in preference to novels – advice which I do not in the least believe they will follow.

January 27th

The Conservative Ministry defeated by about 80 votes. The management of Ireland, that inexhaustible source of trouble to this country, is

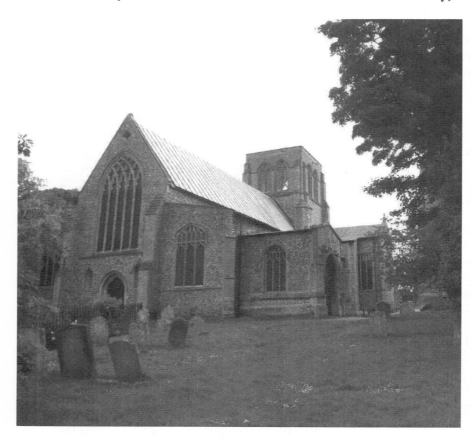

Dereham Church

the cause of this, and it is said that the Conservatives are by no means sorry to be quit of office!

February 8th

Distress everywhere very great in consequence of the continued depression of trade and agriculture. A mob of unemployed hands met in Trafalgar Square London to petition the government for the amelioration of their grievances, and being swelled by 'roughs' they proceeded westwards, smashing not only the bakers' shops but the

310

wine sellers, jewellers etc., as well. It really read in the papers like the outbreak of the French Revolution.

February 15th

Herbert has passed the very last of his examinations and is now at the very top of Captains in his regiment. After all, the Army is not so bad a profession for 'getting on' as some would believe. Unlike the Church it is, at all events, free from religious bias.

February 19th

Was asked to be Chairman at the annual 'Farmer's Tea' at the King's Arms. There was an immense party and 'mine host' had to refuse thirty for want of space, despite the size of the room. Col. Bulwer, Mr C. S. Reade and my old parishioner Everington were there. The speeches were very good, and there were some telling songs, worded to suit the present times.

April 13th

A long gap since my last entry, but nothing has happened worth recording.

Ethel Challice has been here on a visit, her lover, Mr Bidwell, daily and assiduously in attendance. Arthur Nelson here also on a three weeks visit. I am glad to see him with his children, though, but for the children, it is marvellous to me how he can come at all, considering all the circumstances of dear Lilly's unfortunate marriage.

April 28th

I expected the Easter Vestry to pass off quietly as it has in this parish for the last 14 years, but no one can foresee what may turn up at a Vestry, composed, as it is, of Dissenters as well as Churchmen – all who pay rates. I nominated Mr Norgate as my warden and Mr Elvin was proposed, seconded and carried by a majority as the people's warden, when a cantankerous dissenter proposed a Mr Mayes, another of the same sort, and demanded a Poll, which as Chairman I decreed would take place on Monday (though remembering the fatigue of a former occasion I cannot, in my present state of health, take the Chair). This proceeding took everybody by surprise. I do not think Mr Mayes will be elected, but there is no knowing as to what may turn up these days.

April 29th

The Diocesan Conference, but I was too much out of health to attend – physical and nervous debility always attack me at this time of year, and gets worse every season – indicating, no doubt, the beginning of the end, for which may I be prepared.

April 30th

To my great delight Mr Mayes came at 10.00 p.m. accompanied by a friend, and withdrew his demand for a Poll on the condition that the Churchwardens should publish a balance sheet of all the charities. To this I replied that I could not accept any such condition, seeing that the affair was theirs and not mine but that I would mention the matter to them. I concluded that this had stopped the necessity for an adjournment till Monday, and resolved not to attend it. But it turned out that several of the young lawyers were disposed to fight it out, and to put down 'that fellow Mayes'. I adhered to my resolution of not attending, as I had previously declared Mr Elvin duly elected, and the demand of Mayes withdrawn.

May 2nd

A message from the meeting requested me to go there, which I did – an unnecessary action I believe, but the proceeding ended in electing Elvin again. One good thing attended my going, as I was able to contradict a handbill put out by Mayes to the effect that he had consented to withdraw on my promise that a balance sheet would be printed. I reminded the meeting that I always issued a balance sheet of my own desire in matters connected with the parish in my own hands.

May 10th

To Yarmouth with my dear wife and daughter accompanied by the nurse and two granddaughters, together with our manservant, whom I cannot now dispense with. Missed the Officer's dinner and also a dinner to Mr Fellowes, the unsuccessful candidate in the election, to neither of which I felt equal.

May 19th

The inspection of the Norfolk Artillery Militia by Sir Evelyn Wood. It was expected that the Prince of Wales was coming, but, as is so often the case, the lion didn't show. In the afternoon there was a practice for the big guns at targets placed some distance out to sea, but though the balls made an immense noise, and much commotion in the water, I did not see that the target was ever hit, for, when the smoke had cleared, it was just as it was before.

May 23rd
Herbert came on a visit, from Chatham. I should have preferred his deferring the visit till after our return to Dereham, but it seems the Officers always have leave for the Derby, so it was now or never.

May 31st
Returned home and we were all delighted to do so. I don't like fault-finding but we not only had continual bad weather, but a most noisy house, augmented by the arrival of a large family called Small and abominable cooking. All was sacrificed to the splendid sea view.

June 30th
Herbert appears in today's Gazette as Regimental Major. The Sudan, to which we thought it unfortunate that he had been posted, proved to be most fortunate for him.

July 8th
The Committee have resorted to all sorts of devices to pay up the arrears in connection with the restoration of the church, culminating today and tomorrow in a Grand Bazaar on the grounds at Quebec. The ladies were indefatigable in making articles and the townspeople most kind in contributing, but I cannot say I like this way of raising the wind. There was Punch & Judy, theatricals, concerts and a luncheon.

August 20th
Wrote to my niece, Ethel, sympathising with her on account of the separation between her and Mr Bidwell, who, it turns out, has deceived her in regard to his prospects and will not be able to marry for many years. I never thought the engagement would come to anything.

September 10th
Death has been very frequent of late and my old friends and contemporaries are rapidly passing away.

September 16th
John took the choir to Yarmouth for me, as I did not feel equal to the day. 26 of the members went.

January 5th

I thank God for having permitted me to see the beginning of another year which opens, as usual with the ground covered with snow and icicles half a yard long from the bedroom windows, even though there had been a lighted stove all night. At one time the thermometer showed 14 degrees of frost.

February 9th

The annual Choir Supper at the King's Arms. The curates, organist and the old, blind Parish Clerk were all present – the whole choir attended and demolished the very finest turkey I ever saw.

May 12th

It is long since I made an entry, partly from failing health and partly from the absence of anything interesting to record. Last evening the Colonel gave his annual dinner to the Officers of the Battalion but I did not feel equal to undertake it.

EPILOGUE

The diary terminates here. My great grandfather became very feeble in mind and body, and resigned in 1888. He moved with his surviving daughter, Helen, to a small house in Dereham, where he died in 1890, and is buried in the churchyard at Dereham with his wife and the two daughters who predeceased him.

Neither Helen nor Herbert Armstrong married. The latter remained in the army and achieved the rank of Colonel. Helen continued to look after Lilly's children, moving to London following her father's death, and finally buying, with Herbert, a house in Norland Square, where they lived until their deaths, in 1917 and 1912 respectively.

John became Rector of Heydon in Norfolk, and in 1904 Rector of North Tuddenham, where he continued until his death in 1924. His wife, Mary, died in 1927 in Camberwell.

Their son, my father, was ordained in 1901 and after holding curacies at Taunton and Lowestoft became vicar of St James, Norwich, in 1916 and St James, West Hampstead, in 1922. In 1930 he became Rector of

Thorpe St Andrew, and subsequently Vicar of St Margaret's Kings Lynn. He married, in 1931, Ruth Fonnerau Lillingston, whose late father had been the incumbent at Salle, the neighbouring parish to Heydon. He died, in retirement, in Holt, in 1955.

John's daughter, Dorothy, married the Rev. S.J.C.Lucas in 1906.

Of Lilly's children, Helen never married and Margaret married the Revd. G. Remer in 1925. Both sisters spent their later years in the West Country.

C. S. Armstrong

A later photograph of some of the family and friends taken at Heydon in 1897.
John, elder son of the diarist, is on the right of the back row, his wife Mary is front right.
Their daughter, Dorothy, is on the left in the middle row and below her their son,
the editor's father, Herbert Benjamin John.

At the back left, James Gay; centre front Violet Wyllis; back row right Hilda
Wilkinson; centre back Dulcie Stephen.

NOTES

1852

1. The weather vane was in the shape of a deer.
2. The murders involve quite a complicated story. Rush was a tenant of the Jermys and owed them substantial sums which were due for repayment at about the time of the murders. In addition, Rush had sought out potential claimants to the Stanfield Estate and was encouraging them in their attempt to establish their claim. The claim was not likely to be seen as legitimate. Mr Jermy (Snr) was shot first, then his son, his daughter-in-law and finally her servant. The murderer was in disguise, but identified by the maidservant who was wounded, and others, as Rush. Rush's claimed alibi, that he was with his mistress, was denied by her and she was subjected to a 12 hour cross-examination by Rush (who defended himself) when the case came to trial. Rush was found guilty, and hanged at Norwich before a huge crowd many of whom had come by excursion train for that express purpose.
3. Letton Hall is now a Christian Conference and Holiday Centre.
4. The Regiment was re-named The Duke of Wellington's by order of the Queen in 1852.
5. The funeral procession was believed to have been seen by over 1,000,000 people. The lying in state attracted so dense a crowd, that according to one witness, the packed mass of people 'smoked like a lighted haystack' and five people were crushed to death [Source: Frederick Mead on Historic Voices VI, recorded in 1940].

1853

1. Albert Smith had climbed Mont Blanc in 1851, and then having written a book about it, developed an entertainment to describe his experiences. It ran for over 6,000 performances from 1852 & was sufficiently notable for him to give a special performance (at Osborne House) for Queen Victoria and Prince Albert in 1854. The *Illustrated London News* described him as having written 'eloquently, on the sublime'.
2. Wylde's Globe was situated at Leicester Square for about 10 years. It was approximately 20 yards in diameter, and made of Plaster of Paris. Originally Wyld had planned that the globe should be a part of the Great Exhibition, but its size rendered this impractical and he negotiated the use of the Leicester Square site to coincide with the opening of the Exhibition. It was, initially, a huge success but, at the end of the agreed lease, it was destroyed for scrap.
3. Lagley was the home of his wife's family.
4. This Company, the 'Norfolk and Suffolk Company of Comedians' established 13 theatres in East Anglia and toured, playing each for

about 2 months. Fisher is commemorated in Bungay, Suffolk where his original theatre was restored and re-opened in 2006.

5. Franklin's expedition had left in 1845 to navigate the unexplored portion of the Northwest Passage and was not heard of again. In 1848 an expedition was mounted to look for him. A few graves and other relics were discovered.

6. This refers to the day on which (in 1848) the petition to Parliament, with a claimed 6 million signatures, was presented. Great concern was felt by the establishment that this might presage revolution – the Queen was moved to the Isle of Wight, and the Duke of Wellington was made responsible for the defence of London.

7. Headboroughs were the traditional chief officials of a borough – the term dating back to Anglo-Saxon times. In Dereham the Head-boroughs controlled several properties.

8. A 'bagman' was a travelling salesman.

9. A Bill to protect depositors. At the time there were more than 500 individual savings banks.

1854

1. This ship was almost certainly the *Tayleur*, owned by the White Star Line, which was lost on its maiden voyage to Melbourne, on the 26th January 1854. Her loss was attributed to faulty compasses, defective steering and an inexperienced crew.

2. This refers to George IV as Prince of Wales.

3. By 1850, Mormons in Britain outnumbered those in the United States, at over 30,000. By 1854 that number had grown to 54,000.

4. A lawyer & long-term opponent of Armstrong's changes.

5. It appears that, until that time, clergy had been subject to lower annuity rates to reflect their longevity.

6. 'The Wizard of the North' was the name given to John Henry Anderson, a Scottish magician who toured not just Europe, but also in America & Australia. He performed for both Queen Victoria and Czar Nicholas.

7. Dr Cumming was the Minister of the National Scottish Church, Covent Garden, regularly preaching to congregations of more than 500. He was strongly anti-Catholic.

8. The Koh-I-Nor had been acquired in 1849 as part of the treaty whereby the Punjab became part of the British Indian Empire. It was presented to the Queen in 1850, and exhibited at the Great Exhibition of 1851, the *Times* expressing some disappointment with its appearance. The stone was re-cut on the instructions of Prince Albert at a cost of £8,000. Prince Albert was apparently disappointed that the cut reduced the weight by over 40%.

9. Armstrong's father recorded the amounts he advanced to pay Challice's creditors over the period from 1846 until Challice's death in 1863. The

total was £9,636. 2s. 9d. This equates, in current terms, to something in the region of £750,000. In addition he sought to protect his daughter from the bailiffs – his diary entry for 22nd March 1854 reads: 'Dismayed by an early visit from Challice's friend Mr Bicknell to explain the necessity of Challice leaving home pending an arrangement of his affairs. Soon afterwards disturbed by dear Annie coming with the same tale of woe. Sent Annie home with her Mama to bring here all her plate and jewels as advised by Mr Bicknell..........my dear wife returned with Annie, they having previously freighted a large cab with the children's wardrobes. Went off to Jas. Duncombe and left a note begging him to come at 7 this evening to meet Challice & his friend Bicknell. On his coming we went into an examination of Challice's liabilities which he neglected to provide me with until this day at 5 o'clock, although solicited to do so for the last month. The result of this examination was a unanimous opinion that he had to become a Bankrupt and go to the Bankruptcy Court – Duncombe was to introduce Challice to Lawrence & Plews tomorrow to carry out the preliminary measures.'

10. This was the final battle of the first Anglo-Sikh War, fought on 10th Feb 1846.

11. The Minie Rifle was a rifled musket developed by the French in the 1840s. This tale is probably apocryphal as such accuracy was beyond the capability of the Minie.

12. Giulia Grisi left London in 1854, with Giovanni Matteo Mario, to tour the United States.

13. Prices for admission to the Crystal Palace varied according to the day. 1/- days were the cheapest, and the most popular.

14. Armstrong was mistaken – not only did his father promptly obtain such a uniform, but he also arranged to have his portrait painted wearing it!

15. At the time there was a theory that breathing in noxious air spread cholera. This 'miasma' theory was largely scotched by the work of a physician, John Snow, whose detailed investigation of the causes and location of the 1854 outbreaks demonstrated that the cause was contaminated water.

16. Dutch-made gin.

17. There are as many opinions as there are men.

18. John Tawell, a Quaker chemist, having been transported to Australia for forgery, returned to England having made a fortune. On New Year's Day 1845 he poisoned his mistress. He had been seen by a neighbour who raised the alarm. He was easily identified, having committed the crime in Quaker clothes and was arrested the following morning, having been trailed from Paddington Station whence he had travelled from Slough following the murder. The police had been alerted by the use of the telegraph by the Stationmaster at Slough. This is understood to be the first time that a capture was effected using the telegraph.

19. Literally, 'Mirror to the flock'. Generally refers to the notebooks kept by some contemporary clergy in which they recorded the details of their parishioners – an early database.

1855

1. Osborne was, at the time, member for Middlesex. In his speech he was highly critical of the military, though he blamed the Government rather than Parliament as an institution, or the aristocracy, for resisting Army reform.
2. Father Gravazzi was appointed Professor of Rhetoric & Belles Lettres at the University of Naples at the age of 20. Ordained as a monk, he resigned after becoming disillusioned with Popery. When lecturing in Montreal his orations caused a riot in which several lives were lost.
3. James Philippo was a Baptist missionary who was a strong campaigner for the abolition of slavery, upsetting the plantation owners by preaching the Gospel to the slaves. Although Phillipo didn't arrive in Jamaica until 1823, and trading in slaves had been abolished in 1807, the total number of slaves was still about 85% of the pre 1807 number. A church he founded in Jamaica remains today, named after him.
4. Lady Talfourd was the widow of Thomas Noon Talfourd, to whom Dickens dedicated Pickwick Papers.
5. Charles Kean was the Old Etonian son of the actor Edmund Kean. Not at first particularly successful on the London stage, he built a reputation in the United States and in the provinces before returning successfully to London, where he frequently appeared with Ellen Terry.
6. The Diorama, designed by Pugin, was originally built to display dioramic views developed by Daguerre, and originally shown in Paris, opening in 1823. In 1852 it was bought by Sir Samuel Morton Peto, an engineer, railway builder and committed Baptist, and converted to a Meeting House.
7. Dr Landels was a noted Scottish preacher.
8. Richard Cecil was an evangelical Church of England preacher.
9. Lord Robert Grosvenor (an acquaintance of the diarist's father) brought a Sunday Trading Bill to Parliament. It proposed the closing of all shops and beerhouses and the shutting down of all public transport on Sundays. The Bill met great opposition, and Armstrong's experience was typical of the protests. Crowds assembled where there were likely to be carriages to remonstrate with both their owners, and the servants who were themselves 'breaking the Sabbath'.
10. This was Thomas Cook.
11. The Rutland horseshoes are exhibited in Oakham Castle, hung upside down, supposedly to discourage the Devil.
12. Breeze means cinders

1856

1. Concentrated artillery fire.

2. In fact Sir Sandars (sometimes Saunders) Duncombe had held a Royal Patent in respect of sedan chairs. The confusion arises because sometimes these were hired, not owned, and were known as Hackney Chairs.

3. National Schools were ones run in accordance with the teaching of the Church of England, while the British & Foreign Schools were non-denominational. National schools were the more prevalent. From 1833 both benefited from State grants, but became subject to formal inspection.

4. The Caldwells sold Hilborough Hall just 2 years later, to the Duke of Wellington, it having come into the family in about 1765.

5. Celebrating peace in the Crimea.

6. Hudson achieved some distinction in agricultural circles, and was a protégé of Coke.

7. Snapdragon was a popular Christmastide game. Raisins were placed in a shallow dish of brandy which was then set alight, the other room lights being extinguished. The object of the game was to remove and eat the raisins from the brandy without getting burnt.

1857

1. A bag-man in this context was a captured fox, taken in a bag to the location of the Hunt and released, often with its paws cut to increase the scent.

2. Thomas Slingsby Duncombe was a colourful character. His personal style and propensity for gambling led him into such debts that, when he inherited his father's estate in Yorkshire it had to be sold to discharge his obligations. He was the first M.P. for the new constituency of Finchley and remained so until his death 27 years later, being a constant supporter of the Chartists.

3. Roualeyn George Gordon-Cumming was a noted big game hunter, whose trophies were displayed at the Great Exhibition of 1851. Although he didn't return to Africa after 1848 he continued to make capital out of his experiences by speeches and displays. He was the younger son of the 2nd Baronet, and thus the uncle of Sir William Gordon-Cumming, the 4th baronet who was at the heart of the Tranby Croft scandal which caused so much embarrassment to Edward VII.

4. Spurgeon was a Baptist, and probably the best known preacher of his day, frequently attracting congregations in excess of 10,000 before moving to the Metropolitan Tabernacle, which was re-located to a larger site to accommodate his huge following.

5. The diarist is in error. Sir Thomas Bignold, the extremely eccentric founder of Norwich Union, died in 1835. The entry probably relates to his son, Sir Samuel Bignold who succeeded him at Norwich Union when Sir Thomas's fellow directors finally ousted him. It was during Sir Samuel's stewardship that Norwich Union took over the Amicable, the world's oldest mutual insurer, greatly disappointing B.J.A. (Senior)

who was at the time (1866) a Director. He recorded his irritation with his fellow Board Members, whom he described in his diary as 'supine'.

6. There was a protracted legal dispute in Chancery over the building of the Corn Hall. The dispute appears to have been between two rival consortia, and continued even after the building was finished, about whether or not a highway had been built over. Eventually it was decided to allow the building to remain. The dispute was at times heated, and, despite his best efforts to remain impartial, Armstrong was believed by some to be favouring one party over the other, a perception which made his work in the parish more difficult.

7. A Paletot was a double-breasted overcoat

8. This early piece of Direct Marketing got its reward. Armstrong dined there again several times.

9. His cousin had been wounded in West Africa, not the West Indies.

10. The *Leviathan* was so named by Henrietta Hope who was due to launch her, even though throughout the period of build she had been known as *The Great Eastern*, which she was promptly re-named! Her size made it impossible for her to be launched conventionally, so the intention was to launch her sideways. This proved a difficult task and it was only at the fourth attempt that the ship was launched.

1858

1. Phillipo constructed a barn (now a listed building) which carried various inscriptions and protests relating to the game laws. On the South Gable of the barn, the following appears:

'Who can believe it blest with common sense
That taking game in Lent gave God offence
Or that untasted pheasants have the charm
Th'Almighty's fierced's pleasure to disarm
In majesty enthroned supreme-divine
Does he regard on what we chance to dine'

This memorial is erected to transmit to posterity
The fact that in the middle of the 19th Century
The owner of this estate was committed for 14
Days imprisonment in a Felon's jail by two clerical
justices for having taken and eaten his own game
out of season as decreed by English Statute law

(Pevsner and Wilson (2002) Norfolk 1. Norwich and North East, p.377, Yale)

2. A shallow basin used for washing the communion vessels

3. Antoine Claudet was an early photographer, who was appointed, in 1853, as 'Photographer-in–ordinary' to Queen Victoria.

4. Shooting where the game is driven by beating towards the guns.

5.	James Brooke was born in India but sent to school in Norwich, from which he ran away. Setting up as a trader he earned the patronage of the Sultan of Brunei by helping to defeat a rebellion. The Sultan offered Brooke the Governorship of Sarawak, and he was granted the title of Rajah. He proved an effective ruler, but was rumoured to have used excessive force in some cases. He ruled Sarawak until his death.

6.	Cremorne Gardens were situated in Chelsea – they were a less fashionable alternative to the Vauxhall Gardens.

7.	The diarist is mistaken – his cousin lost an arm in West Africa, not the West Indies.

8.	Armstrong was right to be nervous. Being 'capped' meant that the percussion cap was in place so that the chance of an accidental discharge was high.

9.	Dr Gully's establishment at Malvern was very successful; Darwin, Dickens and Tennyson were among his patients. The 'water treatment' certainly lived up to its name. Patients were roused early and wrapped in wet sheets, before being soused with buckets of water, taking long walks via various wells, before returning for breakfast – dry biscuits and water. The rest of the day was spent being immersed in various baths.

1859

1.	Howqua, reputedly one of the richest men in the world, was the senior merchant in Hong Kong and was authorised to trade with foreigners.

2.	George Wombwell was a showman who, having started life as a cobbler, enjoyed enormous success when he turned to showing animals, ending up with three separate shows touring the country. He enjoyed the patronage of Queen Victoria and was consulted by Prince Albert when the Prince's dogs were unwell.

3.	Traditionally, the Church had charged rent for pews, which were then reserved for those who had paid it. This practice continued for centuries. Armstrong's parents paid pew rent in London, as detailed in some entries in his father's diary for 1854:

	27th Jan
	'Went to the Court House in Marylebone to finally engage the best sittings we can obtain in Trinity Church. Finding we were not likely to improve our condition, engaged & paid £2.10.0d for two sittings in Pew 63 for the present year.'
	29th Jan
	'Morning Service, Trinity Church. My dear wife yesterday sent cushions & hassocks to Area Pew 63 and today felt more installed than previously.

4.	Rifle Volunteer Corps were introduced in 1859. Following the Crimean War when it had been necessary to send the militia out to reinforce the army, it was recognised that additional home defence was needed. These units were largely autonomous.

3. The School was founded in 1550, and numbers Sir Thomas Watson, Physician to Queen Victoria, to whom there are a number of references in the diaries, as one of its alumni.

1866

1. Both the illuminated address and the Silver Cup remain in family hands. Sadly of the purse, and its contents, there is no sign!
2. After Lord Armstrong, the armaments manufacturer. 'Armstrong Guns' was a generic title given to the rifled field guns he developed.

1867

1. Many skaters took the opportunity presented by a period of intense cold to skate on an ornamental lake in Regent's Park. On the 14th January there were hundreds skating there when the ice cracked and some 20 people were rescued by stewards. This did not deter other skaters and on the following day the ice fragmented throwing skaters into 12 feet of water. The wearing of skates hampered swimming and some 40 lives were lost.
2. A Roman Catholic religious institute focussing on helping the elderly.
3. The walls of the prison were 3 feet thick. The explosion caused over 100 injuries, many of them children, and 12 deaths, the eventual death toll attributed to the explosion being 30.

1868

1. This refers to the case of the Revd A.H. Machonochie, the perpetual curate of St Alban's, whose adoption of ritualistic practices led to a prosecution supported by the low church 'Church Association' under the Church Discipline Act. The judgement recorded by Armstrong was far from the conclusion of the matter. Prosecutions rumbled on until 1882, when Machonochie resigned, in accordance, it is believed, with the dying wish of Archbishop Tait. By that time he had been suspended on a number of occasions and been required to pay costs.
2. The Duke (Prince Alfred), a Naval Officer, was on a tour of Australia. He recovered in the care of six nurses trained by Florence Nightingale. The affair caused great embarassment in Australia and the would-be asassin, Henry O'Farrell, was executed. The news seems to have taken some time to reach Dereham as the attempt was made on 12th March; the trial started on 30th March and the execution took place on 21st April!
3. King Theodore had requested help from the British in his war with the Moslems. Gladstone's government ignored the request and Theodore responded by taking British hostages, including women and children. Disraeli committed a future Conservative Government to retrieving the situation and on election sent an expedition to do so.
4. No turning back.

5.   This was the first election following The Reform Act of 1867. The total votes cast exceeded a million, nearly three times the number cast in the previous election.

1870

1.   Gurney's took over Harvey's Bank, paying 10/6d in the £ to creditors.

1871

1.   Colonel Duff, later M.P. for North Norfolk, was captured at the Battle of Inkerman and was subsequently mentioned in despatches at the capture of Lucknow during the Indian Mutiny.
2.   Clermont Lodge was purchased by the 2nd Duke of Wellington for £87,000 in 1858. In 1863 he sold the property to John Remington Mills, a brewer, in whose family the property remained until the 1930s.

1872

1.   Now a conservation area.
2.   Founder of the Wallace Collection
3.   The fountain still exists. It was opened by the Princess of Teck and was said to have been given in appreciation of British protection of the Parsi community in India. 'Readymoney' was originally a soubriquet but was adopted by the family as a surname.

1873

1.   A 'Squib' was a brief written note, usually lampooning some event or individual. An alternative usage was a 'fuse'.
2.   Bishop Samuel Wilberforce, the son of William Wilberforce the anti-slavery campaigner, was a High Churchman who became Bishop of Oxford. He was given the soubriquet 'Soapy Sam', reputedly by Disraeli, because of his verbal evasiveness! He was a strong opponent of Darwin's theory of evolution.
3.   Ironically, this parish became the first sole charge of the diarist's grandson.

1874

1.   The tunnel is the Standedge tunnel, approximately 3 miles long and, at the time, the longest in Britain.
2.   Sir Thomas Watson was appointed Physician to Queen Victoria in 1859 and with Jenner and Holland attended the Prince Consort in his last illness.
3.   The start of the partridge shooting season.
4.   The accident was found to have occurred because of a mis-understanding between two railway officials at Norwich. The accident caused 25 deaths and a further 75 injured. It is believed that it was as a result of this accident that the 'tablet' system was devised requiring a driver leaving a section of single track to insert a 'tablet' into a device

which then enabled another train to enter the same line. Each tablet was of a design which would only fit the receiving device for that particular stretch of line and was only given to the driver on entering the line after a system of checks at the next station in each direction.

5. According to some reports, the total compensation paid by the Great Eastern Company was in the order of £40,000.

6. Armstrong's concerns were justified. The *London Gazette* of May 15th 1877 detailed proceedings against Nelson under the Bankruptcy Act 1869.

7. This refers to the emigrant ship *Cospatrick* which, en route from Gravesend to Auckland, caught fire and sank off the Cape of Good Hope, on 17th November 1874. The ship carried 433 emigrants and a crew of about 40, but only two lifeboats. There were only 3 survivors who had kept alive by eating those others who had been picked up initially, but subsequently died in the boat.

1875

1. Annie Emma Armstrong Challice wrote a number of novels and historical books, including that referred to in the diary in Dec 1872/Jan 1873 in connection with the Duc de Rousillon – 'Memories of French Palaces', published in 1871.

2. The Church Association was an evangelical group, founded in 1865, and very active in its opposition to Ritualism and the Oxford Movement.

3. Joseph Arch was a Warwickshire man who became the first President of the National Aricultural Workers Union on its foundation in 1872. In the 1885 election he was elected as a Liberal member for North West Norfolk. He became friendly with Daisy, Countess of Warwick – a long-term mistress of Edward VII, to whom she introduced Arch.

4. He hadn't – he had simply been living beyond his means.

5. This refers to the Kultur Kampf. Bismarck's attack was on the Catholic Church, which he regarded as potentially disloyal to the Prussian state, as its first loyalty was to Rome. The clergy were forbidden to meddle in state matters 'in a manner which might endanger peace'. The Jesuits were banned and the church and clergy put under state supervision.

6. This refers to the annexation of Schleswig-Holstein, Hesse, Nassau and Frankfurt into a Prussian dominated state.

7. The decisive battle of the Franco-Prussian war.

1876

1. Tancred's Charity supported two groups, 12 students were enabled to continue their studies post-graduation for a period of 3 years, and accommodation was provided for 'decayed and necessitated gentleman, clergyman, commissioned officers or sea officers' in Tancred's Hospital, the former home of the benefactor whose will established the

charity, Christopher Tancred. It still exists, though its remit now is only for those over 50.

2. Holt Grammar School became Gresham's School. The School's Register, published in 1955 to celebrate its fourth centenary, quotes this entry in the diary.

3. A Sizar is a student in receipt of some form of financial assistance.

4. Dr Kenealy Q.C. was a renowned eccentric, whose behaviour at the Tichborne trial drew a reprimand from the jury and resulted in his being disbarred.

5. The Tichborne case arose because of the death of Sir Roger Tichborne. He was aboard a ship sailing from Rio to New York which disappeared without trace in 1854. His mother refused to accept that he was dead and supported the claim of an unlikely claimant to the title, a London born butcher from Wagga Wagga in Australia. After a court case in which his claim was rejected, the claimant, Arthur Orton, was convicted of perjury and served 10 years in prison.

6. Maskelyne was an illusionist, Cooke a cabinet maker. Between them they developed a programme of illusions which was so successful that it ran over many years in the Egyptian Hall, Piccadilly. Maskelyne was a man of many parts – he also invented the coin-operated lock for public lavatories, giving rise to the expression 'spend a penny'.

7. This was William Henry Doveton Haggard (an elder brother of Rider Haggard); his bride was Caroline Anna Carroll, whom he married in 1875, but divorced 7 years later.

8. In the 19th century the word 'snob' meant a 'person without breeding'.

1877

1. The Redan was one of the fortified positions defending Sevastopol during the siege

2. A tazza is a shallow dish

3. The siege of Plevna was a major battle in the war. Three times Russian forces were repelled by the Turks and eventually realised the folly of direct assault. With a huge numerical advantage they then encircled Plevna. The Turks, having been refused permission to abandon the city before encirclement, determined on an attempt at breaking through the Russian lines and, despite some early success were driven back into the city and surrendered the following day.

4. This refers to the case of Henry Marsh, an employee of a forge in Wymondham, who beat to death a fellow employee and then the blacksmith, an elderly man who had been on the point of retiring and thus depriving Marsh of his employment. He was hanged in Norwich prison on 20th November 1877.

1878

1. Madame Zazel's feats were the start of a new and immensely popular circus tradition of young female performers who introduced a risqué,

slightly titillating, aspect to the circus spectacular. Madame Zazel (a young girl from Leicester) was stuffed down the barrel of a cannon (actually a spring-loaded catapult) and fired high above the audience at West's Amphitheatre in London. For each performance she received £20 and retired with her fortune two years after this.

2.   The Paris Exposition was intended to demonstrate France's recovery from the effects of the Franco-Prussian war. The site covered 66 acres, of which the French exhibits covered half. Of the remaining space one third was occupied by Britain and its colonies.

3.   H.M.S. *Eurydice* had been designed to operate in shallow water, and, after seeing service in the Caribbean and subsequently in the Crimean War, became a static training ship in 1861. She was re-commissioned, but still as a training ship, in 1877 and was returning from a 3 month tour of the West Indies when she foundered in a snowstorm off the Isle of Wight. Only 2 of the 319 crew and trainees survived. An enquiry concluded that as a frigate of quite radical design, she was not an appropriate training ship.

4.   This refers to the sinking of the *Grosser Kurfürst*, on her maiden voyage, after being rammed by the *König Wilhelm* off Folkestone. The ships were part of a flotilla of three, and the *Kurfürst*, in altering course to avoid a fleet of British fishing boats turned in front of the *Wilhelm* and sank in less than 10 minutes with over 250 lives lost.

5.   Léon Gambetta was a French Republican who, in the Franco-Prussian war, became Minister of the Interior, having escaped the besieged Paris by hot air balloon. A skilful tactician, he is credited with having tempered the extreme views of some republicans and became, briefly, President of the Council.

1879

1.   This refers to the Battle at Isandlwana in which a British force of about 1,200 men was annihilated by an estimated 12,000 Zulus. Only about 60 British escaped. The Zulus had outflanked the British Commander, Lord Chelmsford, who had divided his force. Something in the order of 1,000 rifles and vast quantities of ammunition were lost, but the greatest blow was to British prestige. Chelmsford was unaware of the battle until it was over. The sequel was the famous siege of Rorke's Drift which was the basis of the film 'Zulu'.

2.   Edward Payson Weston was a famous pedestrian, starting his career by walking 500 miles from Boston to Washington to witness the inauguration of President Lincoln. He spent 8 years in Europe successfully challenging other walkers. Even at the age of 67 he once walked 100 miles in less than 24 hours and at the age of 70 he walked the 4,000 miles between New York and San Francisco in 100 days.

3.   Charles Peace had an extraordinary career – he murdered a Mr Dyson, whose wife was believed to have been Peace's mistress. He had a long

history of burglary and led the police a merry dance before he was captured, killing one constable and making fools of several.

4. Willis's Rooms were originally called Almack's Assembly Rooms, a prestigious social club open to both sexes.

5. Christy's Minstrels were an offshoot of an American group of 'blackface' minstrels. In England several groups used the name, the most successful being that which was resident at the St James's Hall for 35 years. Moore was a leading member of the group, which was subsequently called the 'Moore & Burgess Minstrels'

6. Theophilus Shepstone was a Natal based politician whose declared wish was to govern Africans in accordance with their own traditions, a policy popularised in some of Haggard's novels.

7. John Dunn, as the diary entry suggests, betrayed his Zulu connections to fight with the British. His reward was to be appointed to rule the largest of 13 separate territories when Zululand was annexed. His polygamy is evidenced by his having married 48 wives, having a total of 117 children.

1880

1. H.M.S. *Atalanta* was a training frigate which disappeared without trace off Bermuda, causing a great scandal, as the trained crew had been small relative to the 300 trainees. Ironically this ship had been a replacement for the *Eurydice* (see note 2 for 1878).

2. This refers to the Battle of Maiwand where the British suffered a major defeat at the hands of Ayub Khan, the Afghan leader.

3. Baroness Burdett Coutts inherited £1,800,000 at the age of 23, having been selected as the most appropriate heir amongst the grandchildren of Thomas Coutts. The choice was made by his second wife, Harriot Mellon, whom he had married on the death of Baroness Burdett Coutts's grandmother. When Thomas Coutts died in 1822, he left his entire fortune to Harriot, who chose who was to benefit on her own death amongst Thomas's grandchildren. Conditions were attached to the bequest including that Miss Burdett (as she then was) should adopt the surname Coutts and that the legacy was conditional on her not marrying a foreigner. Miss Coutts, as she became known, was a remarkable philanthropist; the Church, the poor, the missionaries, the sick, animals, all benefited from her generosity. Amongst her mentors in her charitable works were Charles Dickens and the Duke of Wellington to whom, somewhat unconventionally, she is believed to have proposed marriage although he was about 40 years her senior – he declined. Made a Baroness in 1871 in acknowledgement of her philanthropy, she married, in 1881, William Bartlett, nearly 40 years her junior and for whose education she had paid. The marriage met general disapproval from the Queen and many others, but it seems to

have been a happy one. Bartlett was an American citizen and she forfeited 60% of her income.

4. William Wynne Rylands was a master engraver, and was appointed Engraver to George III. His business went bankrupt and he was sought in connection with the forgery of Bills of Exchange, the forgery being detected because two such Bills carried identical numbers. Having attempted suicide at the point of arrest Rylands was convicted on evidence that the paper on which the Bill was printed had not been available until after its purported date. He was the last person hanged at Tyburn.

5. The city of Kandahar was besieged following the battle of Maiwand (see note 2 above). The garrison there comprised approximately 4,300 troops who prepared defences and ejected the Afghanistan population. Ayub Khan employed siege guns, but a relief force of some 10,000 men, commanded by General Roberts, was sent to rescue the garrison and Ayub Khan lifted the siege, and took up a strong defensive position; Roberts's force was able to put them to rout, causing more than a thousand enemy casualties and effectively ending the 2nd Afghan War.

6. Thomas Pelham Dale, despite an early leaning to evangelism, became a strong supporter of ritual. He was twice charged under the Public Worship Regulation Act, and, after a judgement against him by Lord Penzance in the Court of Arches (an Ecclesiastical court), he was imprisoned in Holloway.

7. Jonathon Minns was discovered in the presbytery over St Luke's chapel at the cathedral. A coroner's jury found that he had committed suicide while of unsound mind.

1881

1. This was the Battle of Laings Nek, in which the British under General Colley suffered about 200 casualties having allowed themselves to be exposed to fire from both sides. Boer casualties were about 40. A ceasefire was agreed to allow the treatment of casualties.

2. The Battle of Majuba Hill was also a major defeat for Colley, who repeated his mistake at Laings Nek by moving against the Boers without waiting for support which was on its way. Colley himself was killed in the battle.

3. The incident occurred less than 4 months after President Garfield assumed office. The assassin, Charles Guiteau, convinced himself that he had played a major part in Garfield's election and looked for a diplomatic appointment as a reward. Rebuffed, he decided to assassinate the President and shot him twice before he was apprehended. Garfield lingered on, but died from his wounds eleven weeks after the attack. Guiteau was hanged having had his request for an orchestra to play at his execution declined.

1882

1. The Consul was fortunate – 50 Europeans were killed in the riot.
2. The battle of Tel-el-Kebir was fought against a well-entrenched and well-equipped Egyptian force. The British made a night approach to the defences and attacked at dawn, first by infantry and then by cavalry. The victory was substantial – the Egyptians suffered about 2,000 killed, the British less than 60.

1883

1. This copy of the Koran remains in the possession of the Editor.
2. Explosions took place at the House of Commons and at the offices of the *Times*.
3. This tragedy caused the death of 183 children, and led to demands for outward opening emergency doors in places of entertainment. The venue was the Victoria Hall, which was destroyed by German bombing in 1941.
4. A 'wideawake' was a broad brimmed hat, similar to that traditionally worn by Quakers, a pot-hat was similar to a bowler, and a zucchetto is a skull cap of the kind traditionally worn by Roman Catholic priests.

1884

1. There were two battles of El Teb. In the first the Mahdi's forces annihilated a European officered Egyptian army, only about 20% of the total escaping. The second battle, just over 3 weeks later, was fought by British troops and was a total defeat for the Mahdi. After an exchange of artillery fire, the British advanced in a square. The Mahdists tried to break this by attacking with spears and swords but met with a response from Gatling guns. It is estimated that the Mahdists lost 2,500 killed, the British less than 30.
2. Tamai was a more difficult battle for the British. The disciplined squares which had served them well at El Teb were less effective in the face of difficult terrain and attack from the flank at Tamai. At one stage there the square disintegrated and the Mahdists captured both Gatling guns. Fresh forces recovered the situation and the total British casualties of about 110 killed compared with an estimated number of 2,000 Mahdists.
3. The Ras el Tin palace was the location for the signature of King Farouk to the abdication document in 1953.

1885

1. 'Behold how good and pleasant it is for brethren to live in unity'.
2. In this battle, the Mahdists actually managed to break into a British square, but were ejected. It is believed that it was this which inspired Newbolt's poem which begins 'There's a hush in the close tonight'.
3. The day became known as 'Dynamite Saturday'.

4. The Battle of Metemmeh was really a postscript to the Battle of Abu Klea, the following morning. Stewart was killed here, but Burnaby in fact died at Abu Klea. The diarist's description of Burnaby as 'adventurous' is certainly apt. Burnaby had a colourful career and exhibited some bizarre characteristics. On one occasion he carried a pony into the Mess under his arm. In previous battles he had armed himself with a shotgun which he sometimes used as a club in close quarter fighting. He was actually banned by the Duke of Cambridge.

5. The battle of Tofrek occurred when the Arab forces attacked a British force engaged in building defensive positions. After intense fighting they were driven off, with claimed losses of 3,000.

6. The Rev. Bell Cox was another to fall foul of Disraeli's Public Worship Regulation Act. The low church Bishop of Liverpool told Bell Cox to drop his use of lighted candles and incense and not to wear a biretta. With the support of his congregation, Bell Cox refused and was prosecuted by a member of the Church Association in respect of ritualistic practices. Found guilty, he ignored the judgement and was subsequently committed to Walton Prison, where he remained 17 days until released on the order of the House of Lords.

7. This was the first election following 3rd Reform Act which extended the franchise so that most males could vote.

Bibliography - sources consulted

Briggs, Asa , *Victorian Cities* (Odhams Press, London, 1963)

Colloms, Brenda, *Victorian Country Parsons* (Constable & Robinson, London, 1977)

Chadwick, Owen, *Victorian Miniature* (Hodder & Stoughton, London, 1960)

David, Saul, *Zulu* (Viking, London 2004)

Goodenough, Simon, *The Country Parson* (David & Charles, Newton Abbot, 1983)

Janes, Dominic, Victorian Reformation: *The Fight over Idolatry in the Church of England* (Oxford University Press, Oxford 2009)

Norton, Ben, *The History of East Dereham* (Phillimore, Chichester, 1994)

Pakenham, Thomas, *The Boer War* (Weidenfeld & Nicolson, London, 1979)

White, Jerry, *London in the Nineteenth Century* (Jonathan Cape, London, 2007)

Wilson, A. N., *The Victorians* (Hutchinson, London, 2002)

Sources accessed online:

The Oxford Dictionary of National Biography
The Times Digital Archive

www. anglicanhistory.org
www.bbc.co.uk/history/british/victorians
www.churchofengland.org
www.churchunion.co.uk
www.churchsociety.org
www.historyofparliamentonline.org
www.royal.gov.uk
www.victorianweb.org

Index of names and places mentioned in the Diary

338

341

343